Foreign Attachments

Also by Tony Smith

*America's Mission: The United States and the Worldwide Struggle
for Democracy in the Twentieth Century*

*Thinking like a Communist: State and Legitimacy in the
Soviet Union, China, and Cuba*

*The Pattern of Imperialism: The United States, Great Britain,
and the Late-Industrializing World since 1815*

Foreign Attachments

The Power of Ethnic Groups in the Making of American Foreign Policy

Tony Smith

HARVARD UNIVERSITY PRESS

Cambridge, Massachusetts
London, England   2000

Library of Congress Cataloging-in-Publication Data

Smith, Tony, 1942–
    Foreign attachments : the power of ethnic groups in the making of
American foreign policy / Tony Smith.
        p. cm.
    Includes bibliographical references (p.) and index.
    ISBN 0-674-00294-6 (alk. paper)
    1. United States—Foreign relations—20th century.
    2. Minorities—United States—Political activity—History—20th century.
    3. United States—Ethnic relations.   I. Title.
    E744 .S589 2000
    327.73—dc21   00-027288

For the Luebbehusen Family
and
Jose David Ovalle

Contents

Acknowledgments

The origins of this book lie in questions raised by students at Tufts University in a class in the spring of 1995. Looking for information on the role of ethnic groups in the making of U.S. foreign policy, we found only a short list of readings, most of them focused on single groups. The few works that were more general in scope were typically highly contentious in their treatment of the subject, presenting skewed points of view without adequate argument, much less consideration of alternative perspectives. Hence the inspiration for this book.

I was fortunate to be invited in 1997 to the Woodrow Wilson International Center for Scholars housed at the Smithsonian Institution in Washington, D.C., under the direction of Sam Wells and Rob Littwak. While in Washington, I conducted interviews and read what was available in most congenial circumstances. Thereafter, I became the Whitney Shepardson Fellow at the Council on Foreign Relations for the academic year 1997–1998. Under the direction of Nicholas Rizopoulos, assisted by Colin Wheeler, the Council held four seminars on papers intended as drafts for this book.

Jeffrey Berry, David Fromkin, Jonathan Goldin, Samuel Huntington, Miles Kahler, Ronald Steel, and Ibrahim Sundiata offered close readings of the text that prompted useful changes. From sessions at the Council, I would like to thank James Chace, Robert Devigne, Rodolfo O. de la Garza, Inge Hoffmann, Temma Kaplan, Peter Katzenstein,

Barbara Kellerman, Malik Mufti, Sharon Russell, Henry Siegman, Elliott Skinner, Monteagle Stearns, Anders Stephanson, Carol Strauss, Michael Teitelbaum, and Jennifer Whitaker. I have also benefited from the comments of Kareem Al-Bassam, Albert Cho, Elliot Cohen, Will Cruse, Nadia Georges, Joshua Koehler, Mark Krikorian, Jose David Ovalle, Gary Tinterow, Michael Wang, Myron Weiner, Fareed Zakaria, and Henri Zerner. An anonymous reviewer at Harvard University Press encouraged productive changes to my argument about the dilemmas of democratic pluralism, while Jeffrey Kehoe was a superb editor paying special attention to the tone of the book.

It should be obvious that with such a controversial subject, none of these persons agreed with all of my conclusions. Yet these good people expressed basic differences of opinion from mine with a civility and constructive intent that I greatly appreciate, and that I wish could become more common in discussions of multiculturalism in American political life today.

Foreign Attachments

Introduction

> In a political system as large as a country, the plurality of relatively independent organizations is necessary . . . for the democratic process . . . Yet a problem arises—which I have called the dilemma of democratic pluralism—because while necessary, desirable, and inevitable in a democratic order, organizational pluralism may also play a part in stabilizing inequalities, deforming civic consciousness, distorting the public agenda, and alienating final control over the public agenda by the citizen body.
> —*Robert A. Dahl*

> What is clear is that values can clash—that is why civilizations are incompatible. They can be incompatible between cultures, or groups in the same culture, or between you and me. You believe in always telling the truth, no matter what; I do not because I believe that it sometimes can be too painful and too destructive. We can discuss each other's point of view, we can try to reach common ground, but in the end what you pursue may not be reconcilable with the ends to which I find I have dedicated my life . . . These collisions of values are of the essence of what they are and what we are. If we are told that these contradictions will be solved in some perfect world in which all good things can be harmonised in principle . . . we must say that the world in which what we see as incompatible values are not in conflict is a world altogether beyond our ken.
> —*Isaiah Berlin*

> Liberty is to faction what air is to fire.
> —*James Madison*

THE THREE MAJOR propositions I advance in this book are likely to be controversial. First, ethnic groups play a larger role in the making of U.S. foreign policy than is widely recognized. This oversight reflects our poor general understanding of the domestic sources of America's role in world affairs. Yet the success of ethnic activism should not be

1

too surprising. America is a pluralist democracy in which social forces have rather easy access to governmental policy deliberations, hence the country's role in world affairs is bound to express to a substantial degree the opinion of its organized civic actors. This is especially so at times like the present, when no vital threat to the country's security is apparent and a bipartisan consensus on America's proper role abroad is relatively weak.

Second, at present, the negative consequences of ethnic involvement may well outweigh the undoubted benefits this activism at times confers on America in world affairs. To make such an evaluation is only to repeat analogous sentiments often expressed about the efforts of the American business community to have its interests abroad served by policymakers in Washington. And it is to underscore the fact that in a post–Cold War world, where America is the only superpower but lacks a clear agenda in its foreign policy, many interest groups are trying to have their concerns given priority in world affairs. However much we may salute the virtues of a pluralist democracy, its workings can come at a cost.

Third, the contradictions of pluralist democracy are particularly apparent in the making of foreign policy, where the self-interested demands of a host of domestic actors—those in the business community even more than those which are ethnic—raise an enduring problem of democratic citizenship: how to balance the rights and interests of the organized few against the rights and interests of the often inattentive many. For example, how compelling is the claim ethnic groups sometimes make, if only by implication, that they should have a dominant voice in deciding how American power should be used with respect to their kinfolk abroad? Such claims become particularly problematic in cases where these groups—under the ideological mantle of "multiculturalism"—seem to place a higher priority on their sense of ethnic identity than on their sense of identity with the greater American community.

These three findings dovetail nicely: because ethnic group influence is underappreciated and because it sometimes complicates the exercise of American power in the world (issues of practical importance), complex and important questions concerning the character of this country's pluralist democracy and the rights and obligations of citizenship (issues of political ethics) can be raised. While the character of U.S. foreign policy and questions concerning democratic citizenship may fruitfully be related, it is worth underscoring that the latter topic has a vitality all its own. For example, no group of Asian Americans today has an important place at the table in foreign policy discussions as an ethnic constituency. But we can debate what their rights and obligations hypothetically might be at such a table despite their current lack of power. Hence the equal importance of the two themes of this investigation: the one, more empirical, evaluates underappreciated forces at play in the practical world of democratic politics as they affect foreign policy; the other, more theoretical, analyzes the logic of moral arguments concerning the nature of democratic citizenship.

My goal of investigating the practical politics of ethnic influence on U.S. foreign policy derives from observing the frequently formidable roles self-reliant ethnic groups have played in domestic politics and from assuming that their effects need not stop at the water's edge. If domestic reasons are not enough, world affairs can stimulate powerful reactions in American politics thanks to effective transnational connections among kinfolk—networks of communication which may directly and forcibly tie organized American civic associations to peoples and events in the ancestral homeland. Given the openness of the American political process to a wide variety of social interest lobbying in foreign affairs, it would be surprising if ethnic activists were unable to affect foreign policy debates in Washington.

The question of influence raises the question of effectiveness: How efficient is American government, exposed as it is to the policy demands of myriad pressure groups? Can the degree of governmental autonomy necessary for coherent and consistent policy conducted for the common good be preserved in the face of these forces? In the aftermath of the Cold War, at a time when vital national interests in world affairs may be difficult to formulate with precision, a welter of social action groups may subject Washington to demands particularly difficult to reconcile with one another. A study of ethnic group activism alone is not enough to provide a final answer to the question of how policymaking in a democracy may be made more effective, but it can at least be indicative of a response.

My second ambition here is to analyze the logic of ethical questions surrounding arguments specifying the rights and obligations of citizenship in a pluralist democracy. Given the significance of interest group lobbying on all sides—from business associations especially, but also from ethnic and religious communities—questions naturally arise about the justification of a minority's efforts to control policies concerning the American polity in general. Existing theories of democratic citizenship that deal with subnational group politicization are typically far better at defending the rights of ethnic communities to make their voices heard than at indicating the limits on these rights or giving substance to the notion of greater community, or national, interests against which the demands of a subnational group need to be weighed.

The paradox of democratic life is that unity is to be found by respecting, indeed by empowering, social difference. The miracle of democracy is that it can find strength in its diversity and even to a limited degree in social divisiveness. The reality of democracy—one we would be mistaken to forget, flushed with victory over fascism and communism at the beginning of a new century—is that its enormous undertaking may eventually fail not so much because of external challenge as for internal reasons, if social differences legitimized by democracy breed division to such a point that national political cohesion is undone. The study of the domestic sources of U.S. foreign policy leads rather directly, then, to an analysis of the contemporary meaning of democratic citizenship, for it is in the study of America's role in world affairs that the concept of national interests is especially commonplace and thus that the role of particular versus general concerns should be open to fruitful analysis.

Accordingly, in this book I ask the question of who does, and who should, decide this country's foreign policy. Establishing who gives America voice in world affairs is a far more complicated matter than is often supposed. If ultimately a particular presidential administration is generally credited with determining how America acts on the world stage, on closer inspection the roles of the Congress and of popular forces need always to be respected. Indeed, as we investigate the question "Who speaks for America?" it turns out that interest groups (including far more than those ethnically based) frequently write the script, whence the notion of "one nation divisible."

Since the *Federalist Papers* more than two centuries ago, Americans have pondered the ethical and the practical problem in democratic life of particular social interests securing policies of benefit to themselves that may have consequences for the entire citizenry. The Founding Fathers may have feared the "tyranny of the majority" and so provided special protections for minority rights, but in the event, the "tyranny of the minority" became a possibility as a wide variety of civic interests found ways to gain access to power in Washington.

The classic charge against popular involvement with foreign affairs was made in 1831 by Alexis de Tocqueville:

> I have no hesitation in saying that in the control of society's foreign affairs, democratic governments do appear decidedly inferior to others . . . Foreign policy does not require the use of any of the good qualities peculiar to democracy but does demand the cultivation of almost all those which it lacks . . . It has little capacity for combining measures in secret and waiting patiently for the result . . . In politics, the tendency of a democracy [is] to obey its feelings rather than its calculations and to abandon a long-matured plan to satisfy a momentary passion.[1]

Referring to Tocqueville's judgment, George Kennan reiterated the point in 1977, applying it explicitly to ethnic group activism:

> Our actions in the field of foreign affairs are the convulsive reactions of politicians to an internal political life dominated by vocal minorities . . . No one who thinks back over the annals of just these postwar decades will have difficulty bringing to mind a number of prominent instances in which ethnic minorities have brought pressures with a view to influencing foreign policy on behalf of what they perceive as the interests of their former mother country—interests which of course may or may not be identical with those of the United States . . . What has been most remarkable about these pressures has been not so much their existence, for they are in the nature of things, as the degree of their success. Example after example springs to mind where [ethnic groups] have proven more powerful and effective as influences on Congressional decisions in matters of foreign policy than the views of highly competent persons of the Executive Branch who, in contrast to the lobbyists, had exclusively the national interest at heart.[2]

The concerns of Tocqueville and Kennan have a long provenance. Since the writings of James Madison, the man widely agreed to be the chief architect of the political system set out by the U.S. Constitution, theorists of what today is called democratic pluralism have recognized deep strains built into the American political system and looked for ways to reconcile the inevitable contradictions among particular interests and between particular and general interpretations of the good. For our day, Isaiah Berlin is particularly well known for his warnings that there is no magic formula to resolve differences between social forces, that in a pluralistic democracy there will always be tensions among individual and group values and interests and among rival conceptions of the common good.[3] One of the major balancing acts of modern democratic theory involves recognizing the likelihood of ongoing contradictions between two rights—that of the minority and that of the general community. Our hope must be that if we understand the complications of our system of government better, we may deal with its inevitable disturbances more wisely so that democracy may function more perfectly.

Democracy's built-in dilemma is well put by Robert Dahl, the best-known contemporary theorist of American pluralism, noting for our era the inevitable consequences of what Madison called "the mischiefs of faction":

> Whenever democratic processes are employed on a scale as large as the nation-state, autonomous organizations are bound to come into existence. They are more, however, than a direct consequence of democratizing the government of the nation-state. They are also necessary to the functioning of the democratic process itself, to minimizing government coercion, to political liberty, and to human well-being. Yet as with individuals, so with organizations; independence or autonomy . . . creates an opportunity to do harm. Organizations may use the opportunity to increase or perpetuate injustice rather than reduce it, to foster the narrow egotism of their members at the expense of concerns for a broader public good, and even to weaken or destroy democracy itself.[4]

A major difficulty confronting any effort to juxtapose minority to majority rights is the need to specify just what "national interests" are, seldom a matter free of debate. It would be absurd to claim that something called the national interest is obvious at every point in time and that all true Americans should rally round it. All important foreign policy debates should allow for reasonable persons to disagree with one another without any suggestion of disloyalty. Still, the concept of the "common," "collective," "general," or "public" good—that is, the "national interest or interests"—is an essential notion for any democratic people, one that is not suspended by the invocation of special interest rights under pluralism. As even a casual acquaintance with political life will suggest, the effort of the few to commit the many to a course of action designed to benefit only a small sector of the population at the expense of the entire nation is often observed in democratic life. Consequently, a theory of democratic pluralism must have some grounds on which to assert the common cause.

How, then, does the nation limit the demands of a subgroup in a democratic fashion, avoiding the tyranny of the majority? Note that this way of formulating the issue sets the *general* against a *particular* interest; it does not seek to legitimize the rule of the *majority* over a *minority*. In the most influential answer to the problem of pluralism, James Madison, in *Federalist* 10, suggested setting faction against faction, maintaining that through the balance thereby achieved the nation would be protected against the excessive demands of a minority. At times this solution may well be the best practical advice we can follow. Contending interests have contributed to the vitality of American politics with respect to foreign as well as domestic affairs.

But the Madisonian solution is also bedeviled by serious problems. Consider domestic politics: whether we debate affirmative action, tax codes, or education policy, we need some concept of what benefits all of us and not simply segments of the population. To allow taxation or education policy to be decided by whoever has the most clout is to surrender altogether the notion that as a nation we have a moral obligation and a practical interest to protect the weak, provide for the future, and be concerned about how various decisions will serve the entire community. A problem for liberal democratic theory in an era of multiculturalism is the difficulty of defending the moral legitimacy of the "common good," the "general welfare," or the "national interest" rather than letting social interests fight it out in the public arena with the strongest determining policy.

In foreign affairs this Madisonian argument is especially problematic. Here faction may not be so automatically counterbalanced by faction as in domestic life, and here too foreign peoples, movements, and states may call on their American kinfolk in ways that have no domestic parallel domestically. In short, the difficulty of debating what the common good actually is does not mean that the concept itself—America as a community, an *unum* as well as a *pluribus*—can be seen as other than a vital part of the country's collective political discourse.

Ethnic activists often seem to forget or obscure this *unum* in their efforts to aid their kinfolk abroad, giving the impression that they believe national policy toward the Balkans and Turkey should be decided by Greek and Orthodox Americans, toward Africa and the Caribbean by African Americans, toward the Middle East by Muslim or Jewish Americans, toward the Caucasus by Armenian Americans, toward immigration policy by Hispanic Americans, toward Cuba by Cuban Americans, toward Eastern Europe by East European Americans, and the like—and all of this at times based on considerations having to do with demands formulated by foreign leaders or with dilemmas remote from American values or interests. As Samuel Huntington has observed:

> Previous assumptions that the foreign and domestic policymaking processes differ from each other for important reasons no longer hold. For an understanding of American foreign policy it is necessary to study not the interests of the American state in a world of competing states but rather the play of economic and ethnic interests in American domestic politics. At least in recent years, the latter has been a superb predictor of foreign policy stands. Foreign policy, in the sense of actions consciously designed to promote the interests of the United States as a collective entity in relation to similar collective entities, is slowly but steadily disappearing.[5]

WHILE THE TWO major themes of this book—practical politics and democratic theory—are analytically distinct, the study of foreign policy provides a particularly useful perspective from which to become involved in the contemporary debates over the meaning of "multiculturalism." Like the defense of "cultural pluralism" that was sounded earlier in this century, multiculturalism calls for respecting the rights of this country's diverse ethnic communities in our national economic, social, cultural, and political life. But multiculturalism is different from traditional pluralism when it argues that to achieve equality a group must have special treatment: for example, bilingual education in the schools and a rejection of the established intellectual canon; affirmative action and contract set-asides in the workplace; electoral redistricting or proportional representation in the political arena.

What multiculturalism means with respect to the formulation of American foreign policy remains fluid. To some, it means ending the overwhelming predominance of Euro Americans in decisionmaking in Washington. For others, it promises to bring distinctive new ideas to the making of foreign policy, the notion being that groups hitherto marginalized from public life will have a different understanding of national interests than those that heretofore have been in control. Yet a third possible meaning is that ethnic groups will define the nation's policy toward those parts of the world with which they are more intimately connected.

The first claim of multiculturalists seems to me beyond dispute. To the extent that ethnic minorities are underrepresented in the highest councils of government—and this certainly appears to be the case for African, Hispanic, Asian, and Native Americans—the situation should be rectified.

The second claim also has merit: it would be surprising if people with distinctive life experiences did not bring to public life fresh and sometimes discordant perspectives on the proper course of U.S. foreign policy. For example, Randall Robinson, the founder of TransAfrica, gives many instances from his own life story of how the struggle against racial oppression at home has created special concerns in the black community about the U.S. role in world affairs.[6] Or again, the California Representative Esteban Torres may well complain that global economic forces are disproportionately affecting African American and Hispanic American communities, which therefore need to be concerned on an ethnic (not only a class) basis about the effects of the North American Free Trade Agreement (NAFTA) on their economic situation.[7]

Whatever the justice of these two multiculturalist claims, it is unlikely that U.S. foreign policy will undergo a wholesale refashioning as minorities gain power. The objective quality of many American interests in the world, and the ability of domestic values and institutions to increase the sense of national over ethnic identity once power is better shared, should not for a moment be underestimated. In these two domains, the demands of multiculturalists should be accepted, I would argue, as an extension of the promise of democracy in America.

But the third claim seems to me to be unacceptable. American power in world affairs is not something to be divided up among ethnic constituencies to be used as they will; in matters of foreign policy, the greater community should be consulted and its interests protected, while the nation's representatives should determine policy based on some idea of the common good. Although ethnic activists seldom explicitly claim that the self-defined needs of their kinfolk abroad should determine American policies, implicitly this belief is frequently basic to their agenda.

Consider, for example, the possible implications of a statement made by a group of Latino organizations looking forward to the Summit of the Americas that was to be held under U.S. auspices in Miami in December 1997:

> We are united around the principle that, as a "bridge" community, U.S. Latinos have both an interest and an obligation to participate vigorously in the development and implementation of intrahemisphere relations, which are inextricably linked to U.S. Latinos' interests with respect to immigration, trade, economic prosperity, and human and civil rights. We are further committed to achieving recognition of this principle within the policy-making arena. American Jews play an important role in shaping our policies regarding the Middle East, the African Americans play a similarly important role in shaping our policies toward Africa; in this tradition, it is entirely appropriate for U.S. Latinos to help shape our policies within this hemisphere.[8]

Doubtless there are positive or benign consequences that nearly everyone could agree might flow from increased Latino involvement in the making of foreign policy. But other activities might just as obviously be debatable. Take, for instance, the activities of Jorge Mas Canosa and his Cuban American National Foundation, which with associates in other organizations might be said to have gone well beyond being a "bridge" for U.S. policy toward Havana, to running a parallel foreign policy all its own (at least until Mas's death in November 1997). Many Americans might ask by what right as a citizen Mas's conduct could be justified.

More, if Latinos are to play a dominant role in hemispheric relations, does that mean they abdicate to fellow ethnics their rights to be involved in decisionmaking with regard to parts of the world staked out by these other constituencies? One might argue that instead of narrowing their sights on Latin America, U.S. Latinos should better see themselves as citizens of a global power and so recognize that they have an equal, quite possibly even a greater, interest in the nation's policy in the Middle East, East Asia, or Europe. Are Latinos seriously willing to give up their voice toward these critical regions out of deference to other ethnic "bridges," content to control only their own?

Or consider the inferences that might be drawn from related claims made by a largely black group that met at Howard University in May 1996 at a conference entitled "Defining the National Interest: Minorities and U.S. Foreign Policy in the 21st Century." Although participants recognized that ethnic constituencies needed to formulate their concerns in ways that would put them "in synch" with majority opinion, "conferees debated the experience of Jewish Americans and Cuban Americans and sought to extract lessons from the way these two groups succeeded in influencing foreign policy while others failed."[9]

Once again the questions arise: do African Americans understand Cuban and Jewish American influence to predominate in certain domains of foreign policy? Do they approve of this predominance and forswear involvement themselves in debates over proper conduct toward Cuba and the Middle East as well as other areas marked out by ethnic minorities provided their fellow citizens extend to them a similar degree of influence over U.S. policy toward Africa and the Caribbean?

As these comments by representatives of the African and Latin American communities suggest, the question of ethnic group relations with the rest of the national community is not a matter restricted to people of color. Indeed, the claim of these ethnoracial minorities is all too commonly that they are only following in the footsteps of white America when they advance self-interested demands based on feelings of ethnic identity.

Their reaction is to some extent understandable. Asian Americans may have vivid memories of their second-class status in the United States. The Chinese Exclusion Act of 1882 was followed in 1902 by legislation that made Chinese immigration illegal. Chinese remained ineligible for citizenship until 1943. For their part, Japanese Americans can recall restrictions on their owning land in California and their incarceration there during World War II, while Filipino Americans remember a history of labor union opposition to their arrival in California. Restrictions did not apply solely to Asians. During the Depression, perhaps half a million Mexicans were deported. And it has only been since the 1970s that African Americans have achieved an effective voice in foreign policy deliberations.

Yet as the immigration quotas enforced after 1924 indicate, "white" America itself was divided, for Jews, Slavs, and Southern Europeans were thereafter sharply restricted in coming to America by a quota tied to the population according to the census of 1890. "White" America might thus appear to mean Northern Europeans. But Irish Americans, though not affected by the quota of 1924, could with justice maintain that they had been discriminated against earlier by Protestant America. Even German and Scandinavian Americans, although largely Protestant, could themselves claim to have been marginalized by those of English descent.

"White" America thus came to mean Anglo America. No one has yet convincingly demonstrated that this group has ruled in foreign affairs on the basis of a sense of ethnic identity, however much this claim may suit certain prejudices. To be sure, the author of the only book-length history of the ethnic impact on America's role in world affairs manages to recount virtually the entire history of the foreign policy of the Republic (prior to the rise of multiculturalism in the 1960s) as if it were nothing but the saga of white Anglo-Saxon Protestants acting in a pro-British fashion thanks to their ethnic heritage. Debatable as this historical account is, it nonetheless unfortunately serves to legitimize contemporary multicultural demands on the making of foreign policy, sanctioning the expression of particularistic demands by racial minorities (or hitherto silent European Americans) as nothing more than business as usual in America and hence as the fulfillment of the democratic promise.[10] Already, in the words of one Harvard professor in 1963, for example:

Jews are not the first ethnic or religious group in America that has sought to influence American foreign policy in favor of kinsmen or coreligionists . . . Ethnoreligious politics, like the politics of interest groups in general, have been an inescapable consequence of the pluralism and multiplicity of interests in American life and are therefore a fact to be reckoned with . . . the desire of minority groups to promote their particular views and interests, and the efforts of politicians to organize a variety of such views and interests into a winning majority are integral aspects of the American democratic process today. To exhort the voters to put the national interest above their particular group interest and the candidates to put integrity above the desire to catch votes is often insulting and always futile.[11]

Writing nearly twenty years ago, then Maryland Senator Charles Mathias offered what until now has been the only sustained criticism from a democratic pluralist viewpoint of the mischiefs of faction in the making of U.S. foreign policy:

There are two basic problems, the lesser being the imbalance between competing groups so that some exert disproportionate influence at the expense of those who are weaker in numbers, unity, and resources. The greater problem is the loss of cohesion in our foreign policy and the derogation from the national interest when, as Washington and Madison feared, factions among us lead the national toward excessive foreign attachments or animosities. Even if the groups were balanced—if Turkish Americans equaled Greek Americans or Arab Americans equaled Jewish Americans— the result would not necessarily be sound, cohesive foreign policy because the national interest is not simply the sum of our special interests and attachments. It is not, to be sure, wholly separate from these, nor can the national interest be antithetical to the strong preferences of large segments of the population, but the overall requirements of the United States—strategic, economic, political, and moral—constitute a whole larger than the sum of its parts. Ethnic preferences figure in that whole but cannot be permitted to preempt it.[12]

We need not look far to find ethnic groups collapsing ethnic and national interests into one. For example, Armenian groups often stress their diasporic character, and since the establishment of an Armenian state in 1991, some of their publications have repeatedly referred to the United States as a "host country" and to Armenia as the "homeland" or the "Mother country." In its issue of July 31, 1998, to cite but one instance, the *Armenian International Magazine* printed a long article dedicated to rallying the Armenian diaspora to the defense of the homeland. As one contributor declared in terms implicitly echoed throughout the edition: "We in the Armenian Diaspora have a unique opportunity to exercise our dual allegiance to our host country and to Armenia. We should take advantage of our rights as citizens of the host country [the United States] to gain its support of Armenia."

In its January 3, 1998, edition, the *Armenian Reporter International* gave an example of what this commitment meant, citing as "a major victory for Armenia and the Diaspora's lobby" the achievement of $87 million of U.S. foreign aid for Armenia, $12.5 million more for Nagorno Karabakh, and the blocking of the Clinton administration's effort to repeal Section 907 of the Freedom Support Act, which barred foreign aid to Azerbaijan in retaliation for its embargo of Armenia. Later in the year the lobby registered another win. In a press release of September 18, 1998, the Armenian National Committee of America saluted its victory the day before in the House (by a vote of 231 to 182) over efforts to repeal Section 907, a measure backed not only by the Clinton administration (in the person of Madeleine Albright, who launched a vigorous critique of the Armenian lobby), but also by fourteen oil companies with interests in Caspian Sea oil (and so in Azerbaijan), an impressive assembly of Jewish organizations (concerned to solidify Israel's relations with Turkey), and a segment of the Republican leadership in the House including the head of the Appropriations Committee.[13]

In fact, the Armenian American victory probably involved a trade-off. By the end of the year, the American government and oil companies were close to announcing the construction of an oil pipeline from the Caspian through Georgia to a Turkish port on the Mediterranean, meaning that Iran, Russia, and Armenia would all be bypassed (except for the petroleum the former two directly controlled in the region) and Azerbaijan enormously enriched as a result. Depressed prices for petroleum through most of 1999 may have in turn put a check on the construction of such a pipeline, but the point is that the Armenian "victory" of September 17, 1998, was not quite as it seemed. A combination of oil company, Jewish, and Turkish lobbies appeared ultimately to have far more clout even though the Armenian lobby had been rewarded with a large foreign aid package.

American Jewish groups celebrated their strength (as well as the growing strategic alliance between Israel and Turkey) in a November 8, 1998, advertisement published in the *New York Times*, paid for by the American Jewish Committee, the American Jewish Congress, and the Anti-Defamation League:

> Congratulations! Mazeltov! Tebrinkler! As Americans and Jews, we join in celebrating the 75th anniversary of the Turkish Republic. We especially applaud Turkey for: its democratic and secular values; its close and mutually beneficial ties with the United States; its invaluable strategic role as a NATO partner; its ever deepening relations with the State of Israel; its historic tradition dating back more than 500 years, as a haven for Jews fleeing persecution. We join with the Turkish people in celebrating this milestone, and we look forward to continued flourishing ties in the years ahead among Turkey, the United States, and Israel.

Within days, representatives of Greek American associations had made public their displeasure with this advertisement—not speaking as representatives of anything that might be construed as American national interests (an approach seldom followed by Greek American activists) but instead listing Greece's complaints against Turkey. Months later, as the United States bombed Serbia, Greek Americans made their dissatisfaction with U.S. foreign policy in the Balkans and with respect to Turkey evident once again in terms that made no effort to speak of a collective American purpose but instead spoke of concerns that were uniquely Greek or Orthodox Christian.[14]

So the question arises of whether this is how American foreign policy is best determined: by Greek, Armenian, Kurdish, and Arab Americans on the one side opposing Jewish and Turkish Americans (along with oil companies) on the other, each with a self-interest in mind that aligns these Americans with ancestral kinfolk while paying no apparent heed to American national interests? Perhaps in a situation where the two sides balance each other some concept of the common good for America can be advanced, but as I will show in Chapter 3, the lobby for the common cause is not particularly strong, and to assume that it can only emerge from a standoff between rival social forces is surely an imperfect way to defend national interests.

The point is not to debate one by one the merits of particular ethnic groups' proposals for U.S. foreign policy. One may agree that the building of the Caspian Sea pipeline through Turkey or the embargo on Iran is in American national interests (or that Washington should support democratic governance in Haiti, the peace process in Northern Ireland, efforts to isolate Castro's government in Cuba, the expansion of NATO to include Poland, Hungary, and the Czech Republic, or the cause of Cypriot reunification) without at the same time agreeing that the way these policies are formulated in Washington—in substantial part at the insistence of ethnic lobbies—is the best way for the United States to decide its role in world affairs. In a democracy, policy is made legitimate not only by being effective but also by being the collective expression of the will of the people and bearing some relationship to their general interests. Yet, in a pluralist polity, it is far from clear that foreign policy is either optimally effective or morally legitimate when a minority gains enough influence to commit the entire community to a policy from which that minority alone may benefit, potentially at substantial cost to the country as a whole.

How do we reconcile the rights of an ethnic minority with the rights of the greater national community? In terms of the history of democratic argument in the United States, my perspective in this book may properly be called pluralist. I accept the multiculturalist argument that ethnics have a legitimate right in a democratic order to speak out on public policy in a way that corresponds to their values and interests. But I insist as well that democratic citizenship involves obligations on the part of ethnics to the national community of which they are members, obligations that may often override for moral and practical reasons their right to insist on the priority of furthering the interests of their kinfolk abroad. Pluralists do not doubt the cogent historical and moral grounds on which ethnoracial communities join together politically, but we do believe that in debates about the formulation of American foreign policy, national identity, values, loyalties, and obligations must be placed above ethnic ones. Pluralists therefore stand at an intermediate point between those who denounce multiculturalism in all its guises and those who unselfcritically embrace it in all its manifestations. Pluralists are the natural bridge between multiculturalists and their nationalist critics, for we respect the cogency of each side's position but believe that a credible middle ground can be staked out, even if with difficulty.[15]

At the opening of this Introduction I predicted that certain of my conclusions would be controversial. But to say they are controversial is not to say that they are alarmist. Thus to argue that on balance ethnic groups today have a negative impact on American foreign policy is not to say that this has always been the case, nor that it always will be, nor is it to doubt that in many instances ethnic internationalism has been salutary in its consequences. Even less am I suggesting that America is today in serious danger of internal fragmentation or external disaster because of ethnic group influence. Although I do believe that because of these influences our foreign policy is less coherent and consistent than it might be, and that to follow certain ethnic preferences would be unfortunate for America's role in the world, I am not saying that the house is on fire or that the sky is ready to fall.

What I am calling for instead is an effort to lay out the framework on which ethnic group preferences for American foreign policy can be subjected to open and rational debate. Yet, because of historical memories of oppression and marginalization, ethnic groups are often understandably hostile to those who criticize their policy recommendations. They may suspect those who argue against their preferred policies on grounds of national interests of questioning their patriotism or loyalty. Let me, then, repeat that I believe ethnic groups have a basis in liberal democratic theory to organize to promote their values and interests. I do not intend to impugn their patriotism when they demonstrate a deep and legitimate concern for their kinfolk abroad. Rather, my point is to remind them that on occasion America may have values and interests not only different from but actually opposed to the expressed values and interests of their ancestral homelands. To say this is to call attention to the way ethnic groups (like most of us in many situations) often appear to compartmentalize their political identities, resisting the notion of tensions and contradictions among their multiple loyalties, preferring to see a close convergence of interests between the United States and their kinfolk abroad. And it is to argue that for Euro Americans especially, all of whom were voluntary immigrants to this country, their national identity should take priority over their ethnic identity if ever a divided loyalty becomes a serious political matter.

In his second administration President Bill Clinton made progress in improving ethnoracial relations the centerpiece of his domestic agenda. During his State of the Union address on February 9, 1997, Clinton declared: "We must never believe that diversity is a weakness—it is our greatest strength." Yet less than six months later, on June 14, 1997, the President implicitly recognized that "our greatest strength" also contained serious problems as he called for an "honest dialogue" about race in the country. Both the *New York Times* and the *Washington Post* criticized Clinton for being vague on specifics, long on good intentions. Haven't we been talking about this issue for generations, they asked? Are we any closer to agreement today on these complex and vexing questions than we were in the 1960s when Presidents Kennedy and Johnson launched a renewed national debate?

The focus of Clinton's remarks had to do with domestic relations, in education and jobs especially. But his words could be applied equally well to international relations in a manner that transcends his own presidency:

> Can we be one America, respecting, even celebrating our differences, but embracing even more what we have in common? Can we define what it means to be an American, not just in terms of the hyphens showing our ethnic origins, but in terms of our primary allegiance to the values America stands for?

Trying to answer this question with respect to ethnic involvement in the making of American foreign policy is the purpose of this book.

Multiculturalism and U.S. Foreign Policy

All over the world, people are being torn asunder by racial, ethnic, and religious conflicts that fuel fanaticism and terrors. We are the world's most diverse democracy. And the world looks to us to show that it is possible to live and advance together across those kinds of differences.

America has always been a nation of immigrants . . . We started as an experiment in democracy fueled by Europeans. We have grown into an experiment in democratic diversity fueled by openness and promise . . . We must never believe that diversity is a weakness—it is our greatest strength.

—President Bill Clinton

TODAY, THE MOST contentious issue fueling debates about the rights and obligations of citizens in democracies has to do with the call of what are usually referred to as social identity groups—ethnic and racial groups in particular but also those based on religion or gender—to have collective political voice, claims sometimes summed up as "group differentiated citizenship rights." Here is the issue concerning the meaning of citizenship that President Clinton correctly asserts is an unresolved ethical matter of vital daily significance confronting not only America but democracies everywhere. Both from the viewpoint of practical politics and from the perspective of democratic theory, the nature of "multicultural" citizenship (a term virtually synonymous with multiethnicity and to be defined below) is for American policymakers today at the forefront of the political agenda.[1]

To be sure, the most dramatic cases of ethnic demands raising issues of historical and humanitarian importance do not concern the world's democracies. As the momentous collapse of first the Soviet empire, then the Soviet Union itself once again underscored, ethnic solidarity and ethnic hatreds were among the most critical political facts of the twentieth century. Ethnicity was an important part of the dynamic of both world wars and of decolonization, as well as of the collapse of Soviet communism. The ethnic murders in the former Yugoslavia (Bosnia and Kosovo especially) and several parts of Africa (most notably Rwanda and Burundi) are unsurpassed in recent times. They immediately recall the Jewish Holocaust and the Armenian genocide, the most tragic examples of race murder in the twentieth century.[2]

Yet despite winning the wars against fascism and communism, the democratic world has no clear answer either to many of the difficult questions raised by multicultural citizenship. India remains plagued by problems of ethnic violence and separatist movements. No one is sure what will happen due to ethnic tensions in South Africa with Nelson Mandela not in power. As if Israel's antagonism with the Muslim world were not enough, now cultural differences suggestive of ethnic cleavages within Judaism are seriously straining politics there. So, too, as democratic transitions gain strength in Latin America, long-suppressed racial issues concerning African and indigenous populations quickly become matters of passionate political debate.

Even in prosperous and consolidated democracies like Canada and Belgium, ethnic cleavages threaten national partition. Or again, the many millions of migrants from North Africa and Turkey entering Germany and France, from the Caribbean and South Asia entering Great Britain, and from Southeast Asia, Mexico, the Caribbean, and Central America entering the United States create issues that are new and volatile in all these countries. In short, while democracies have shown themselves to be considerably better than totalitarian or authoritarian orders at handling internal ethnoracial differences, they nonetheless confront serious long-term problems that cannot be avoided. The very dynamic of democratic citizenship that empowers all elements of the population—the right to freedom of speech, assembly, and election—has now brought these problems to the fore. It may be true that to date democracy's strengths have blunted the edge of ethnic hatred, but do the democracies know how to overcome their internal divisions, how, indeed, to empower themselves in the process? It is prudent to be modest in reply.

The Question of Definitions

Given the conflicts over the definition of "multiculturalism," we need to look more closely at other terms basic to its meaning. I propose to define *ethnicity* as a voluntary organization of people with a collective identity based on an intellectually formulated and emotionally felt assertion of their distinctiveness from other peoples. Such a sense of togetherness is typically expressed in an account of a people's common history, their common culture (a variable mix of language, symbols and ceremonies, religious beliefs, and family practices), and their common destiny—all felt with enough intensity to give this community the unity and purpose to seek to be politically represented for the sake of demands specific to their group identity at the level of the state. The cultural component of ethnicity allows us in common usage to treat the terms *multiculturalism* and *multiethnicity* as synonyms.

A sense of ethnic identity or consciousness is not identical with the related term *nationalism*, although the two are related and often conflated. I thus propose to define *nationalism* as a politically more demanding variant of ethnic consciousness, one that calls for the existence of a state on a designated territory to give sovereign political form to the collective life of an ethnically described people.

A country like the United States is thus *multiethnic* or *multiracial* but not *multinational*, because the various peoples composing it find their major political concerns satisfied by the existing social contract and are willing to coexist with other ethnicities under a common state. A multiethnic people moves in the direction of multinationality when various ethnicities begin to ask for their own states—as Quebec separatists have proposed in Canada, or as the Slovaks claimed when they set themselves up independently from the Czechs, or as occurred when the Soviet Union and Yugoslavia disintegrated. By contrast, American ethnic groups may properly be called nationalist only in their demands abroad, as when they agitated for statehood for Ireland, Poland, the countries of colonial Africa, or Israel in the past century.

The term *race*, like the term *gender*, adds to the notion of ethnicity a common physical similarity. Given the greater intensity of issues concerning African, Native American, Hispanic, and Asian populations in multiethnic politics and normative discourse today in the United

States, there is a meaningful distinction to be made between race and ethnicity. Hence the necessity of the term *ethnoracial*. Similarly, given the critical role religion often plays in ethnic group culture and political solidarity—as with the African, Armenian, Greek, Mexican, Irish, Jewish, and Polish American communities particularly—the term *ethnoreligious* is also useful. Theologies are the founts of unique symbols, values, and ceremonies surrounding individual and group identity, making the association of strong feelings of ethnicity and religion understandably close for many.

It stands to reason, given these considerations, that when an ethnic group can also be distinguished by a racial or religious distinctiveness (or by both), it is likely to demonstrate a greater sense of its separation from the rest of society and correspondingly a higher degree of political solidarity. Degrees of intensity in ethnic group feeling must therefore be appreciated. For example, the term "Euro American," while sometimes useful, is far less socially and politically meaningful than the term "African American."

In three circumstances especially, the term *ethnic* may remain confusing. First, the distinction between ethnic and national identity allows us to appreciate that many Americans may feel little or no ethnic identification although they identify closely with their national designation as Americans. In the process of writing this book, I was surprised at how often people who think of themselves ethnically, and particularly ethnoracially, have difficulty accepting the idea that some of their fellow citizens are altogether lacking in such a sense of roots, thinking of themselves instead as Americans, pure and simple. While this sense of national, not ethnic, identity may be more likely among Euro Americans, its existence reflects not so much the power these people possess to speak in a nationalist voice which disguises ethnic biases (as their critics often allege, mistakenly imputing to "whiteness" an ethnic meaning) as quite simply the absence of an ethnic identity in the terms used to define it above.

People without a strong ethnic identity may not have a family history of political struggles different from those of the United States as a nation, they may not belong to a distinct religious tradition that overlaps with an exclusive set of cultural practices, they may not find that their racial or linguistic identifying marks give them a particularistic sense of self. Thus, in the domestic American context, their identity is national, not ethnic: they have assimilated; the proverbial melting pot has had its effect.

Despite the attacks by many multiculturalists on what they sometimes call the myth of the melting pot and the coercive aspects of assimilation, there are in fact many Americans who are more aware of their national, class, or religious identities than they are of what it means to be an ethnic. As Seymour Martin Lipset reports, polls of positive associations of the American public with a national identity show a higher level of patriotism in the United States on most questions than in other comparable countries. Or consider as another index that children of racially mixed marriages numbered 500,000 in 1970, but 2 million in 1990 and 3 million by 1998. Given that the 1990 census figures show a marked increase in interracial marriages over the last forty years (and especially in two bellwethers: in the military and in California), the dulling of ethnoracial feelings may be proceeding apace, despite the efforts of some multiculturalists to promote a sense of self and a form of group loyalty apart from associations that are national.[3]

A second and related way the term *ethnic* can be confusing occurs when it obscures more than it reveals about a people's internal political cleavages, suggesting a monolithic, static entity never subject to change. For example, black Americans may differ widely among themselves in terms of basic questions of identity. Those of West Indian origin may feel very differently from those whose ancestry for generations back is in the United States. Yet as the closing of ranks to demand U.S. action to reverse the military coup against Jean-Baptiste Aristide in Haiti in 1991 illustrates, these contrasts, which at times may make these two groups seem so distinct that they might be considered different ethnicities, are better understood as intra-ethnic differences. Similarly, Jewish Americans differ markedly among themselves, such that one may sometimes wonder if it is meaningful to classify, for example, secular and Orthodox Jews as belonging to the same political world. The point is that while the term *ethnic* is a useful designation, allowing us to categorize groups that are politically active in terms of like characteristics, ethnics themselves are seldom as homogeneous as the term may suggest.

A third and final way the term *ethnic* can be confusing is when it is juxtaposed to the term *nation*. As I suggested above, the terms *ethnic* and *nationalist* relate to the formulation of individual and group political identities based on a sense of common history, culture, and future purpose, the difference between the two lying in the demand by those who are nationalists to live together under a sovereign state. But ethnic and national identities can clash, especially when ethnic kinfolk abroad make demands, or find themselves in circumstances, that rally ethnic groups in the United States in a way the greater national community may be slow to endorse or may actually oppose. The result can be conflicted loyalties, a situation ethnic activists are almost sure to dispute by claiming that what is good for their kinfolk abroad is good for America as a whole.

I refer to *conflicted* rather than *divided* loyalties because the latter term summons up painful historical memories. For example, Japanese Americans were falsely accused of divided loyalties during World War II and interned on the West Coast as a result. The concept of divided loyalties is one that understandably might make them nervous. Or again, American communists (and by extension leftists in general) were accused of divided loyalties, especially during the early 1950s when Senator Joseph McCarthy conducted a witch hunt in Washington that raised nationalist fears by exaggerating the degree of communist penetration in Washington.

By using the term *conflicted* rather than *divided* loyalties, we avoid impugning the patriotism of those who have a strong sense of ethnic identity and we can perceive more readily the similarity between conflicted ethnic allegiances and those of business, religious, or other citizen action groups. When charges are made, for example, that corporations are conflicted in their loyalties between seeking profits and doing what is arguably better for the greater community (charges that they are exporting jobs, evading tax or environmental regulations by activities abroad, or selling technology to countries potentially hostile to the United States), we should understand that only in times of war can the question of patriotism legitimately be raised. Religious or human rights activists may also have loyalties that at times put them into conflict with what many other Americans believe is best for the nation without the question of their right to advocate their values in foreign affairs being doubted. In all of these circumstances, we accept a division of interests and values as part of what it means to live in a pluralist society and so deal with contradictions as best we can, and first of all by avoiding inflated rhetoric.

Multiethnicity and World Affairs

Today, the problem of achieving multiethnic harmony within a single state is everywhere a complicated affair. Hence it would be parochial to see the question of multicultural rights and obligations in America strictly in terms of the character of this nation's founding. To be sure, coming to this country as slaves or as immigrants, members of many of the various groups that peopled the United States found in ethnic kinfolk structures systems of mutual support in an America that was often discriminatory and always difficult. Indeed, the argument is commonly made that American ethnicity is in many respects a domestic invention, a response to a specifically American experience that creates a different kind of group membership and identity—one might almost say a different kind of ethnicity—from that which existed prior to arrival in this country. Yet it has also been remarked that the study of American foreign policy is often ethnocentric: that it is standard to look at the dynamics of America's behavior in the world from the "inside out," from an America-centric point of view as if no other forces were at work.[4] We may thus understand this country better if we take a moment to see matters from the "outside in," for from such a perspective we will recognize that issues of ethnic identity have a wider and longer pedigree than we might realize if we took, for example, the rise in ethnic group consciousness that began in the 1960s as our base of departure, or even if we returned to the times of the Founding Fathers.

Let us then recall the rise of modern, mass-based political participation in the eighteenth century, seeing in global forces the birth of many popular forces, one of which we today call multiethnicity. As we have seen, the core concept of nationalism is that a "people" created by a common history and culture that can be identified ideologically have the right to a sovereign state with authority over a specific territory. Ethnicity is similarly an ideological construct of a distinct people's shared history and culture, virtually identical to nationalism except for the important difference that it stops short of nationalism's demand for a separate state.

Defining *ethnicity* and *nationalism* in ways that make them related if distinct terms allows us to see the question of ethnicity, which is often thought of predominantly as a matter of domestic politics, as linked to the question of nationalism, a subject more obviously central to world affairs. By underscoring the linkage, we may perceive more clearly that many of the current issues related to American multiethnicity did not arise overnight in this country alone, but bear a direct relationship to one of the great subjects of global history over the last two hundred years: the rise of mass participation in the political process.[5]

The American and French revolutions were thus nationalist in origin (though they had related dynamics such as those based on class interest as well), and their success gave rise to a host of imitators. In the nineteenth century, nationalist passions and thinking related to themes of ethnic notions of cultural and historical distinctiveness brought about Latin American independence from Spain and Portugal, the "springtime of nations" associated with a crisis of German and Austro-Hungarian imperial orders in 1848, the unification movements in Italy and Germany, the efforts to modernize defensively the governments of Japan, Turkey, Russia, and China in reaction to the onslaught of the Western world, and the birth of Zionism. In the twentieth century—the "people's century"—nationalism spurred on both world wars, the Arab Awakening, the decolonization of European empires in Africa and Asia, the Mexican, Chinese, Cuban, and Iranian Revolutions, and the collapse of the Soviet empire and the Soviet Union itself.[6]

These nationalist demands of the past 225 years engendered what can be called with no exaggeration "a crisis of political modernism," for they spelled nothing less than the eventual end of the millennia-old authoritarian and imperial state. With its appeal for popular sovereignty reflecting an upsurge of mass political participation, nationalism spawned debates over new forms of citizenship—including the place of ethnic minorities—new ways of organizing the state, and new kinds of political legitimacy.

But if nationalism over these years has been a solvent of authoritarian and imperial political orders, it has been far less good at specifying how the modern state should be constructed and how it should relate to the international community. In these circumstances, the task of the twentieth century would be that of substituting a new form of relationship between the state and society, an undertaking that necessarily involved governments basing their control of the population on political parties, complete with new symbols and ideologies of political legitimacy based on wholly new ideas of civil society and basic human rights for the individual.

Unavoidably, therefore, the twentieth century was destined to be highly charged ideologically. Many variants of modern government capable of responding to nationalist demands were proposed, but only three universal blueprints emerged: liberal democracy, communism, and fascism. (While "modern" in the sense of meeting the nationalist demands laid out above, both the Mexican Revolution, which ended in 1917, and the Iranian Revolution, which ended in 1979, had no more than national significance so far as proposing a new form of government was concerned.)

In time, these three ideologies came into conflict, each bidding to be the blueprint that would organize the politics of twentieth-century nationalism. Each proposed new institutions of government, new forms of state legitimacy, and new bases for citizenship. All of these processes involved nation building in multiethnic environments, which came to mean very different ways of constructing ideologies of national unity.

Of course there were differences within each of these three ideologies: fascism in Germany and Italy differed markedly, just as did democracy in Britain and the United States or communism in the Soviet Union and China. But the family resemblances within each ideological camp were so unmistakable, while the differences among the camps were so pronounced, that there should be no difficulty recognizing the profound distinctions among them. Because adherents of these three ideologies could be found in every industrial state, and because these adherents came to dominate the governments of rival major powers, the crisis of modernism—related as it was to issues of ethnicity and nationalism—contributed directly to both world wars, to decolonization and the Cold War, and to many civil conflicts that never reached the international arena.

Yet whatever the important differences among them, neither fascism, communism, nor liberal democracy had a compelling answer as to how to deal with history's legacy of ethnic privilege or victimization and the deeply felt personal and group antagonisms that the past bequeathed to the present. Fascism's solution—the politically enforced superiority of some ethnic groups defined in racial terms, the subordination of others, and the physical elimination of still more—ended in 1945, even if disturbing variants of its theme emerge from time to time in different parts of the world. So far as liberal democracy was concerned, the struggle against fascism heightened as never before an

awareness of the evil of ethnic stereotyping and of the need for a just
and free political order to recognize the essential dignity of all peoples.

For its part, communism had traditionally denounced racism as a
maneuver of the ruling class to divide the weak, and it had mocked nationalism (and by extension multiculturalism) as a form of bourgeois
class consciousness destined to disappear under the dictatorship of the
proletariat. But in taking power in 1917, Lenin cleverly exploited the
nationalities question to gain support for the Bolsheviks in Russia immediately after the Revolution and to encourage allies for the country
in foreign affairs thereafter by firmly embracing the slogans of national
self-determination. Nevertheless, Lenin in power found himself atop a
multiethnic empire whose differences had to be recognized. His solution was to promote a degree of local autonomy kept soundly in place
under an authority ruling through a communist party that was highly
centralized and at its higher levels overwhelmingly Russian.[7]

With the end of the Cold War, small wonder that this Rube Goldberg construction quickly collapsed. As the reforms launched by
Mikhail Gorbachev gained momentum, the Soviet Union not only
proved unable to maintain its multiethnic empire against powerful nationalist forces within it, but its own internal multiethnic composition
turned in a nationalist direction as well, leading to the breakup of the
country in 1991. The irony is apparent: in specifically discounting ethnicity and nationalism as political forces in favor of class interests as the
principal dynamic of history, Soviet rule was undone by its own ideological blindness.

Yet despite the collapse of communism and fascism as compelling
ideologies of state power, liberal democracy remains bedeviled by the
ethnic question. In theory at least, democracy is unlike fascism in that it
rejects ethnoracial hierarchy; unlike communism, it recognizes that
ethnic differences are a reality with political strength that cannot be reduced to class interests. That said, the most powerful currents of the
liberal democratic tradition in the twentieth century tended before the
1960s to resist the incorporation of groups based on ethnic identity
into the political arena. Rather than viewing ethnics as similar to economic actors with a right to political voice, democratic politics viewed
the matter of ethnicity as rather like religion, a private matter that
should not be explicitly politicized. The implication was that national
identity superseded ethnic identity, as if democratic membership in the

nation gave individuals adequate cultural and historical bearings for political loyalty in the public arena without the need to politicize more parochial attachments like religion and ethnicity.

But because not all ethnicities were equal—because some felt themselves to have been marginalized, indeed victimized by other ethnics—the fiction that depoliticized ethnicity could not long sustain itself in the second half of the twentieth century. Democracies have tried to deal with deep-set civic differences by allowing these groups to share power through federalist practices (most notably in India), or through consociational arrangements (as in Switzerland), or through proportional representation (as in Israel). Where these methods have failed, democracies have even offered to partition themselves, allowing the creation of new states (as in the division of Czechoslovakia). In the United States, the Civil Rights Movement eventually resulted in other democratic innovations such as affirmative action or work set-asides combined with educational reforms designed to enhance ethnic awareness. What all of these measures (many of them novel in democratic life although consistent with its basic logic) have in common is the empowerment of ethnic groups politically in ways that respect their rights yet (with the obvious exception of partition) try to maintain national unity as well.

Democracies have, then, come up with serious answers over the last thirty years to the taxing question of ethnic coexistence. Indeed, we should be careful not to exaggerate the strength of the ethnic challenge to national unity. Many Americans have weak ethnic identities. Many more privilege their national (or class or religious) loyalties over attachments to their ethnic origins. Many who have a strong sense of ethnoracial allegiance nonetheless feel that this commitment is in no way incompatible with an equally strong sense of American patriotism.

A sense of common citizenship in the United States today arises from a variety of sources: from a widely shared appreciation of national political values and institutions with their demonstrated capacity to handle the demands of the people and to provide a high standard of living for the great bulk of the population; from the strength of religious interfaith dialogues; from the wide appeal of interethnic artistic accomplishments and sports teams; and from the lack of a strong sense of class differences as well as a general acceptance of diverse lifestyles. There is a robust sense of American national identity—allegiance

to what Gunnar Myrdal called the "American Creed"—that I expect
should prove resistant to being torn apart by multicultural demands,
many of which should in any case contribute to making the country
even more inclusive and hence stronger in its unity than it already is.[8]

In attempts to arrive at a balance in democratic life between ethnic
rights and obligations, one thing is clear: the wholesale depoliticization
of ethnicity is no longer possible, particularly in the United States. The
immigrant experience has created solidarity groupings of mutual assistance that for generations have had basic and explicit political consequences at the state and local levels especially. The black experience
even more profoundly has marked American politics. The end of the
Cold War has weakened the American state relative to the society so
that in many domains interest groups are gaining in strength. And conflicts in the world outside have repeatedly reminded many American
ethnics of their transnational identities, their multiple loyalties as "peoples." The primary question of democratic citizenship for today is that
of multiculturalism: What rights and obligations should individuals in
subnational ethnic groups possess as citizens of a liberal democracy?

The Right to Voice in American Democracy

The promise of democratic government is to establish political freedom by empowering the citizenry, allowing them to control their state
by the free exercise of their rights of assembly, speech, and the election
of public officials who will determine the law and enforce it subject to
the consent of the governed. The structure of political institutions var-
ies rather widely among the world democracies, but in all of them leaders govern through representative institutions with power delegated to
them by the citizenry, which retains sovereignty through these freedoms of speech, assembly, and election.

Who, then, is a citizen and what are his or her rights? The history of
democracy is the story of the progressive evolution of that term, where
in the American case, for example, race, economic status, religion, gender, and ethnicity (sometimes as overlapping categories) have all been
grounds at one time or another for arguments against extending the
franchise and hence full citizenship. At the very beginning of this nation's existence, John Jay may have declared in *Federalist* 2 that "Provi-
dence has been pleased to give this one connected country to one

united people, a people descended from the same ancestors, speaking the same language, professing the same religion, attached to the same principles of government, very similar in their manners and customs." But the reality was that the Founding Fathers determined that black slaves—close to 20 percent of the total population at the time—were not citizens, in the process beginning the country's longest and most serious debate over the meaning of democratic citizenship.

The debate was not limited to questions of race. Even among white Protestants, immigration could raise questions that in effect were those of multiethnicity and what it meant to be an American. Thus the same Benjamin Franklin who authored the confident national motto *e pluribus unum*—out of many, one—wondered whether Germans should not be kept out of Pennsylvania, where their numbers were fast increasing: "Why should Pennsylvania, founded by the English, become a colony of *Aliens*, who will shortly be so numerous as to Germanize us instead of our Anglifying them? . . . [They] will never adopt our language or customs, any more than they can acquire our complexion."[9] So too, Thomas Jefferson was concerned about the noxious affect that immigrants to this country from absolutist European monarchies might have on a people whose government presupposed a culture composed "of the freest principles of the English constitution, with others derived from natural right and natural reason":

> To these nothing can be more opposed than the maxims of absolute monarchies. Yet from such, we are to expect the greatest number of emigrants. They will bring with them the principles of the governments they leave, imbibed in their early youth; or, if able to throw them off, it will be in exchange for an unbounded licentiousness, passing, as is usual, from one extreme to another. It would be a miracle were they to stop precisely at the point of temperate liberty. These principles, with their language, they will transmit to their children. In proportion to their numbers, they will share with us the legislation. They will infuse into it their spirit, warp and bias its direction, and render it a heterogeneous, incoherent, distracted mass.[10]

Misgivings over the impact of ethnic factions on the young nation's foreign policy similarly led George Washington to be concerned about a tide of immigration that might disrupt the sense of national identity. "I want an *American* character, that the powers of Europe may be convinced we act for *ourselves* and not for others," he declared to Patrick Henry. As he put it in a May 1796 draft of his Farewell Address (given that September) stating the "most ardent wishes of my heart," Washington asked:

> That every citizen would take pride in the name of an American, and act as if he felt the importance of the character by considering that we ourselves are now a distinct nation the dignity of which will be absorbed, if not annihilated, if we enlist ourselves . . . under the banners of any other nation whatsoever. And moreover that we should guard against the Intrigues of any and every foreign Nation who shall endeavor to intermingle (however covertly and indiscreetly) in the internal concerns of our country—or shall attempt to prescribe rules for our policy with any other power . . . as one of the greatest evils that can befall us as a people.[11]

As these lines from Franklin, Jefferson, and Washington indicate, the Founders were alert to the dangers for the system they were creating of the social divisions a democratic political order not only permitted but actually encouraged. What of national unity and strength? How could such a people survive in a world of hostile, authoritarian powers? Yet if democracy means popular self-government, then how could the divisions of the people not be reflected politically?

The most famous answer at the time came from James Madison in *Federalist* 10, warning that the problem of what he called "factions" would never cease to bedevil the life of a democracy. How, then, would the perils of pluralism be best managed?

> There are two methods of removing the causes of faction: the one, by destroying the liberty which is essential to its existence; the other, by giving to every citizen the same opinions, the same passions, and the same interests. It could never be more truly said than of the first remedy that it was worse than the disease. Liberty is to faction what air is to fire, an aliment without which it instantly expires. But it could not be a less folly to abolish liberty, which is essential to political life, because it nourishes faction than

it would be to wish the annihilation of air . . . because it imparts to fire its destructive agency.

The second expedient is as impracticable as the first would be unwise. As long as the reason of man continues fallible and he is at liberty to exercise it, different opinions will be formed . . . The latent causes of faction are thus sown in the nature of man.

To control for the inevitable existence of factions and the danger that they might breed either the tyranny of the majority or the tyranny of a minority, Madison proposed representative government, in which wiser minds could deliberate popular passions; a federal system that would decentralize social interests and so minimize their presence at the center; and an expanded democracy that would multiply interests, setting them against one another in a cross-checking way that could finally produce the best outcome. The tenor of Madison's remarks is the heart of the matter: to avoid the power of factions that might either tear a people apart or else subordinate the interests of the whole to those of the few, openness and vigilance are called for combined in a system of government that commands the general allegiance. But no solution could be perfect. The effort to achieve social justice with unity and political freedom with strength will be the never-ending struggle of liberal, pluralist democracy, its irresolvable tension.

Within a decade of Jefferson's death, the question of how to ensure national unity despite social division surfaced anew with the argument that Catholic immigrants, though white and Christian, were culturally too foreign to be permitted to become citizens. John Higham has recounted how, from about 1830 to 1860, American "nativism" was equivalent to anti-Catholicism. In 1790 only 35,000 Americans were Catholic, but by 1860 they numbered some 3.1 million and were the largest religious denomination in the country. Alleging the subordination of this population to an authoritarian clergy and the Pope, and distrusting a Catholic concern for the separate education of their children, Protestant fundamentalists launched a mighty evangelical revival to ward off what they perceived as the Catholic menace to American democracy.[12] It was also in the 1840s that persecution of Mormons reached its peak, resulting in their migration to Utah beginning in 1846.

By the late 1850s what today would be called multicultural differences over religion were replaced by even greater multicultural sectional tensions and the debate over the abolition of slavery. While the first issue was resolved by the Civil War, Reconstruction ultimately failed to establish the rights in practice of the freedmen despite the Fourteenth and Fifteenth Amendments to the Constitution. Under the Jim Crow laws passed after 1890, blacks were excluded from power. In Louisiana in 1904, for example, only 1,342 blacks were registered to vote, although they constituted some 660,000 (47 percent) of the state's population of 1.4 million. Still today, the greatest questions of multiculturalism remain those concerning race in America.

In colonial America, property qualifications restricted the right to vote of those who were propertyless. But with the Revolution, restrictions based on property and religion were virtually everywhere abolished (although Rhode Island was a holdout favoring property restrictions until the 1840s). As a result, a principal reason the U.S. labor movement did not become bound up in a struggle over citizenship is that the coming of universal male suffrage in this country handily predated the growth of the working class as a major actor in American social and economic life. Nevertheless, what well may be called working-class citizenship rights had to be established, and labor conflicts with capital exceeded in duration and bloodiness those of any other industrial nation in the period from the 1880s through the 1930s. Ultimately the organization of the unions into national confederations, and the involvement of the government in national labor relations, took much of the edge off the conflict with capital. But as the continued polarization of wealth and globalization of capital indicate, class differences remain very much alive in America today.

Greatly increased immigration from Southern and Eastern Europe after 1879 (still more marked after 1903), and the growing involvement of the United States in world affairs beginning with the Spanish-American War in 1898, brought up yet a new kind of ethnic issue, popularized as "hyphenation" by Theodore Roosevelt (who deplored such people) in 1895 and gaining general currency by World War I. The concern now principally was the division between those Americans of German, Scandinavian, and Irish descent—the first favoring Germany in European quarrels, the Irish hating all that was British, and the Scandinavians, like American Jews, opposed to Russia—and those of Anglo stock in combination with most immigrants from Eastern Europe, who favored a continued American tie with Great Britain. Neither the immigration law of 1924, which severely limited access to this country to peoples not already well represented here, nor America's victory in the war settled the national debate, however, and ethnicity continued to have a marked electoral impact, in the Midwest especially, during the interwar period.[13]

Immigration has reemerged as a divisive political issue today, when the United States is experiencing the largest immigration wave in its history, one which is likely to make some 20 percent of the country of Mexican ancestry by the year 2050. In many of its particulars the current debate is unique, but its general content reflects once again the question of what it means to be an American in terms of the social contract involving the rights and responsibilities of American citizenship.[14]

Race, religion, and economic position were not the only deeply felt differences democracy had to compose. Efforts to enfranchise women began in the nineteenth century, with the formation of the New England Woman Suffrage Association in 1868 and the rival National Woman Suffrage Association in 1869—and their eventual merger in 1890. Thirty years later, in 1920, the Nineteenth Amendment to the Constitution became law, granting universal suffrage to women. Yet the struggle to define the citizenship rights of women continues today, for there are unsettled questions as to the kinds of jobs and the treatment on them that continue to be widely debated as basic gender concerns.

During Wilson's presidency and that of Theodore Roosevelt before him, issues of class division were addressed more frankly than at any earlier time in American history. Wilson was in office when women gained the vote (although he had not supported the measure). And he was the first American president to see the importance of nationalism as a global political force.

Yet although Wilson recognized the power of nationalism and sought to tame it through democratic institutions, his blueprint for domestic life never satisfactorily addressed the problems of multiethnic life for peoples who could not live under governments that reflected their own nationalist aspirations. To be sure, in thinking about conditions in Eastern Europe after World War I, Wilson asked that national minorities be permitted cultural freedoms and the right to organize freely and to participate in politics democratically. But as the first president from the South since the Civil War (he was nine years old when that War ended), as a leader who had had to strive mightily to take his country into war against the pull of Irish, German, and Scandinavian American organizations that bitterly opposed him, Wilson clearly lacked all the answers.

More to the point of our concerns, Wilson never frankly confronted the reality of the United States as a multiethnic nation. When it was in his interest, Wilson cultivated the support of Polish, Czech, Slovak, or Jewish Americans on the basis of their ethnic interests, but he insisted that the Irish, German, and Scandinavian Americans who opposed him should drop their ethnic consciousness. As he put it rather courageously on May 14, 1914, to a largely Irish American audience that he knew would disagree with him:

> And the test for all of us—for all of us had our origins on the other side of the sea—is whether we will assist in enabling America to live her separate and independent life, retaining our ancient affections, indeed, but determining everything we do by the interests that exist on this side of the sea. Some Americans need hyphens in their names, because only part of them has come over; but when the whole man has come over, heart and thought and all, the hyphen drops of its own weight out of his name.[15]

Even more critically, Wilson was a segregationist. The apostle of national self-determination for others, he was notably unable to address the problems of multiethnicity at home. The paradox of Wilsonianism, then, was that while it recognized the power of nationalism internationally it made little attempt to answer the question of how to organize democracies internally in terms of their multiethnic groupings.

Wilson's failings were not remedied by his presidential successors during the interwar years. Instead of dealing forthrightly with its multiethnic character, the United States continued to discriminate against blacks, drastically curbed immigration, and accelerated its efforts at "Americanizing" those newcomers, from Eastern and Southern Europe especially, deemed in need of rapid assimilation. Articulate protests might be heard from certain Jews, blacks, partisans of separate education for Catholic youth, or the likes of John Dewey—voices resisting the ideology of the melting pot by pointing to the integrity of minority cultures, the cruelty and futility of assimilationist tactics, and the value of diversity as an aspect of the national identity. But these were voices before their time, whose statements are more widely studied today than in those years.[16]

Still, the most direct pre–World War II ancestors of today's argument in favor of multiculturalism come from the period around World War I and the legitimacy then given to ethnic diversity in democratic theory by the use of the concept of "pluralism." Shocked by the nationalist excesses of the war, American social scientists began work on ethnic studies that was eventually to contribute to ending efforts to "Americanize" the population in a way that meant denying the value and importance of ethnic difference. John Higham has traced the intellectual roots of these dedicated academics to the teachings of William James at the end of the nineteenth century and his impact especially on two of the most articulate voices talking about "cultural pluralism" before 1918, the black American leader W. E. B. Du Bois and the American Zionist (who coined the term) Horace Kallen. By 1944 these various efforts had established a receptive intellectual climate for what was arguably the single most influential work on American multiethnicity, a massive project on African Americans headed by a Swedish social scientist, Gunnar Myrdal's *An American Dilemma.*

Race, ethnicity, religion, class, gender: all of these categories have had to struggle to be recognized as social groupings having political weight in U.S. history, and the terms under which each has its rights and obligations defined continue to be debated today, as they will so long as democratic government exists. Here are the origins of today's struggle over multiculturalism, a history that shows that struggle for the recognition of group rights based on cultural distinctiveness, which in practice means the political organization of ethnic and ethnoracial communities, has a distinguished provenance in the American democratic discourse.

Multicultural Citizenship Today

Despite the abundant evidence that multiculturalism is a logical extension of the history of the American democratic experience and the normative arguments in favor of social pluralism, many of its most salient features are relatively new, dating from the 1960s. While Nathan

Glazer reports that the term itself did not appear on his Nexis search before 1989 (when it had only 33 entries, rising to 1,500 in 1994), he is right to point to the Civil Rights Movement of the 1960s as the most important single antecedent of today's debate.[17] Although affirmative action and discussions of political redistricting obviously grow out of this group's concern, it was demands of many women that equivalent considerations apply to them (underrepresented as they were in the workplace and political office), the immigration reform legislation of 1965 (the Hart-Celler Act), Jewish American reaction to the 1967 War in the Middle East, and demands by homosexual groups that broadened the movement. In short, *multiculturalism* is at once a term that relates to the long history of debates over the meaning of citizenship in the United States and a notion whose contemporary meaning has been with us scarcely a single generation.

Exactly what it means to be a multiculturalist today obviously remains open to divergent definitions. At one end of the spectrum are those who treat ethnic organizations much as religious organizations are treated—as self-organized groups operating with their own resources outside the public sphere under a presumption that the state will not interfere with them, nor they with the state, except under the most extreme circumstances. I term such people "soft multiculturalists," for while they acknowledge the rights of citizens to organize themselves on whatever grounds they see fit, while they put a high value on tolerance and the benefit of diversity in civil society, and while they appreciate the particular historical imperatives that have led ethnic and ethnoracial groups to organize politically, they are reluctant to see these groups empowered by direct government action, preferring instead to draw an analogy between the position of religion in American public life and ethnicity. For them, the national motto *e pluribus unum*—out of many, one—stands unchallenged.

At the other end of the spectrum are those we might call "hard multiculturalists," those who make demands on government so as to increase the presence of ethnoracials hitherto discriminated against in education, the workplace, and political life. Given their frequent opposition to efforts to insist on the psychological or ethical priority of national over ethnic allegiances, they might be understood as adopting for their motto *ex uno plures*—out of one, many. Perhaps we can better say that whereas the soft multiculturalist emphasizes the *unum*, the hard multiculturalist champions the *pluribus*, in a contest of genuine importance to the meaning of citizenship in America.

Yet what is common today is not to point out the diversity among multiculturalists but instead to lump them together and contrast them with those who oppose them, who for lack of a better word might be called nationalists, uniculturalists, or assimilationists. Such a reduction is regrettable, at times simplifying history in a way that distorts it, as in the writing of Ernest W. Lefever, who laments that "the American idea and experience are under siege by multicultural advocates, historical revisionists, and outright nihilists whose views have abetted the decline of the American family, public education, and the place of religion in the public square."[18] James Kurth similarly vilifies all multiculturalists: "The multicultural coalition and its feminist core despise the European version of Western civilization, which they see as the work of 'dead white European males.' They also despise the American version of the American Creed, particularly liberalism, constitutionalism, the rule of law and free markets . . . [and have] succeeded in marginalizing Western civilization in its very intellectual core, the universities and media of America."[19]

Can we not improve on this debate? Perhaps no amount of discussion will change minds like Lefever's or Kurth's, but multiculturalists themselves can begin the effort by being more self-critical of the way in which they talk about democratic citizenship. Accordingly, my effort in this book is to stake out some kind of "moderate" middle ground—a more difficult job in the current intellectual environment than it might seem—between the misleading dichotomy often drawn between multiculturalism and assimilation. Such an intermediate position might favor proactive state policies to promote hitherto marginalized ethnoracial communities so as to exchange a policy of exclusion for one of inclusion, but set limits on who is helped and how. Its goal would be to recognize group differentiated citizenship rights because of democratic principle and in order to increase the cohesion of the greater community by reinforcing a sense of national identity. Moderate multiculturalism might therefore be seen as a throwback to early-twentieth-century pluralism, for both see the recognition of distinct ethnic group identities as compatible with, indeed a precondition for, national unity—the one need not deny the other.

An interesting case that adopts the difficult middle ground is Nathan

Glazer's *We Are All Multiculturalists Now* (1997). Glazer is generally recognized as one of the major voices in ethnic studies in the United States, a man who originally (in 1975) called for "benign neglect" of ethnic differences along the lines of the separation of church and state, much the traditional pluralist point of view. He has been critical of affirmative action, for example, as well as developments within ethnic groups (such as Afrocentrism) that he sees as historical misrepresentations that may ultimately prevent our ability to act in a unified way on the basis of shared values and institutions that have contributed much to human freedom and that should continue to be seen as the foundation for a shared American identity. Yet in his most recent work, Glazer reports that despite his continued reservations about many aspects of the multicultural agenda, and his concern that the tradition of national values and institutions be respected, he has concluded not only that ethnic group unity is a deep, perhaps permanent, characteristic of American political life but that certain measures have to be taken by the state for the sake of justice, liberty, and equality (with respect to African Americans particularly) that mean state-sponsored empowerment of identity groups.

For this revision of his former position—what I would term a movement from soft to moderate multiculturalism—Glazer has been attacked by conservatives warning that the Union itself is imperiled by such demands. So Linda Chavez in a review of Glazer's book declares that multiculturalism has the "potential to tear the nation apart," that "in fact, and in practice, multiculturalism has nothing to do with inclusion": "Proponents of the doctrine favor the notion that no single common culture unites all Americans. They argue as well that whites, especially white males of European ancestry, must give up cultural, economic and political dominance, and they are anxious that the surrender commence immediately."[20]

Another well-known conservative critic of multiculturalism is Thomas Sowell, who in reviewing Glazer's book wrote:

> It was precisely when blacks began to be treated as mascots of sympathetic whites—whose "help" included largess, excuses, double standards of performance and behavior, and an undermining of law enforcement—that a major retrogression began in the black community in crime, violence, family disintegration, and moral

squalor in general . . . As for the inevitability of multiculturalism, within living memory, Nazism, Communism, apartheid, colonialism, Jim Crow and numerous other once apparently impregnable evils have all collapsed. Why then are we to believe that multiculturalism is carved in stone and invincible?[21]

Since the eighteenth century, democracy's critics have accused it of fomenting internal divisions that would sap the unity and hence the strength of a people—whether by empowering the poor, women, or religious, racial, geographic, or ethnic difference through a competitive party system that selects the officials to run a government itself divided in its powers and based on the rule of law. Common sense seemed to many to support these critics. Whether in the family, religious associations, the workplace, or the political arena, the cost of empowering fundamental social division seemed self-evident—a challenge to the unity of society and to the strength of the state that could only lead to weakness and possibly even conquest by outsiders less given to ideas of freedom, equality, and fraternity that meant government for, by, and of the people.

But whereas previously democracy's critics invoked society's need for established order based on tradition reinforced by hierarchy, today the critics invoke national unity and strength. Here is the common concern, one that contemporary experience around the globe with the catastrophic consequences of ethnic conflict reveals to have some foundation, be it expressed by Kurth, Lefever, Chavez, or Sowell.

In his widely read book *The Clash of Civilizations and the Remaking of World Order*, Samuel Huntington has made much the same charge on a substantially broader scale. Huntington subsumes the issue of ethnicity under that of civilizations, which become the carriers of culture and history that create individual identities and group solidarity. He then declares that "culture and cultural identities, which at the broadest level are civilization identities, are shaping the patterns of cohesion, disintegration, and conflict in the post-cold war world":

The most important distinctions among peoples . . . are cultural. Peoples and nations are attempting to answer the most basic question humans can face: who are we? And they are answering it by reference to the things that matter most to them. People define themselves in terms of ancestry, religion, language, history, values, customs, and institutions. They identify with cultural groups: tribes, ethnic groups, religious communities, nations, and, at the broadest level, civilizations.[22]

In my opinion, the boundaries Huntington draws between civilizations are too arbitrary (separating Eastern from Western Europe and Latin America from Western civilization are highly debatable decisions, for example), and the significance he attributes to culture relative to other factors motivating the behavior of peoples (from a concern for survival to an urge to dominate) is too strong. Nevertheless, Huntington recognizes through his discussion of culture that nationalism and ethnicity are primary forces locally and globally.

More specifically for our purposes, however, Huntington sees Western civilization essentially from a unicultural perspective that emphasizes the difficulties that arise from its ethnic complexity. Given the seriousness with which he views the coming cultural wars, Huntington emerges as a demanding assimilationist, raising serious doubts as to the wisdom of the current flows of Muslims wanting to emigrate to Western Europe and of Latin Americans wanting to come to the United States, and warning of the possibility that American ethnics acting transnationally may erode our capacity to have an effective foreign policy.[23] Specifying the rights and obligations of democratic cultural pluralism is not a subject he means to address. Yet even if there is a good case for stricter immigration controls and for insisting that ethnic groups place their national obligations over ethnic ones, the real issue for practical politics and moral debates today is how to address the rights and obligations of multiethnic citizenship.

The nationalist critics I have reviewed appear to underestimate the practical and ethical power of multiculturalism and to overestimate the danger to national unity posed by social pluralism. Yet these nationalists are correct to be concerned that the potential for serious social divisiveness is contained in many hard multiculturalist demands. For if multiethnicity is a practical reality whose recognition in some ways is a moral imperative, debate is not ended. If the Devil is in the details, then here is where debate will begin in earnest, and multiculturalism's nationalist critics well may be on firmer ground, for there is nothing at all inevitable about how a package of measures a special interest calls for in any domain of political life will ultimately be treated politically.

Surely the role of ethnics in the formulation of American foreign policy will be open to debate and modification as other ethnoracial demands have been. Consider, for example, the status of many domestic claims: in the school, ethnic insistence on basic curriculum reform in the humanities and social sciences and calls for multilingual education; in the workplace, practices such as affirmative action (including measures to ensure gender equality) and contracting set-asides for minority businesses; in the political arena, the question of electoral redistricting to secure higher ethnoracial representation. As these topics indicate, the power and the legitimacy of ethnic political voices are real, but this reality does not mean that ethnic groups have free rein in formulating public policy, for they may themselves alter their claims as time passes, and their fellow citizens may have good reason to conclude that some of their demands are unacceptable.

Multiculturalism and Foreign Policy

What is it, then, that multiculturalists want from American foreign policy? If they are concerned that members of ethnic minorities are seldom represented at the highest level of government, then surely their concern is valid. To the extent that the making of foreign policy has been the preserve of Euro Americans, the door has to be opened to new talent.

But many multiculturalists say more. They often assert that black, Asian, or Hispanic Americans may have very different agendas for U.S. foreign policy from that which Euro Americans have established as in the national interest. Indeed, they may contest the notion of "the national interest" itself, alleging that it is permeated with ethnoracial considerations that are often not shared by Americans of color.[24]

Unfortunately, we lack data to substantiate the assertion that ethnic minorities are markedly different from their fellow citizens in their outlook on world affairs. To be sure, there is limited evidence that African Americans see foreign affairs differently from their fellow Americans.[25] And Randall Robinson persuasively argues that the black American experience creates strong bonds of solidarity with Africa and the

African diaspora, as well as with issues of human rights and resistance to racism everywhere.[26] Still, in many other cases it may be that political marginalization, rather than ethnic difference, best explains differences in world outlook. To the degree that the United States has objective national interests irrespective of class, ethnic, or gender perception, the integration of hitherto excluded minorities into positions of power should bring a change in the perspective of these ethnic groups more than a change of interpretation as to the meaning of American national interests. In short, the assertion that multiculturalism will entail a radically different U.S. foreign policy is difficult to accept without qualification.

A third claim by multiculturalists is more contentious: that in effect ethnic familiarity through kinfolk ties with certain areas of the world confers on them a special authority to define American foreign policy in those areas. Just as Euro Americans have determined policy in Washington on the basis of ethnic considerations (or so the argument goes), so now other minorities will take their turn using the country's power as they see fit.

The basic objections to ethnic demands for such influence are three: that an interest group is asking the entire country to serve its purpose when the policy it seeks may not serve the common good and indeed may endanger it; that ethnics may sometimes act at the behest of foreign movements or governments whose agendas they place ahead of American interests or Washington's established agenda; and that the religious core to many ethnic cultural groupings means that the essential arguments in favor of the separation of church and state should be seen to apply to ethnic group activism in foreign affairs. In a world where American foreign policy needs to be coherent and consistent and to take serious account of community-wide, national interests in its formulation, the increased legitimacy of ethnic lobbying deserves closer scrutiny. Where better to begin than with the classic warnings about the character of the making of foreign policy in American democracy made by Alexis de Tocqueville in 1831 and repeated by George Kennan in 1977 (both of which I quoted in the Introduction)?

Consider, for example, the concerns of two prominent thinkers on American foreign policy, Samuel Huntington and James Schlesinger. In an article published in 1997, Huntington worried that ethnics place the demands of foreign governments ahead of American considerations so that national interests are subordinated to foreign interests, and like his fellow conservatives he painted a single portrait of all multiculturalists: "They deny the existence of a common culture in the United States, denounce assimilation, and promote the primacy of racial, ethnic, and other subnational cultural identities and groupings."[27] Similarly, Schlesinger wrote in that same year:

> In the past, those who pushed an ethnic agenda were defensive and somewhat sheepish about it. There were lots of explanations and even a touch of an apology. Now, however, such groups are persuaded that they have the right to demand that the power of the United States back their parochial claims. Demands on behalf of particular ethnic agendas have been legitimized. Too many politicians seek legislation to satisfy those demands. Ethnicity has become the norm. To speak of the national interest in the abstract is to invite rebuke.[28]

Whatever the overstatement in Huntington's and Schlesinger's remarks, these nationalist critics of multiculturalism have made important contributions to the contemporary debate over the meaning of citizenship in a democracy with respect to the making of foreign policy. At present many multiculturalists do indeed stress the rights of one's ethnic allegiance over any clear notion of one's obligations to the national community—a subject that they often seem to ignore altogether. Rather than closing their minds to their nationalist critics, multiculturalists might consider examining their own position more critically. In the process they may realize that many of their efforts amount to using their rights as citizens to advance agendas that correspond neither to the wishes nor to the interests of the bulk of the American citizenry.

Who speaks for America? The notion of a unitary government expressing the combined wishes of all Americans consonant with a single conception of the national interest becomes harder to imagine with the end of the Cold War and the weakening of the American state relative to society. Does this mean that interest group lobbies will come to have even more power in the making of foreign policy than they have had in the past, so that they will speak for America? Does it mean that we will increasingly become "one nation divisible"?

One reply is optimistic: If particularistic social forces write the legislation, are matters really much different than they have ever been? And will the general interest really suffer, or may the national community actually benefit from this activism? Others are more pessimistic, concerned that foreign governments will find ways to exploit Washington's power thanks to their domestic kinfolk, making America less the master of its destiny in world affairs and more ungovernable domestically. Or perhaps we would best be stoic, believing that we are simply going through a brief historical period in which the rise of ethnoracial activism in the United States coincides with a moment when this country faces no vital threats to its security from abroad and the power of the state relative to society is in decline. Perhaps as integration and assimilation proceed domestically, and as new external threats to the nation's well-being arise, the ethnic group moment will pass.

For today, the question may not be *whether* we should be multiculturalists but *how* we should be. The imperatives of history, both international and domestic, as well as the logic of the democratic way of life, properly demand that we respect the right to voice of ethnoracial groups in American political life. What must be hoped is that the greater national community will assert the legitimacy of defending its rights and interests, and that ethnic actors will temper their rhetoric and demands as they find their national identity in a community with other Americans in "one nation indivisible." Should this occur, then in this domain of civic life as in so many others the promise of *e pluribus unum* will be reaffirmed.

Three Historical Stages of Ethnic Group Influence

My order is that an Italian citizen must remain an Italian citizen, no matter in what land he lives, even to the seventh generation.
—*Benito Mussolini, 1940*

When we land, we will meet German and Italian soldiers whom it is our honor and privilege to attack and destroy. Many of you have in your veins German and Italian blood, but remember that these ancestors of yours so loved freedom that they gave up home and country to cross the ocean in search of liberty. The ancestors of the people we shall kill lacked the courage to make such a sacrifice and continued as slaves.
—*General George S. Patton on the eve of the landing in Sicily, 1943*

ETHNIC GROUPS have long exerted influence on U.S. foreign policy. The history of that influence in the twentieth century can be divided into three periods. In the first stage, from the 1910s through the 1930s, the most active ethnic groups—German, Scandinavian, and Irish, and later Italian—acted as a drag on American involvement in world affairs. These groups may not have been primarily responsible for U.S. neutralism at the onset of World War I, the failure to enter the League of Nations thereafter, and the isolationism of the 1930s, but they were of more than marginal importance to the positions Washington took on the world stage.

During the Cold War, or stage two, by contrast, virtually all American ethnic groups concerned about foreign policy were internationalists, backing an assertive American effort to stand up to Soviet communism, most often by promoting national self-government abroad. Americans of West European, East European, or Balkan ancestry feared Soviet communism. Jewish Americans supported the creation of Israel. African Americans called for the decolonization of Africa. Later other groups—such as Cuban or Armenian Americans—would be added to the list. In contrast to the first stage, when ethnic and national loyalties could stand in stark contrast, during the Cold War ethnic and national identities tended to coincide. While an exception should be made in this generalization for African Americans, here too, during the Carter years, there was a blending of ethnic activism with policy decisions taken in Washington with regard to America's role in world affairs.

Since the end of the Cold War, we have entered what might be called a third stage, in which ethnic group internationalism has remained pronounced. The creation of new states abroad following the implosion of the Soviet empire and the Soviet Union itself has called forth a sympathetic response among their American kinfolk. Moreover, all ethnic groups are more than ever aware of the extent of American power in world affairs. At the same time, the decline of a sense of clear U.S. national interests since the disintegration of Soviet communism has engendered an erosion of bipartisanship on foreign policy. The lack of consensus on foreign policy priorities, combined with the reassertion of the power of society relative to the state ("the era of big government is over," as President Bill Clinton twice put it in his January 1996 State of the Union address), has facilitated the access of American ethnic lobbies to policymaking in Washington to an unprecedented degree. Today more than ever is the ethnic group moment in the making of American foreign policy.

Of course, ethnic politicking with respect to U.S. foreign policy did not begin in the twentieth century. In this immigrant nation, many constituencies were in close touch with kinfolk abroad, and frequently their concerns had a direct impact on American policy and thereby on world events. In the nineteenth century, the most clear-cut example of an ethnic group's trying to influence American foreign policy involved Irish Americans. In their determined opposition to anything British— especially after the potato famine of 1845–1847, which the Irish charged was a British attempt at genocide—Irish Americans repeatedly sought to involve Washington in conflict with London, hoping thereby to secure Ireland's independence.[1]

Efforts to create a revolutionary movement in Ireland after 1847 were paralleled in the United States (as well as in France, Canada, Australia, and Britain itself, where there were also large numbers of Irish immigrants). A major opportunity came with the Civil War, with some 150,000 Irish Americans mustered into the Union and Confederate armies, often in Irish-only regiments. In addition, some 50,000 Irish came to the United States to fight—some at the suggestion of Northern or Southern officials who wanted their manpower, others because they wanted the training warfare could give them, their idea being to return to Ireland to fight for its independence.

The Irish Revolutionary (later Republican) Brotherhood (or Army, as the IRB called itself briefly) or the Fenians, as they were known in the United States, eventually claimed several hundred thousand members. Their most audacious plan was a project (attempted in 1866 and again in 1870) to challenge Britain through an invasion of Canada from American soil. They hoped that by gaining at least a part of that country the IRB would obtain further international support, or could exchange the territory seized for Irish independence, or perhaps could even provoke war between the United States and Britain (a recurrent hope of this community during the nineteenth century), the eventual outcome of which would be a British retreat from Ireland.

But while the Fenians disappeared shortly after the failure of their second attack on Canada in 1870, their conviction that only armed force could finally persuade the British to leave Ireland could be felt thereafter in the United States through the Clan na Gael (or United Brotherhood) and later in the Irish Republican Army, which until the Good Friday 1998 peace accords traditionally had significant support from a part of the Irish American community (especially the Irish Northern Aid Committee, or NORAID, and the Friends of Sinn Fein). Of course there were moderate Irish American groups as well, who opposed efforts to free Ireland by force (and whose primary leader today is Senator Edward Kennedy). What all of these groups nonetheless shared was an intense sense of their Irishness born of a continued loyalty to the struggle of their kinfolk in the Old Country.

Aside from the extraordinary efforts of the Fenians, nineteenth-century Irish Americans agitated against a wide range of agreements with London, from fishery accords in the Northeast to boundary settlements in the Northwest, from American policy toward the Venezuelan boundary dispute to American neutrality with respect to the Boer War, in the process contributing handily to Grover Cleveland's defeat in the election of 1888.

But in the nineteenth century this example of ethnic group activism was a relatively isolated case. It took a massive wave of European immigration in the late nineteenth and early twentieth centuries and the entry of the United States onto the world stage with the Spanish American War of 1898 for the ethnic factor to become a general aspect of the making of American foreign policy.

Stage I

Between 1900 and 1914 some 13.4 million persons emigrated to the United States, in the greatest wave of newcomers relative to the established population in the country's history. Accordingly, as Europe moved toward war after 1912, ethnic constituencies rather naturally divided, some favoring American involvement in Europe's struggles, others (which were much better organized) calling for a policy of neutrality. Americans of German, Scandinavian, and Irish ancestry tended to favor American neutrality in the war and isolationism thereafter, while those of British, Russian, Polish, Yugoslav, and Czechoslovak descent tended to favor American participation in the war and involvement in world affairs after 1918. (Over 40,000 Greek Americans had fought in the Balkan Wars that immediately preceded World War I. More than 30,000 Polish Americans would later fight under French officers in World War I before America's entry into the struggle in 1917.) The problem of "hyphenation" was therefore acute, as the dual loyalties of many American citizens were under terrible strain, first as the country moved toward war, then as it tried to help organize the peace.[2]

As a result of the efforts of those who either opposed war with Germany (German Americans, who had become significantly more aware of events in Europe since the unification of Germany in 1870) or opposed alliance with Britain (Irish Americans chafing at London's abuses of Irish Catholics) or opposed alliance with Russia (Scandinavian and initially Jewish Americans with memories of Czarist expansion and pogroms), the United States was slow to enter the conflict. But President Woodrow Wilson, in league with those who favored American participation in the war, played an active role in the peace settlement that followed and was seen as a founding father of the Polish, Czechoslovak, Yugoslav, and Albanian republics, as well as saluted for his support for a Jewish homeland in Palestine and for an American mandate (that never materialized) for Armenia.

The literature on U.S. reaction to the war seldom devotes much attention to activism by domestic ethnic groups. Yet demographic statistics make Wilson's dilemma clear. Of a total U.S. population of 92 million in 1910, 13.5 million were foreign born, of whom some 12 million came from the belligerent or strongly partisan countries in the Great War—including 1.2 million Americans of British birth, 1.4 million born in Ireland, 1.3 million of Scandinavian origin, 2.3 million of German birth, 1 million born in Poland, 1.3 million of Austro-Hungarian origin (perhaps half of whom were of subject Czech, Slovak, Romanian, and Yugoslav birth), 1.4 million of Russian origin (including some 200,000 Balts), and 1.3 million born in Italy. Another approximately 17 million Americans had been born here of at least one foreign-born parent from a country involved in the war or with decided sympathies in the struggle, including 2.4 million of immediate British descent, 3.1 million of first-generation Irish stock, 1.9 million of Scandinavian parentage, 5.7 million of German parentage, 1 million of Polish descent, and 1 million of Austro-Hungarian ancestry.[3]

Troubling as these figures showing roughly one-third of Americans directly concerned by the conflict had to be to Washington, still other considerations gave them even more political weight. For one thing, those born abroad in countries involved in the hostilities—some 13 percent of the entire population—were significantly more likely to be of voting age than the general population. For another, these immigrants had not dispersed uniformly throughout the United States but were concentrated in specific geographic regions, increasing the likelihood of a strong ethnic identification and giving them more electoral clout. Thus, of 25.4 million whites in the Northeast in 1910, 6.6 million were foreign born (26 percent); of 29.3 million in the North Central states, 4.7 million were foreign born (16 percent). Finally, Wilson had probably won the election of 1912 because of a split within the Republican ranks, as a result of which they ran two candidates for president. The Democrats had good reason, in short, to take the ethnic vote most seriously even if we cannot be sure at just what rate these groups naturalized and then went to vote.

Walter Lippmann believed that Wilson's proposals for multilateral institutions after the war reflected in part America's need to satisfy all its ethnic constituencies with the peace in Europe. Because an alliance system based on a traditional balance of power would favor some

Americans' countries of ancestry over others, the domestic sources of U.S. foreign policy preconditioned American leaders to think in terms of organizing European politics in a way that would ease the tensions of governing a multiethnic America. Given the consistent efforts of foreign governments to influence Washington through their kinfolk in the United States, Wilson had reacted prudently in 1914: "We definitely have to be neutral since otherwise our mixed populations would wage war on each other."[4]

Another critical factor complicating Wilson's decisionmaking was that foreign leaders and governments believed ethnic constituencies could influence Washington's course of action and took steps to rally domestic American support to their side in a fashion that George Washington had explicitly warned against in 1796. Germany was particularly successful at mobilizing the German American community on its behalf. The British were well aware of these forces at work. Their ambassador to the United States, Cecil Spring Rice (failing to appreciate the strong pro-British sentiments of the great bulk of American Jewry, newly arrived from Russia, and focusing instead on the Jewish American financial elite of German descent), wrote to London that Jewish Americans had surpassed American Irish in lobbying effectiveness and that:

> The President [Wilson] seemed to fear that the methods of the Germans here were having an extremely exasperating effect upon American public opinion and that this government was in some danger of having to face a violent racial division which has hitherto been avoided on this continent. Once racial animosity breaks out the position of the government here will be one of great difficulty. The President said that his main and paramount duty was to preserve peace at home and abroad . . . There seems to be no doubt whatever that the Germans took a very strong part, both in votes and money, in the last elections and this part was one hostile to this administration . . . The Jews show a strong preference for the [German] Emperor and there must be some bargain. Since Morgan's death the Jewish banks are supreme and they have captured the Treasury Department by the simple expedient of financing the bills of the Secretary of the Treasury . . . the President

quoted to me the text "he that keepeth Israel shall neither slumber nor sleep." One by one the Jews are capturing the principal newspapers and are bringing them over as much as they dare to the German side.[5]

In issuing the Balfour Declaration late in 1917, with its promise of a Jewish homeland in Palestine, Great Britain had its eye at least in part on Jewish American sympathies best expressed by Wilson's friend the Supreme Court Justice Louis Brandeis (British eyes were also on the sentiments of Russian Jews). And a long list of East European nationalist leaders—most notably the Czechoslovak nationalist Tomas Masaryk and the Polish pianist Ignace Paderewski—hoping to rouse American support for eventual statehood for their peoples traveled through the country with great success.

During the interwar period, ethnic differences continued. Irish Americans (supported by other domestic ethnic constituencies disgruntled with the outcome of the Versailles Conference) were especially effective at blocking American participation in the League of Nations (so Woodrow Wilson repeatedly declared that "hyphens are the knives that are being stuck into" the peace treaty).[6] German Americans moved toward the Republican party. The result was to play a role in the election of the Republican Warren Harding in 1920. Somewhat later, Italian Americans, many of them proud of Mussolini, who had come to power in 1922, contributed to the isolationism of the 1930s.

The concern to "Americanize" the immigrant population and to remain isolated from conflict in Europe could not insulate the country from the impact of world affairs on domestic ethnic relations, however. The rise of Bolshevism and fascism after World War I raised the question of racial segregation in the United States in the interwar years—the communists excoriating America for it, the fascists in warm support. To be sure, the failure of Marxism was its inability to see that racism is to an important extent independent of class conflict. But given that the two issues do interrelate, and that the status of blacks in the United States was in flagrant contradiction with what Gunnar Myrdal called in 1944 the American Creed, Moscow found in American race relations a strong ideological argument against the United States. Meanwhile, given fascism's embrace of racist thinking, the United

States was forced to distance itself for yet another reason from its treatment of its citizens of African and Jewish heritage were it to make clear
the moral basis on which World War II was to be fought.[7]

In the election of 1940, Republicans looked forward to picking up
votes among Italian and German Americans as a result of their continued dislike of Wilsonianism and concern again to stay out of war. By
contrast, those ethnic groups which, like Polish Americans, saw in the
rise of communism and fascism threats to their kinfolk abroad maintained the internationalist commitments they associated with Wilson
and the Democratic party. One need not argue from these observations
that ethnic prejudices were the primary, much less the sole, determinant of much of American policy to conclude that they nonetheless had
an important influence, usually neglected in the literature, not only on
American policy toward specific countries but on the general cast of
America's role in world affairs. As Walter Lippmann put it in 1937, although the United States needed to become involved in European affairs, the dilemma was that Americans could not "fuse as a nation if
they are not secure against the divisive passions of the European ancestors . . . Our dealings with the European nations instantly raise issues
which divide us at home." The result was a substantial drag on American involvement in European affairs from the 1910s through the 1930s
that it is impossible today not to find regrettable.[8]

Stage II

The divisive impact of European affairs on American domestic politics
changed completely after 1945. Not simply the national unity created
by the war, but even more importantly the struggle with the Soviet Union that broke out thereafter, served to blur distinctions between ethnic
and national identity and to fuse the European Americans together in a
common national identity, whose absence due to divisions in Europe
Lippmann had earlier lamented. Internationalism, not neutrality or
isolationism, became the hallmark of this new stage of ethnic activism,
providing a firm domestic underpinning to U.S. steadfastness in fight-
ing Soviet communism.

Of course, not all problems were settled by this sea change. During
the war Ireland had remained neutral, despite a group of prominent
Irish Americans who visited the island in a vain effort to persuade Dub-

lin to change its policy now that it was an independent country. Nevertheless, the problem of Northern Ireland had not been settled, so that Anglo-American differences remained in this score, meaning that the Cold War did not end the division between ethnic and national consciousness so far as many Irish Americans were concerned.

Moreover, just *how* to be internationalist could be a matter of bitter partisan debate. Prior to the 1944 election, FDR misled Charles Rozmarek of the Polish American Congress as to his engagements with Stalin so as not to lose the support of this constituency. Thereafter, the Republican charge that the Democrats had "given away" or "sold out" Eastern Europe to the Soviets at Teheran and Yalta succeeded in moving large numbers of these ethnic constituencies, who had previously voted solidly for the Democrats, the party of their hero Woodrow Wilson, into voting for Republicans who would "roll back" Soviet control of their ancestral homelands. In the 1950s Eisenhower faced serious objections from the right of his party, which had promised East European Americans more action, when he would not confront the Soviets more aggressively over their control of Eastern Europe.[9]

Yet these domestic tensions have to be weighed against the far greater benefits that flowed to Washington from ethnic group activism in world affairs. For example, the Truman administration, aided by the Catholic church, encouraged tens of thousands of letters from Italian Americans to their relatives in Italy warning of the danger of communism and urging a vote for the Christian Democrats (who won the election). Again, in the Truman Doctrine, many Greek Americans could see a defense of Greek independence and anticommunism, which they heartily supported. For their part, Jewish Americans saw the security of Israel as linked to an active American concern with stability in the Middle East. All three of these groups voted for Truman in 1948 partly because of these issues. Although the Republicans, in an effort to pander to the Italian vote, actually said in their 1948 platform that they would work for the return of Italy's African colonies to that country, they failed to appreciate either that African Americans would take offense at this pledge or that Italy itself would not be interested in such an offer. More significantly, the Republicans, apparently not understanding the dynamic of ethnic group voting at the time as clearly as the Democrats, failed to make a strong pitch to East European Americans in the 1948 election that their kinfolk had been betrayed by Roosevelt at Yalta.

But a more important consideration points not so much at U.S. relations with specific countries but rather at how containment managed to bring closer together Euro American ethnicities in a common bond of anticommunism and American patriotism. For the Cold War had the general effect through the Marshall Plan and NATO of creating a more united Western Europe, increasingly linked by economic and security ties, reconciling in substantial degree thereby British, French, and German rivalries in Europe, and opening the door for the membership of Italy, Spain, Portugal, and Greece first in NATO and later in the European Union. American policy thus contributed not only to the creation of a stronger ally in a more united Western Europe across the Atlantic but also to the reconciliation of differences among Euro Americans at home. American ethnic communities, seeing that their kinfolk abroad were establishing harmonious relations, came more easily to cooperate with one another in terms of their common American identity.

The situation was somewhat similar for the many millions of East European descent, for they too found that their ethnic and their American identities coincided so far as the basic anti-Soviet thrust of U.S. foreign policy was concerned. True, the bipartisanship displayed toward the integration of Western Europe was not so much in evidence over policy toward the East. Although the Republicans understood the importance of the ethnic vote after they analyzed the results of the 1948 election and elements within the party wanted to push the issue hard as a way of winning power, Eisenhower was initially reluctant to endorse "rollback" to the extent many Republicans wanted for the sake of electoral gain in 1952, especially if it meant explicitly repudiating wartime agreements with Moscow and raising the specter of armed confrontation. Moreover, given U.S. failure to act meaningfully with respect to the Hungarian uprising in 1956, the Democrats could claim that they better represented the interests of freedom in Eastern Europe. In 1959 the Congress passed a "captive nations resolution" marking the third week in July each year as a period of remembrance, but in due course the occasion was forgotten until resurrected in 1982 by Ronald Reagan. Nevertheless, one hears repeatedly of nationalists in the Baltic Republics, Poland, Hungary, or Czechoslovakia encouraged by U.S. support for their eventual independent self-government.[10] It is not difficult to conclude that for Americans of East European ancestry, even more than those from the West, the Cold War permitted the fusion of their ethnic and national identities.

The role of Polish Americans in the eventual breakup of the Soviet empire in Eastern Europe deserves special attention. At an early date this ethnic community became involved in helping Washington in a difficult and delicate process of engaging the Polish government. The essential strategy was one of cooperating with and rewarding Warsaw when it was independent of Moscow, but of withholding approval if either communist government moved to diminish whatever measure of freedom Poland enjoyed. At the same time, the strategy dictated covertly helping those sectors of Polish society—the Catholic church and later Solidarity especially—that were slowly creating a new social contract and basis for state power in Poland. Experts may disagree on the relative contribution of Polish Americans working with the American government to the eventual coming to power of Solidarity and on the meaning of this development, in turn, for the fate of the Soviet empire in general. But there should be little doubt that Polish nationalism enormously complicated Soviet political life, and that the influence of the Polish American community on both Poland and Washington was real.[11]

During the Cold War, American liberals typically lamented the visceral anticommunism of East European ethnic groups as an impediment to better relations with Moscow. And not only liberals: Henry Kissinger's effort to establish détente with the Soviet Union in the early 1970s by finally accepting the division of Europe decided at Yalta is a good part of the explanation as to why he had so little influence over Ronald Reagan's wing of the Republican party when it took power in 1981. Indeed, might not Soviet-American differences have been more likely settled in favor of a great power condominium over the world had it not been for the steady pressure of Americans descendant from Eastern Europe to give these countries their freedom and the eventual decision of the Reagan administration to push this policy more forcefully than it ever had been pushed before?[12]

A major legacy of World War II for international affairs was the revelation of the Holocaust. The result was widespread sympathy among most Americans for the creation of Israel in 1948 and a new commitment to Zionism on the part of the American Jewish community. It is often argued that the 1967 War was the most important watershed for

Jewish American activism with regard to world affairs, but in either case the primary motivating factors for a heightened sense of group loyalty and political concern were essentially international, not domestic. Indeed, prior to World War II, Zionism had been actively opposed by segments of the American Jewish community who favored downplaying specifically Jewish demands on Washington. But the birth of the state of Israel and the challenges that country has faced since 1948 have contributed much more than anything in American domestic life to the Jewish American sense of ethnic solidarity.[13]

In the first two years of its existence, Israel's leaders were unsure how to react to the increasing tensions of the U.S.-Soviet rivalry. Many Israelis were socialists, many Jews still lived in the Soviet Union, and neutrality in any case seemed a prudent course of action. But in internal debates between mid-1950 and 1951 Israel decided to seek its security in aligning with the United States.[14] For the American Jewish community, then, to defend Israel was not simply to work against Arab efforts to undermine the Jewish state but to counter Soviets efforts as well. In working with the United States thereafter, Israel appeared helpful in reducing Soviet influence in the Middle East, as the Nixon administration recognized in expanding military support for the Jewish state.

The impact of American Jewry on the prosecution of the Cold War was not limited to the Middle East. In the aftermath of the 1967 War, Soviet Jews increased their political activism, eliciting a powerful positive response from their American kinfolk. While American Jewish leaders continued for the most part to be liberal in domestic affairs, a growing number of them (styled the "neoconservatives" who had once been liberal, but including Orthodox and Zionists as well) became more hawkish in their feelings toward the Soviet Union and worked with conservative members of Congress to stymie détente. In 1974 Senator Henry Jackson and Representative Charles Vanik proposed to deny the Soviet Union most-favored-nation trade status so long as it restricted the emigration of Jews and certain other categories of dissidents. Kissinger complained mightily that this kind of public censure only complicated a Jewish exodus from the Soviet Union and in the process was wrecking the spirit of détente that he had labored so mightily to engender. But to no avail. Again, in 1977, President Jimmy Carter could complain that Jewish Americans had derailed U.S.-Soviet efforts to establish a joint framework for a Middle East settlement between Israel and the Arabs, Israel claiming that this would be an "imposed solution" of the sort it had always opposed. During both the Nixon and the Carter years, then, Jewish Americans played a role (one which should not be exaggerated, however) in breaking up what might otherwise have been a budding relationship between Washington and Moscow.[15]

The imponderable question is the extent to which the confluence of ethnic group commitment to the Cold War fueled Washington's determination to stay the course, driving the competition to a successful conclusion that made impossible a global condominium with Moscow. Surely many factors other than ethnic considerations were involved in prolonging the superpower contest, including the basic dissimilarities between Soviet and American economic, social, and political systems, the stakes in world affairs ranging from the nuclear balance to regional conflicts, and a Soviet unwillingness to try to make détente workable in the 1970s. But it must be remembered that Moscow, too, had its ethnic problems, and one reason it continued the conflict with the United States as long as it did was its well-founded fear that should the struggle end it would be unable to impose its authority so easily on foreign peoples, who might well use détente to turn against Moscow's influence.

Even if we cannot measure with any precision the contribution of American ethnic groups to the conduct of the Cold War, the usual failure in the literature even to mention the subject needs to be corrected. From Washington's perspective, the Cold War in Europe allowed East and West European Americans to feel a solidarity with one another as well as an end to any tension they might have felt between their ethnic loyalties and their identities as Americans—the problem that had bothered Washington between the 1910s and 1941. A similar process was at work with Jewish Americans: one could proudly affirm one's ethnic affiliation to kinfolk abroad without in the slightest way contradicting one's loyalty to the United States. Indeed, activist elements among East European and Jewish Americans were influential in their different ways at upsetting efforts at détente and so forcing the Cold War to a conclusion ultimately favorable to the United States.

If Euro American ethnic communities were increasingly comfortable with the congruence of their ethnic and national identities thanks to the Cold War, the same cannot be said of the black community. African American hopes for U.S. foreign policy did not meld with geopolitical thinking in Washington as easily as did the concerns of Jewish or Euro Americans. For many blacks, the problem of racism and white rule in Africa outweighed concerns about the dangers of communism and Soviet expansion in that region—a perspective not shared by many others in Washington for whom the communist threat reigned supreme.

The consequence was continued black frustration with American foreign policy. The Cold War was far from the first time the African American community became interested in world affairs. In 1898 there was black American support for U.S. involvement in the Spanish American War, based on the hope that war would bring liberty to blacks in Cuba. By 1918 Jamaican-born Marcus Garvey was championing the idea of Pan-Africanism in his newspaper appropriately entitled *The Negro World* and through his Universal Negro Improvement Association. At the same time, perhaps the greatest of the black internationalists, W. E. B. Du Bois, was insisting on the interrelationship among challenges to peoples of African heritage throughout the world. But at Versailles in 1919 Wilson had turned a deaf ear to appeals from African American leaders for an end to imperialism in Africa based on the President's own support for national self-determination.

During the 1920s black leaders became acquainted with the teachings and practice of nonviolence under Gandhi's leadership in India. The influence of Gandhi's thinking about the practical political utility of nonviolence was later evident in the Montgomery bus boycott of 1955 and apparent thereafter in a host of measures taken by African Americans and their civil rights supporters (although some blacks did advocate violence). In 1935 black American leaders, supported by the widest and deepest upsurge of sentiment within the African American community to that time toward world affairs, deplored the Italian invasion of Ethiopia. In 1945 Du Bois became president of the Pan-African Congress (headquartered in Manchester, England). Du Bois's internationalism was such that Martin Luther King Jr. could claim in 1967, in a salute to Du Bois on the centennial of his birth, that Du Bois's insistence that black Americans feel their kinship with the black diaspora could be translated to Southeast Asia, for Du Bois "would readily see the parallel between American support of the corrupt and despised Thieu-Ky regime [in South Vietnam] and northern support to the southern slave-masters in 1876."[16]

It is surely no accident that the American Civil Rights Movement emerged during the Cold War and that it grew in strength from contact with the rise of African nationalism and the coming of decolonization to Africa, beginning with Ghana in 1957. Many black Americans perceived themselves to be part of an African diaspora linking them to events elsewhere, as suggested by the prestige of the Ghanaian leader Kwame Nkrumah, who had attended Lincoln University in the United States (as had the future Nigerian leader Nnamdi Azikiwe). And the international connections of the NAACP (the National Association for the Advancement of Colored People) allowed it to ask for the Soviet Union's sponsorship of a petition to the United Nations in 1947, whose title summed up its message: "An Appeal to the World: A Statement on the Denial of Human Rights to Minorities in the Case of Citizens of Negro Descent in the United States of America and an Appeal to the United Nations for Redress."[17]

Nevertheless, sensitivity to world affairs within the black community had to be weighed against domestic concerns. After a brief period following World War II during which African Americans' anticolonialism was joined to the call for civil rights in the United States, the coming of the Cold War obliged this community to promote the latter struggle over the former if they were to have much influence in Washington. Only with the emergence of the powerful Civil Rights Movement in the 1960s were critical voices again heard from African Americans concerning world affairs, voices denouncing the murder of the Congolese leader Patrice Lumumba in 1961 with CIA participation, calling for an end to U.S. involvement in Vietnam where black servicemen were dying in numbers disproportionate to their part in the population, and urging that Washington respect African nonalignment and oppose white minority rule in southern Africa. While King was a leader in this development, so were members of the black left. In 1963–1964 Malcolm X reported the encouragement he got for black liberation in the United States from the Bandung Conference and the Non-Aligned Movement and from the creation of the Organization of African Unity.[18]

In retrospect, it is still surprising that these differences between white and black perspectives on policy toward Africa did not disturb domestic politics more than they did. Part of the reason was the growing willingness of the American political system to accommodate black demands; part of the reason was that the Cold War never exploded with the force in Africa that it did in Southeast Asia or even Latin America.

By 1969 Charles Diggs had become head of the House Foreign Affairs Subcommittee on Africa, and two years later he created the Congressional Black Caucus (CBC). By 1972 divestment from South Africa began to be discussed in the Congress, and the Reverend Leon Sullivan proposed his influential principles for businesses wanting to invest in South Africa, asking them to guarantee schemes for the integration and promotion of black employees in exchange for the right to do business there. At about the same time, as the Republican administration weakened, Democratic liberals in the 94th Congress, elected in 1974, held repeated hearings on human rights violations in countries friendly to the United States, including those in Africa.[19]

But the willingness of mainstream black leaders to work through the American system to influence foreign policy, and not to remain hostilely outside, increased substantially with the election of Jimmy Carter, who took office in 1977. For the first time blacks had direct access to the White House for foreign policy deliberations. Within months of Carter's election, Andrew Young became U.S. Ambassador to the United Nations, Randall Robinson (who had worked with Representative Diggs) founded TransAfrica, and Vice President Walter Mondale was in South Africa, telling Prime Minister B. J. Vorster that the U.S. looked forward to a regime in Pretoria based on the principle of "one man, one vote." Mondale reported that he had communicated to the South African "the profound commitment that my nation has to human rights, to the elimination of discrimination, and to full political participation . . . we believe that perpetuating an unjust system is the surest incentive to increase Soviet influence . . . They know we will not defend such a system."[20] In regard to Rhodesia/Zimbabwe the cooperation of the Carter White House with black Americans was strikingly successful, securing the repeal of the Byrd Amendment that had allowed the United States to import Rhodesian chrome and refusing to recognize the government of Bishop Abel Muzorewa because of the control local white officials had over him.

The experience of African American activism during the Carter years set the stage for this ethnoracial group's leadership on legislation imposing economic sanctions against South Africa during the 1980s. As with other ethnic lobbies, measuring the extent of African American influence on U.S. foreign policy, and of this policy in turn on events in South Africa, is impossible to do with any precision. There was a coalition of forces within the United States that opposed apartheid, and forces far greater than simply those that were American combined to bring about the dramatic end of apartheid and the inauguration of Nelson Mandela as that country's president in 1994. But that black Americans were a significant element determining both the pace of this process and its democratic outcome seems unquestionable.[21] Yet if the black role in ending apartheid indicated the degree to which African American influence was now part of mainstream bargaining over foreign policy, black Americans' opposition to the American coup against the communist government of Grenada in 1983 demonstrated the extent to which they nonetheless remained outside the prevailing Cold War consensus.

Greek American opinion evolved in a reverse direction from African American during this period. In the early years of the Cold War, Greek American sentiments were closely congruent with those in Washington in the belief that communist expansion had to be stopped, and the Truman administration received the support of this community when the president announced his "doctrine" to achieve this end in 1947. Later, however, relations between the community and Washington became strained. Concern with Turkey repeatedly led Greek governments to insist that NATO come to Greece's assistance, with Athens enjoying the hearty approval of the Greek American community. The most serious problems involved Greek-Turkish relations after the Turkish invasion of Cyprus in 1974 and the unstinting support Greek Americans gave to Athens despite the facts that the government there in 1974 was hostile to democracy, that Greeks had been the initial disrupters of the peace on Cyprus as right-wing militia terrorists deposed Archbishop Makarios in the name of union (*enosis*) with Greece, and that Turkey was altogether more important to American interests in the region than was Greece.

The danger was that NATO's eastern flank would disintegrate if Greece and Turkey went to war—a danger the United States had to work hard to avoid. It was not aided in its efforts by the unrelenting Greek American support of Athens's cause in Washington, which resulted in a three-year embargo on military sales to Ankara, the retaliatory closing of NATO listening stations in Turkey, and the obligation to provide military appropriations to Greece thereafter that still today equal 70 percent of anything given to Turkey. It may well be, as then-U.S. Ambassador to Greece Monteagle Stearns has concluded, that American military aid along the lines of that the Greek lobby secured was what the United States should have wanted for its own purposes in order to secure an Aegean balance. But this outcome nonetheless was more a fortunate outcome of events than any consequence expressly desired by either Greece or its kinfolk in the United States with their ceaseless efforts to cripple Turkish power.[22]

Stage III

Since the end of the Cold War, the influence of American ethnic lobbies on foreign policy may be said to have entered a third stage. Its most important feature is the continued commitment to internationalism. If American public opinion remains committed to an active role in world affairs, one may assume that communities that are ethnically organized are even more committed, at percentages that may equal those of the political elite.[23] Greek American organizations keep a sharp eye out for events in the Balkans and the Aegean; Jewish Americans remain attentive to the Middle East and the fate of their kinfolk in Russia; African Americans are involved in monitoring the occupation of Haiti and the future of democratic government in and U.S. economic relations with Africa; Armenian Americans closely follow events in the Caucasus; Irish Americans worry about the peace process in Northern Ireland; East European Americans work for the enlargement of NATO; and new groups, of which the most prominent is Mexican American but which include Asian Americans as well, are active regarding immigration legislation, adding an important new dimension to ethnic group politicking with respect to America's role in world affairs.

The end of the Cold War has given rise to two interrelated developments so far as the influence of American ethnic groups in Washington is concerned: the rise of ethnonationalist conflict abroad stemming from the collapse of Soviet power and the withdrawal of American support has alerted American kinfolk to the need for action; and the decline of any obvious threat to U.S. security has weakened the American state relative to social forces at home, which in turn has increased the openness of our political system to interest group influence.

Of course, in important ways, Washington and ethnic groups can act together for related ends. The post–Cold War call by the Clinton administration to replace containment by efforts to enlarge the number of democratic states worldwide well suited a host of ethnic groups, giving them the right to champion their kinfolk abroad by appeals to America's democratic and human rights traditions. For instance, in Africa and Latin America the end of the superpower contest created a new opportunity to make the effort to create democratic governments, often favored by American ethnic communities. In addition, the creation of new states from the disintegration of the Soviet empire, the Soviet Union, and Yugoslavia meant a new source of demands in foreign capitals to which American ethnic groups have been responding.

But an identity of purpose between Washington and ethnic activists is not always apparent. The end of the Cold War has contributed to a change in the domestic American political process that has served to increase ethnic group influence. In a situation where the country is under no threat to its vital security interests, where the once "imperial presidency" is in retreat before Congress, and where the Congress itself is increasingly subject to partisan rivalries, social forces have correspondingly more power to influence foreign policy than they did during the Cold War. Given the rising legitimacy of multiculturalism in domestic American life, it seems fair to conclude that, powerful as ethnic sentiment may have been in shaping U.S. foreign policy during the Cold War, it is even more influential today.

As the debate over the enlargement of NATO showed in 1998–99, the end of the Cold War did not stop some Americans of East European descent from mobilizing to influence the fate of their ancestral homelands. In 1994 the Central and East European Coalition was formed by members of various American ethnicities whose ancestral homelands had once been under Soviet domination. To underscore their political clout, they pointed out that for the 1996 election their fellow ethnics represented at least 10 percent of the vote in North Dakota, Nebraska, Minnesota, Wisconsin, Illinois, Michigan, Ohio, New York, Massachusetts, New Jersey, Delaware, Maryland, and (the highest, at over 18 percent of the total) Connecticut and Pennsylvania.[24]

It should thus come as no surprise that President Clinton delivered all his major addresses in 1996–97 on NATO enlargement in cities like Detroit, Chicago, and Milwaukee, where large ethnic communities would be attentive to the message and likely to rally in support.[25] In my opinion, it was not Americans of East European origin alone, or even principally, who were driving the decision to expand NATO; instead, long-standing decisions to combine as much of Europe as possible in ways favorable to American interests dictated Washington's policy. Still, the perception that Clinton was angling for votes was widespread, as was illustrated in the comment by Canadian Prime Minister Jean Chrétien (who thought his microphone was turned off) to the Belgian Prime Minister about NATO's three new candidate members in August 1997: "All this for short-term political reasons, to win elections. In fact [American politicians] are selling their votes, they are selling their votes . . . It's incredible. In your country or in mine, all the politicians would be in prison."[26]

With East European governments now free of Moscow's control, leaders of these countries have become more active in soliciting the support of American ethnic communities to whom they are culturally related. Much as Masaryk or Paderewski visited the United States to encourage both the American government and their kinfolk here to come to the aid of the ancestral homeland, so the leaders of the Czech Republic and Poland come today, to be entertained at the White House and to address Congress, while at less publicized moments also meeting with Czech or Polish American groups to coordinate their positions on world affairs.

The result has been a triple alliance involving the Clinton administration (with its activist Secretary of State Madeleine Albright, of Czech birth), East European governments, and American ethnic constituencies in a common cause to bring the new countries of this region into Western-dominated economic institutions and NATO. The success of these ambitions with respect to Poland, the Czech Republic, and Hungary in March 1999 crowned more than eighty years of effort, beginning with the activism of East European Americans, East European political leaders, and Woodrow Wilson during World War I. Nothing could have been more Wilsonian than Albright's speech at Harvard University in June 1997, on the fiftieth anniversary of the announcement of the Marshall Plan, in which she declared that "American security and prosperity are linked to economic and political health abroad":

We must take advantage of the historic opportunity that now exists to bring the world together in an international system based on democracy, open markets, law and a commitment to peace. To-day the greatest danger to America is not some foreign enemy; it is the possibility that we will fail to heed the example of [the post-war] generation; that we will allow the momentum toward democracy to stall, take for granted the institutions and principles upon which our own freedom is based, and forget what the history of this century reminds us: that problems, if left unattended, will all too often come home to America. A decade or two from now, we will be known as the neo-isolationists, who allowed tyranny and lawlessness to rise again, or as the generation that solidified the global triumph of democratic principles.[27]

Yet in the spring of 1999 the easy association of those who were now calling themselves Central (no longer Eastern) European American groups with the expansion of NATO ran into opposition from other Orthodox Americans, who were alarmed at Washington's attempts to curtail Serbian power first in Bosnia then in Kosovo. When bombing runs on Serbia began at the end of March 1999, the first to protest were Serbian Americans, located in many eastern cities but especially in Chicago (where some 250,000 of them make up the largest Serbian community outside Serbia proper). By April other Orthodox communities in the United States began to criticize the attacks, as the Serbian Americans were joined by U.S. communities of Greek and Russian descent. The ethnic patchwork quilt of the Balkans, where Western Christianity and Islam were in conflict with the world of Orthodox Christianity, suddenly revealed itself to be present in the United States as well, where congregations of Muslim (and not only Albanian) Americans could be seen mobilizing in favor of the war effort. "President Clinton, why do you ignore the suffering of Orthodox Christians," ran a full-page ad in the *New York Times* on May 2, 1999, which recounted oppression against the Orthodox in Cyprus, Southern Albania, Croatia, and Turkey, before concluding: "Why is Washington more tolerant when the victims are Orthodox Christians? Why is American foreign policy slanted against Orthodox Christians wherever we turn?"[28]

Similarly, the end of the Cold War opened up new possibilities for peace in the Middle East, which Jewish Americans working with the government of Yitzhak Rabin in Israel were vital in promoting. With the eclipse of Soviet power and the defeat of Iraq in the Gulf War in

1991, radical Arab rejectionists had been weakened to such a point that it appeared that a process could finally begin of exchanging recognition of Israel for the independence of occupied Arab territories on the West Bank of the Jordan River. The result in domestic American politics was for the first time a collaboration between mainstream Arab and Jewish Americans for a goal they all shared.[29]

Of course, it was also necessary that Israel and the Palestine Liberation Organization be willing to exchange territory for peace. The coming to power of a Labour government under Rabin in Israel (in 1992) and a Democratic administration in the United States (in 1993) facilitated the task that the Bush administration had begun, leading to the signature of a peace settlement between Israel and the PLO in September 1993 and its extension to Israel and Jordan a year later.

What neither Rabin nor Clinton nor the end of the Cold War could bring about, however, was the acceptance of the peace process by Iran and certain Arab states and movements. As a result, the United States sponsored a "double containment" of Iran and Libya (which was actually "triple" because of an embargo on Iraq). The American Jewish community was basic to the U.S. decision in August 1996 to extend a full commercial embargo on Iran, with penalties on third parties investing more than $40 million in that country. In addition, the American Israel Public Affairs Committee (AIPAC) played a leading role in seeing that Russian firms were penalized if they helped Iran to improve its missile technology.[30]

The end of the Cold War also facilitated efforts by the World Jewish Congress, in alliance with the U.S. government, to pursue claims on behalf of victims of the Holocaust against the Swiss banking system. Tens of millions of dollars in accounts once belonging to European Jews had in effect been confiscated by Swiss banks. Prominent Jewish Americans like Stuart Eizenstadt and others in the Clinton administration assembled the evidence, which was brought to the Senate floor by the head of the Senate Banking Committee, Alfonse D'Amato, with the implied threat that Swiss banks in the United States might be closed if the matter were not satisfactorily addressed (a threat that was first realized in October 1997, when the Union Bank of Switzerland was barred from participation in a New York state bond project because of the negative attitude of its leadership toward the investigations).[31]

An equally impressive example of ethnic group lobbying for a trade embargo came when Cuban Americans allied in the Cuban American National Foundation (CANF) persuaded Congress to pass, and President Clinton to sign, the Helms-Burton bill in February 1996, extending the jurisdiction of American courts over suits brought by American citizens to defend property rights that the Castro government had nullified after 1959. To be sure, the Cuban American sponsors of this bill were working closely with powerful Cold Warriors like Senate Foreign Relations chairman Jesse Helms, who were determined to complete the American triumph against the Soviet Union by destroying the Castro government, and by economic interests that wanted either compensation or protection from competition from Cuba. And they were fortunate in that Castro proved once again to be his own worst enemy, easing the task of his American opponents by shooting down unarmed Cuban American planes that were dropping anti-Fidelista pamphlets over Cuba while a Cuban human rights organization in Havana was holding its first meeting, which Castro then shut down.

The result of Helms-Burton was a major row in U.S. relations with its best trading partners, including not only all the members of the European Union but Canada and Mexico as well. Perhaps these countries should agree with the United States, as conservative Americans often say, maintaining that a regime like Castro's would only be emboldened if relations with it were normalized. Perhaps Castro would be better "killed with kindness," as more liberal Americans argue, claiming that his government could not withstand the upsurge of confidence Cuban society would experience if its isolation were ended. For our purposes, the point is rather that CANF demonstrated real power over American foreign policy in these debates, and that through the trade bill's impact on U.S. relations with all its trading partners in the World Trade Organization, this ethnic group has had an impact on matters far beyond the Caribbean.[32]

While the internationalism of Jewish and East European Americans is now several generations old, and that of Cuban Americans begins with the Bay of Pigs in 1961, the end of the Cold War has allowed other ethnic communities a new role in American foreign policy. Thus Armenian Americans gained critical influence on U.S. policy in the Caucasus by virtue of the creation in 1991 for the first time of an Armenian Republic. It is widely agreed that the high level of U.S. aid to Armenia (the second highest per capita in the world, after Israel) and the embargo of official assistance to Azerbaijan (which sits alongside massive amounts of oil in the Caspian Sea) would be inconceivable American policy were it not for this ethnic American community and its determination that the Armenian population of Nagorno Karabakh, a province of Azerbaijan, be given home rule if not united with Armenia itself. By Section 907 of the Freedom Support Act of 1992, Armenian American lobbyists managed to exclude Azerbaijan from receiving aid intended to support newly independent former Soviet states, despite the fact that the Armenian government was highly authoritarian, that it was an aggressor state, and that it was friendly with Iran and Russia, the two rivals of the United States in the region.[33]

In their efforts, the Armenians have been aided by Greek Americans, who for over two decades have successfully mitigated what would otherwise surely be, in the minds of most observers, a much more pro-Turkish policy on the part of Washington. While all ethnic lobbies have an understandable tendency to exaggerate their strength in order to increase their membership and their clout in Washington, the assessment of the 104th Congress by Aram Hamparian, the executive director of the Armenian National Committee of America, was probably close to the mark: "The Armenian lobby enjoyed unprecedented success during the 104th Congress. The Radanovich-Bonior, Visclosly, and Porter Amendments sanctioning Turkey for their ongoing denial of the Armenian Genocide, continued blockade of Armenia and human rights abuses—each passed by an overwhelming margin. At the same time, U.S. aid to Armenia steadily increased . . . We owe these successes to the tireless efforts of countless Armenian Americans."[34]

To be sure, the Armenian lobby could make only limited gains as the oil industry rallied to break its hold on U.S. policy in the Caucasus for the sake of getting access to the estimated 50–200 billion barrels of oil under the Caspian Sea. In late 1997 these reserves were estimated to be worth some $4 trillion at current prices, not counting another $4 trillion in gas reserves (making the area second only to the Persian Gulf, which has at least three times more energy resources underground).[35] As I indicated in the Introduction, the Armenian lobby also had to contend with the American Jewish community, which rallied to the side of Turkey in the petroleum dispute in its ambition to defend the growing Turkish-Israeli relationship. Still, it is well worth noting that for years the Armenian lobby has had a remarkable degree of control over

American policy in this region, and that in September 1998, even as the tide was turning against this lobby over the direction of U.S. policy in the Caucasus, the Congress approved $100 million in aid to Armenia and Nagorno Karabakh.

The end of the Cold War has also seen a continuation of African American involvement in the formulation of U.S. foreign policy. Black Americans were critical in determining a policy toward Haiti that ultimately led in October 1994 to that country's military occupation by the United States, with the expressed purpose of restoring it to democratic government under its duly elected president Jean-Baptiste Aristide. Perhaps the United States would have acted without this pressure, for there was opposition to the arrival of Haitian refugees, and the government of Raoul Cedras had repeatedly humiliated the Clinton administration by reneging on its commitments. But given widespread public opposition to military intervention there (polls showed 80 percent in opposition at one point), the principal force behind the U.S. occupation was the demand by black Americans (the political elite especially) on a president whom they had done much to elect that decisive action be taken to restore Aristide.[36]

Subsequently, black Americans became leaders in defining administration policy toward sub-Saharan Africa. A particular ambition of TransAfrica was the restoration of democratic government in Nigeria, as well as the promotion of human rights elsewhere on the continent. In December 1997 Jesse Jackson visited Kenya to back the idea of democratic processes there in light of upcoming elections. At the same time, black entrepreneurs, apparently working through the Congressional Black Caucus (CBC), were influential in persuading legislative forces and the administration to combine behind new initiatives for trade and investment throughout the region, which were announced in June 1997 (and passed in the House in March 1998 under the name Africa Growth and Opportunity Bill).

This recital of events should not obscure the complexity of black involvement in American foreign policy. Apparently, Nigerian pressure eventually forced TransAfrica to back off from its campaign to promote democracy there. Disagreements between the CBC and Randall Robinson over trade with and aid to Africa ultimately stymied the legislation. Still, the importance of promoting the participation of African Americans in the making of U.S. foreign policy—and not just toward the Caribbean and Africa—can be seen by Minister Louis Farrakhan's attacks on America's role in the world. In a trip through the Middle East and Africa in 1996, Farrakhan was reported to have called for the destruction of this country by the Muslim world and to have accepted $1 billion from the Libyan leader Muammar Qadaffi for his political activities within the United States. Better by far the role played by the Reverend Jesse Jackson in world affairs, most Americans would agree, than that played by Minister Farrakhan.[37]

As in Haiti, so in Northern Ireland, the end of the Cold War allowed the Clinton administration to take initiatives at the behest of an American ethnic community. Late in 1968 "the Troubles" began in Northern Ireland, as police attacked a Catholic civil rights march. The following summer riots escalated and British troops arrived; by 1970 the IRA had split and the Provisional IRA, using the threat of force, was renewing a traditional effort to get the British out of the six provinces and reunify the island. The IRA effort was backed in the United States by NORAID, the Irish Northern Aid Committee, which formed the same year. Shortly thereafter prominent Irish Americans like Chicago Mayor Richard Daley and Senator Edward Kennedy called for withdrawal of British troops and unification of the island, but denounced the use of violence to achieve these goals.[38]

In the 1992 election Clinton sought to gain the Irish vote by promising to encourage a peace process in Ulster. Given British objections to American involvement, it seems unlikely that he would have undertaken this initiative had he not been advised by the Irish American Senators Daniel Patrick Moynihan and Edward Kennedy that it would aid the return of so-called Reagan Democrats (largely blue collar, white Catholics) to the Democratic party.[39] In the event, it appears the initiative paid off; for the first time a presidential candidate pledged to try to end the sectarian struggle in Northern Ireland and set out to do so. According to the polls for the 1992 and 1996 elections, the only groups of white Americans who voted more for Clinton than for his rivals were Jews and Catholics, the Catholics returning to the Democratic party in a presidential election for the first time since 1977 and presumably including many Irish and East European Americans (the latter pleased by the prospects for NATO's expansion as the former were by his positions on Northern Ireland).

Well before the signing of the Good Friday peace accord on April

10, 1998, there was general agreement—even among those British who at first deplored Clinton's invitation to Sinn Fein leader Gerry Adams to visit the United States and Clinton's follow-up trip to Ireland late in 1995—that the American role in the peace process, under George Mitchell's leadership, had been positive and substantive. Had it not been for the activism of Irish Americans, little of this might have happened—neither direct presidential involvement, nor participation in the International Fund for Ireland, which funnels nearly $20 million yearly from the United States to the North to assist investments in areas that might otherwise be shunned or in companies that agree to abide by the MacBride Principles, designed to promote equality for Catholics in the country. During his involvement, Clinton changed from an apparently opportunistic to a seriously committed partisan of a just peace in Ulster. He said on his visit to Belfast on November 30, 1995: "Because [America's] greatness flows from the wealth of our diversity as well as the strength of the ideals we share in common, we feel bound to support others around the world who seek to bridge their own divides. This is an important part of our country's mission on the eve of the twenty-first century, because we know that the chain of peace that protects us grows stronger with every new link that is forged."

One ethnic issue related to foreign affairs that originated during the Cold War but only became politically sensitive thereafter involves Mexican Americans. Three areas of foreign policy preoccupy this group: NAFTA, the prospects for democratic government in Mexico, and U.S. immigration law. While the Mexican government has played a role in mobilizing Mexican Americans in support of NAFTA, the results of these ties to date do not seem to have been more than marginal (indeed, of late some Hispanics have charged NAFTA with taking jobs away from poor Americans). The same is true of Mexican American efforts to promote democracy in Mexico.[40]

Concern among Mexican Americans has run wide and deep, however, about measures like Proposition 187 in California, designed to end all public assistance to undocumented aliens, and thus about immigration law more generally, believed by many in this community to be an assault on their dignity as Latinos and their rights as Americans. With the Immigration Reform Act of 1965, the United States ended its forty-year system of ethnic quotas, opening its doors to immigrants from any country so long as they had family members here, job skills in demand, or refugee status. In short order the reform allowed an influx of immigrants second only to the great wave of the early twentieth century (perhaps greater when one adds illegal immigration) as well as unprecedented in that it was overwhelmingly (over 80 percent) composed of Latin Americans and Asians, who previously had been a relatively small percentage of the American population. Current estimates are that immigration patterns should reduce the American population of European stock to just over half of the total by the middle of the twenty-first century, when the country should be approximately 25 percent Hispanic, 8 percent Asian, 14 percent black, 1 percent Native American, and 52 percent white.[41]

In 1965 immigration to this country totaled just under 300,000. By 1981 immigration had doubled, and by 1991 it had risen sixfold to 1.8 million (with a record 1.2 million naturalized in 1997). Of the approximately 10 million legal immigrants arriving between 1980 and 1994, only some 1.5 million (15 percent of the total) were of European descent; of the approximately 4 million illegal immigrants in 1992 (estimated at 5 million by 1996), only 10 percent were of European descent.[42]

To some extent, the surge in immigration has been domestically driven, by employers wanting cheap or skilled labor or by immigrants already here wanting to be reunited with family members. But these immigration flows in recent times have been largely dependent on events outside the United States, especially on high demographic expansion and poor economic opportunities in Latin America and Asia, and on political turmoil, as in the Horn of Africa after 1989 or in Haiti between 1991 and 1994. External push more than internal pull is the primary dynamic currently at work.

The effect of this great wave of immigration on multiethnic life in the United States is the subject of heated debate. Those who favor the flows point to the energy of the youthful immigrant population, deny that it depresses wages for native-born Americans, and maintain that welfare cost increases in specific states like California and Florida should in fairness be offset by the federal government, which is enjoying the tax receipts these newcomers generate.[43]

Those who oppose the flows are concerned about how unskilled many of the migrants are and worry in particular that the Mexican and Central American immigrants, with their high numbers and their relatively low rates of economic success and the difficulty their children have had in doing well through education, will soon slip into an underclass whose proportions will threaten future political stability. Of the 13.5 million legal immigrants to this country between 1981 and 1996, over 3.3 million came from Mexico. Of the 916,000 persons naturalized in 1996, 164,000 were Mexican. Of the estimated 5 million illegal aliens in the United States in 1996, 2.7 million were estimated to be Mexican. For our purposes, however, the point is to indicate once again that global forces are deeply influencing multiethnicity within the United States while domestic ethnic groups, in turn, are having a decided impact on America's place in world affairs.[44]

Observers agree that Mexican Americans were active in shaping the Immigration Reform and Control Act of 1986 and the Immigration Act of 1990, measures that despite their names effectively blocked meaningful changes in these migration patterns and that indeed by amnesty provisions surely substantially accelerated them. To be sure, in testimony before the House Judiciary Committee in June 1995, Raoul Yzaguirre, president of the most important Latino political group in the country, the National Council of La Raza, declared that "the U.S. has a right and a duty to control its borders . . . the critical question is not 'Should the U.S. control its borders?' but rather 'How do we achieve this goal?'" Yet Yzaguirre went on to criticize (1) efforts to create a national identification card or establish some alternative form of employer verification code; (2) measures to expand or enforce "deeming" obligations (by which U.S. citizens who want to sponsor family members coming to this country legally commit themselves to support their relatives for a given period); and (3) such sanctions against illegals as permanently denying them immigration rights or streamlining measures for deportation.[45]

In the fall of 1996 an immigration reform law passed the Congress and was signed by the President that measurably increased the difficulties faced by those who would come to the United States illegally. But if this could be seen as a defeat for the Mexican American lobby, the fact that the guidelines for legal immigration remained unchanged should be seen as a greater victory, for it meant that Mexican Americans' numbers would continue to swell, through family reunification provisions especially, far past what critics of the law deem desirable. Moreover, the impact of Mexican and Central American voters on the

1996 elections (essentially in California, Arizona, New Mexico, and Texas, where in each state they made up over 11–15 percent of the vote—a percentage that is growing by about 1–2 percent annually—and thus provided at least a quarter of the votes Democratic candidates received) means that this ethnic group has come of age politically throughout the Southwest, from Texas to California.

In a more general sense, the change in the ethnoracial structure of the United States caused by large-scale immigration since the late 1960s may eventually have a dramatic impact on this country's foreign policy by realigning domestic concerns about foreign affairs. "The immigration process is the single most important determinant of American foreign policy," declared Daniel Patrick Moynihan and Nathan Glazer in 1975, and if the statement is surely exaggerated, the point is nonetheless well taken:

> It is odd how little this phenomenon figures in American public discussion; it is neither hailed nor challenged, but simply ignored . . . This process regulates the ethnic composition of the American electorate. Foreign policy responds to that ethnic composition. It responds to other things as well, but probably *first of all* to the primal facts of ethnicity . . . Foreign policy will be affected in diverse and profound ways. Yet oddly, the United States Department of State almost wholly ignores the immigration process. The fact that immigration policy is foreign policy is a seemingly inexplicable thought in Foggy Bottom.[46]

Who Speaks for America?

This third, post–Cold War stage of ethnic involvement in U.S. foreign policy is like the second stage that existed during the Cold War in that most organized American ethnic groups are proudly internationalist. But what is strikingly different today is that in many, if not most, cases their activism no longer coexists with a strong bipartisan sense of national purpose in Washington. As a result, whereas ethnic groups from the 1940s through the 1980s tried to make their goals harmonize with those of Washington, today the situation is reversed, with Washington increasingly playing court to ethnic group lobbies.

As we shall see in more detail in the next chapter, since the end of the

Cold War the national government has become weaker in three respects. First, the executive and legislative branches have become less likely to be in agreement, so that government is more often divided on issues of foreign policy. Second, at the party level, bipartisanship is declining, making Congress more divided. Third, at the level of state-society relations, organized civic interests are gaining new power over the state as "the era of big government" is pronounced finished. The first two of these trends make it increasingly difficult for the country to define a coherent foreign policy and defend it with some account of the national interest. The third trend means that in the absence of clear government leadership, American foreign policy is increasingly being defined by organized social interest groups, many of which are ethnic. The problem that arises in these circumstances is not simply that the real power of the United States to influence local events is limited but also that the structure of American government makes the power it does have subject to a host of internal constraints.

Who, then, speaks for America in world affairs? How politically positive or morally legitimate is it that ethnic or business interests increasingly determine major aspects of American foreign policy? A principal question, long familiar to theorists of democratic pluralism, is the status in right of the organized few to decide policy for the many. A second question is the more practical one of costs and benefits: is America better off when a few activists decide policy, or instead does foreign policy become inconsistent, incoherent, capricious, and conceivably even dangerous to the national community?

We should not suppose there is any easy or obvious answer to the question of the merits of the influence of ethnic groups on U.S. foreign policy. Surely there is much to approve in the range of initiatives Washington has undertaken largely at the behest of ethnic lobbies, be it participation in the peace processes in Northern Ireland or the Middle East, in the expansion of NATO in 1999, in the revelation of Swiss banking scandals, in the military occupation of Haiti, or in the expanded embargoes on trade with Cuba and Iran. Such activism counters the trend to neo-isolationism which lurks as an ever-present danger in the American public while it also promotes democratic governments compatible with U.S. interests. Still, many observers might well find something to fault among such policies, arguing that they contribute to incoherence or inconsistency in the U.S. role in the world, or that they commit this country to complicated and dangerous involvements abroad at the urging of determined minorities who are unconcerned with promoting American national interests in the agendas they pursue.

We confront here the question of the effect of democratic pluralism on the conduct of American foreign policy. To be sure, there are those who may deny that the question is meaningful, either because ethnic groups are too weak for their activism to be a telling test of the character of pluralism, or because their impact has been so overwhelmingly positive that the benefits of pluralism are obvious. But the most insightful students of democratic pluralism have always realized that the benefits of democratic government come at a cost, that democracy has tensions within itself that must be frankly confronted if the virtues of the system are not to be undone by its inherent contradictions.

Without, then, either questioning the right of ethnic groups to have positions on American foreign policy or denying that ethnic activism can be beneficial to American interests in the world, let us consider what case can be made that this domestic influence exacts its price. Critics cite examples of controversial policies strongly promoted by ethnic groups: influenced by the Greek American lobby, Washington has allowed Athens to hobble U.S. relations with both Turkey and the former Yugoslavia; beholden to the Armenian American lobby, U.S. policy in the Caucasus was long rigid and shortsighted; unable to buck the Israel lobby, the United States failed to pressure the Netanyahu government despite its undermining of the Oslo peace accords; giving in to the Cuban American lobby, Clinton slapped an economic embargo on Cuba that provoked outrage from our closest trading partners; bowing to the African American lobby, Washington launched what initially looked like a high-risk occupation of Haiti that in the event did little to help that benighted land.

But more than specific policies, critics of ethnic group activism point to the generally incoherent and contradictory character of American foreign policy in the post–Cold War years that has exacted its cost on American national interests. Perhaps the most obvious arena is U.S. international economic policy. It is widely agreed that the greatest success of the Clinton administration has been in foreign economic policy. The World Trade Organization, the North American Free Trade Association, and Asia Pacific Economic Cooperation may all have started during the Bush years, but they were brought to fruition by Bill Clinton and are generally considered his most important legacy in foreign policy.

However, various measures supported by ethnic group activists to employ economic sanctions not only against unfriendly countries but actually against allies of the United States threaten to cripple these important initiatives. What are we to think, for example, of American leadership of the world economy when in November 1997 the U.N. General Assembly voted 143–3 in favor of a resolution calling on the United States to terminate the Helms-Burton sanctions on Cuba, the three votes in the negative being the United States, Israel, and Uzbekistan?

Prior to 1996, American ethnic activists who succeeded in getting economic sanctions imposed on foreign regimes were able only to punish American businesses which flouted the law, and even here the penalties were minimal. For example, blacks were successful at restricting trade with Rhodesia and at working against apartheid in South Africa by these means (the so-called Sullivan Principles and later the call for "divestment") and again at isolating Haiti after Aristide's overthrow in September 1991. Using the MacBride Principles, Irish Americans persuaded, as of 1997, sixteen states and thirty-one municipalities not to do business with and to withdraw pension funds invested in U.S. corporations that failed to protect equality for Catholics in enterprises in Northern Ireland. But these measures pale in comparison to the sanctions that could be meted out thanks to the embargo on Cuba, backed by the Cuban American National Foundation, or those to be levied on companies doing business with Iran, promoted by the American Israel Public Action Committee. For with these measures, signed into law by President Clinton in 1996, businesses and individuals in countries that have long been close economic partners of the United States can be severely penalized for failing to comply with U.S. embargo legislation.

The question is not whether in principle these embargoes are good policies. The notion of a club of democratic states acting together to protect their interests or to promote their values is an appealing one in theory. Many Americans still want to settle scores with Castro. And the state-sponsored terrorism of Iran, compounded by the possibility that by 2005 that country may have missiles capable of carrying nuclear weapons, is a serious matter that the international community needs to

deal with collectively. But the rub comes not in principle but in practice. Efforts to create a democratic club and maintain its cohesion are
never easy, and in the case of the U.S. embargoes against Cuba and
Iran, Washington's allies are angered that the measures were taken uni-
laterally without their being consulted, that they are punitive in severe
and novel ways, and that they therefore contravene basic procedures of
the very international trade and investment mechanisms—especially
the World Trade Organization—that presumably were to be the hallmark of American leadership in world affairs after the Cold War.[47] In
short, in Washington it would appear that the proverbial right hand
(wielded by the ethnic groups and elected officials) does not know what
the left hand (wielded by business interests and most of the government bureaucracy) is doing.

A related issue is the power of states and municipalities effectively to
legislate foreign economic policy (a right reserved to the Congress by
Article 1, Section 8 of the Constitution) with the myriad of boycotts
these jurisdictions regularly enact through their pension funds and
public purchasing decisions to influence the behavior of firms doing
business with foreign governments. The success of the anti-apartheid
movement in the 1980s, when twenty-three states and eighty cities
used economic means to protest racial segregation in South Africa,
prompted imitators among Irish, Jewish, and Cuban activists especially.
As a consequence, in November 1999 the Supreme Court finally decided to take up the question of the constitutionality of such practices
when it agreed to review whether Massachusetts had exceeded its powers as a state by requiring its agencies to boycott firms doing business in
Myanmar. The hope of business groups that opposed such legislation
was that the Court would rule such practices unconstitutional and
make the ruling binding on the entire country.[48]

A nearly equivalent degree of incoherence in U.S. foreign policy can
be argued to exist in the field of military aid. During the Cold War, instances abounded of the United States helping its Arab clients arm
themselves against potential enemies only to find the Israelis understandably worried about the consequences. Part of the solution to the
problem was to involve the Israelis more closely in weapons development efforts so as to reassure them of their military superiority in the
Middle East. But in November 1999 Pentagon officials criticized the
Israeli sale of an advanced airborne radar system to China that would

give China important military abilities in the Taiwan Strait. The Israelis insisted that the radar system was their own fabrication, a claim disputed by American officials, who maintained that after such a long and close collaboration, separating what was Israeli from what was American was often quite difficult to do and in the case of this sale impossible.[49]

Similarly, U.S. policy in the eastern Mediterranean was bedeviled by the Greek concern that military aid to Turkey to build up NATO's eastern flank might embolden Ankara in its dealings with Athens. In the aftermath of the Cold War, neither of these dilemmas has disappeared while still others have been added, as in the agitation of Indian and Pakistani Americans with respect to military sales to their ancestral homelands.

As special interests of a variety of sorts proliferate—and the primary activists are not necessarily ethnic—American foreign policy appears more and more to be up for grabs, not only lacking coherence and vision but on occasion seemingly impelled by self-defeating forces that no one can master. So Samuel Huntington deplores "the disintegrative effects of the end of the Cold War," noting that both the attacks by anti-government militias on the right and "the rise of the cult of multiculturalism" have part of their roots in world affairs. Former CIA Director and then Secretary of Defense James Schlesinger makes much the same point:

> The weakening, if not the disappearance of the time-honored concept of America as a melting pot has reinforced these tendencies [to disdain the idea of a national interest]. The new fashion among the academics of multiculturalism and what is called "ethnic consciousness-raising" serves to legitimize further the demands of ethnic constituencies to have the world's leading power back their special agendas. But in terms of its impact on foreign policy, it is hard to find the benefit of multiculturalism or "ethnic consciousness-raising." To sustain an effective and reasonably consistent foreign policy requires a national consensus, which in turn depends on a sense of common purpose. The new intellectual fashions weaken and, in a sense, delegitimize the search for that common purpose . . . This is not the foundation on which the American democracy can sustain its role as world leader.[50]

One concern of Huntington's and Schlesinger's is that the appearance of new states after the Cold War raises more clearly than heretofore the question of how American ethnic groups in league with foreign popular movements or governments will try to influence Washington's role in world affairs. The problem is not a new one—Tomas Masaryk had tremendous success mobilizing Czech and Slovak Americans and lobbying President Wilson for the creation of Czechoslovakia in his trip to the United States in 1918, preparing the way for Vaclav Havel to appeal to Czech Americans to support the enlargement of NATO in 1997–1999. Before both world wars, the German government sought to rally German Americans in its support (and were notably successful before World War I), and Mussolini received strong support from Italian Americans prior to World War II. During the Cold War, both the Israeli and the Greek governments found that their American kinfolk could be valuable political resources. This recognition is now shared by the new governments in Warsaw, Kiev, Prague, Budapest, Yerevan, and elsewhere, while foreign leaders from Nelson Mandela to Gerry Adams directly address ethnic constituencies in the United States. A case that could be of particular importance in the future would involve Taiwan acting with and through Taiwanese American organizations to promote U.S. defense of the independence of that island. In an era when America's sense of purpose in the world is declining, while these various other states are well aware of the regional dangers that continue to confront them, foreign governments working through American ethnic organizations—whose activities they will do all they can to stimulate—may expect to gain an important extra measure of influence in Washington.

How may a democracy safeguard its pluralism while addressing its challenges? At least four courses of action (perhaps in a blend) are conceivable. The first suggests that, faced with the proliferation of domestic demands, the United States would be well advised to limit its commitments abroad for fear of unwise choices made under pressure from special interests. This is the counsel of Samuel Huntington, who writes in favor of "a policy of restraint and reconstitution aimed at limiting the diversion of American resources to the service of particularistic subnational, transnational, and nonnational interests . . . [that will lower] American involvement in the world in ways that will safeguard possible future national interests."[51] The objection to this proposal, however, is that it might lead to neo-isolationism, a development to be avoided.

A second course of action would be to put an informal moratorium on ethnic group politicking in foreign affairs in much the same way that religious organizations have traditionally been constrained (often without success) from taking political positions. Ethnic caucuses in the Congress and ethnic PAC money designed to influence U.S. foreign policy would henceforth be discouraged. Here, however, the problem is how to safeguard ethnic activists' civil rights to be involved in domestic politics and to maintain direct relations with their kinfolk abroad. A related way to act would be to reform campaign finance so as to reduce the role of interest group money in elections; changes that strengthen party discipline might also reduce interest group influence (both matters are discussed in Chapter 3).

A third course of action would be to increase government's independence from the demands of social forces by providing government officials with more autonomy to act. For example, the Hamilton-Crane-Lugar Sanctions Reform Bill introduced in the House of Representatives in October 1997, with thirty-seven Democrats and fifty Republicans as cosponsors, had a variety of clauses to restore more credibility to Washington's role in world economic affairs. The bill proposed that the Congress would have to determine the domestic economic and foreign humanitarian price of any unilateral economic sanctions engaged in by the United States; the President would have increased authority to waive such legislation once passed; and sanctions would have to be renewed every two years.[52] The virtue of the proposed legislation was its effort to increase the power of centralized leadership in Washington relative to social forces.

Yet a fourth course of action would be to rely on the Madisonian formula of setting social interest groups against one another as countervailing powers. So far as ethnic groups are concerned, their major antagonists are usually business interests and sometimes other ethnic actors. As economic sanctions based on ethnic demands have proliferated in the aftermath of the Cold War, commercial groups have pointed out that the targets of the sanctions have seldom been affected, but that American business has suffered greatly. By the middle of 1998 the American Chamber of Commerce, USA Engage, and a variety of legislators and commentators had accumulated enough power substantially to reverse many of the punitive efforts of American ethnic lobbies to use trade legislation as a stick against regimes abroad.[53] In these circumstances of antagonism between social forces creating a political standoff, the state rather automatically becomes more autonomous.

Of these four possible courses of action, the most likely is a blend of the third and last, or essentially things much as they are now, "business as usual." We should not rule out campaign finance reform that would result in public underwriting of elections, however, nor underestimate how great an impact on the way Washington determines policy such a reform could produce. In order to explore the character of business as usual more closely, let us now turn from an historical survey of what has happened to a political analysis of how interest group power has been accumulated. By looking more closely at the ways ethnic groups have organized themselves as effective lobbies in terms of the structure of American politics, we can hope to acquire a better appreciation of just how strong they truly are.

THREE

Gaining Influence in Washington

Today, as people have become ever more doubtful of the ability of the Government to deal with our problems, we are increasingly drawn to single-issue groups and special interest organizations to ensure that whatever else happens, our own personal views and our own private interests are protected. This is a disturbing factor in American political life. It tends to distort our purposes, because the national interest is not always the sum of all our single or special interests. We are all Americans together, and we must not forget that the common good is our common interest and our individual responsibility.

—*President Jimmy Carter*

As we saw in Chapter 2, at different periods in the twentieth century ethnic group activism had different effects on U.S. foreign policy. In a first stage, from the 1910s through the 1930s, ethnic pressure contributed to American neutrality before World War I, the failure to enter the League of Nations thereafter, and the isolationist feelings of the interwar years. During the Cold War—the second stage—ethnic lobbies tended, by contrast, to be internationalist, as Euro Americans surmounted their differences and any tension between their ethnic and national identities by joining together in the struggle against Soviet communism. In the third stage, which followed the Cold War and is not yet over, ethnic group internationalism has continued, now well-instructed in clothing itself in the national interest; but with a decline in Washington in recent years of a clear sense of national interests, the struggles among business and ethnic interests for influence have contributed to an increasingly incoherent and contradictory foreign policy.

But this version of the historical record may not satisfy everyone. Setting an account of ethnic group activism alongside an account of what actually happened may be deceiving, some may say, for the former may only coincide with, without actually causing, the latter. More evidence is called for to show how ethnic groups translate their preferences into policy. The purpose of this chapter is a closer analysis of the dynamics of ethnic group politicking, centered mainly on the third historical stage.

A major conclusion is that the structure of the American political system, as much as the character of particularistic social forces, explains the importance of ethnic groups in the formulation of American foreign policy. But to leave the matter there is to fail to investigate why some ethnic organizations (or other interests groups) have more influence than others. Accordingly, this chapter falls into two major parts, the first focusing on the structure of the American political system that allows social forces the degree of influence they have on foreign policy, the second analyzing ethnic group organizing itself to see why some organizations are especially effective at getting their agendas adopted in Washington.

The Structure of American Politics

Is it essentially because America is "a nation of immigrants" that ethnic and racial groups have had so much influence on U.S. foreign policy? The slave and the immigrant experiences have been so individually and socially powerful that it may seem self-evident that they would have significant political results. The United States is a democracy, and if its government is rule of, for, and by the people, then how could ethnic communities fail to demand that their government behave in world affairs as the people would have it? Or so the small literature that exists on ethnic groups or diasporas in the United States commonly sees the matter.

Yet surely the political context in which ethnic lobbies act determines the outcome of their efforts too. It is not only the social character of America as a nation of immigrants that makes for the prominent role ethnic actors play in foreign policy deliberations; it is also the structure of American democracy that allows ethnic communities, and a much wider range of civic interest groups in general, access to policymaking. By shifting the focus from the interest lobby to the structure of American politics—or better yet, by analyzing each in terms of the other—we can achieve a fuller account of how foreign policy is made.

The chief feature of American politics to keep in mind here is that relative to other democracies (although perhaps more like certain multiparty parliamentary systems) the American state is comparatively lacking in autonomy because it is highly penetrated by interest groups that are capable of making their agenda that of the government.[1] The key feature of American democracy that explains this greater penetration of governmental decisionmaking by social interest groups is to be found in the structure of state-society relations, which in comparative historical terms has put decided limits on concentrated, autonomous state power.

At the founding of the republic, a variety of considerations argued for the creation of a weak central government. Some favored strong states' rights in recognition of the different personalities the colonies had acquired under long British rule. A federal organization of power was the consequence, which by the late 1990s was experiencing a vigor it had not felt since the civil rights legislation of the 1960s restricted local authority in favor of national legislation. Others were concerned to preserve private property, and especially slaveholding, from public expropriation. Later, the manner in which American capitalism grew up independently from the state meant that the market and society in general opposed regulation to a degree unfamiliar in most other democracies (as in Scandinavia, France, Germany, or Japan). Still others had religious grounds to limit state power. The separation of church and state, along with an ethic of tolerance, preserved an important sphere of social life from government interference. And yet others feared the accumulation of power itself as a threat to freedom (and so, for example, opposed the creation of a standing militia or insisted on trial by jury). The result of all these forces was a society vigilant in reserving power to itself by circumscribing the role of the state—a degree of pluralism that was distinctively American.

Accordingly, the Founding Fathers deliberately created a series of institutional checks and balances that resulted not so much in a *division* of power as in a *sharing* or *overlap* of responsibilities that works to see that no single branch, much less individual, can monopolize power and so convert democracy into tyranny. Hence in foreign policy, which is more controlled by the presidency than by the legislature or the courts, and where by general agreement bipartisanship is supposed to reign, the power of the purse and the right to ratify treaties and declare war remain with the Congress, which also has the ability to conduct log-rolling between domestic and foreign programs and the right to independent public scrutiny of the executive.

Because the Congress and the President can be of the same mind or the same party, it is conceivable that the institutional struggle built into politics by the Constitution might not occur and thus the government would enjoy relative autonomy in the face of social pressures. But in the American system of government the likelihood of any such outcome is significantly reduced by a system of political party organization that enormously empowers social forces. Thus candidates for public office are not named by the party (as in so-called disciplined party systems such as those of Great Britain and France) but nominated through primaries (which began in western states in the late nineteenth century, and were used everywhere by the beginning of the 1970s) whose results are decided by local electorates. The consequence of such party discipline is that in practice public officials may well be as responsive to their constituents as to their party leadership. Given that the Congress is also a decentralized entity, with many points at which legislation can be either initiated or blocked, even civic interests operating on a small social base may find their concerns being reflected in legislation.

As a consequence of the country's political structure, social forces have two principal sources of entry into the system: first, at the local, grassroots level of party selection of officeholders during primaries; and second, not only in the divisions that naturally open between the executive and the legislature, but also (indeed, especially) in the divisions within the legislature itself in Washington during the course of political deliberations.

But how much is enough? In 1997 I several times asked experts on the American system what kind of access an ethnic group able to muster at least $1 million in targeted campaign contributions and 250,000 votes in a selected number of congressional districts could buy (roughly the clout of the Cuban American National Foundation—CANF—in the 1992 and 1996 presidential elections). The reply was always that the influence of such a group might well be "considerable," providing that the group had no powerful enemies, a clear agenda, and the capacity to find at least some credible allies. The price of access has doubtless risen since 1997, yet given what a low percentage of the electorate or of total campaign contributions these figures represent in the United

States, I would conclude that this is a very low threshold of entry indeed into policymaking.

Consider, for example, a report by Tim Weiner in the *New York Times*, January 6, 1999. Despite an array of forces favoring a liberalized U.S. policy toward Cuba, including the Chamber of Commerce and the Catholic church, the Clinton administration would embrace only hesitant measures toward an opening, fearful of a political backlash from intensely concerned elements in the powerful Cuban American community in New Jersey and Florida in the elections of 2000. Again, with its eye on elections, a report in the same newspaper by Michale Janofsky on January 25, 1999, explained the Clinton administration's efforts to increase social welfare programs for legal immigrants because of pressure "from states with large immigrant populations, like New York, New Jersey and California, where Hispanic residents and Asians are voting in ever increasing numbers." Not coincidentally, Vice President Gore presented details of the administration's immigrant welfare program during a swing through California, the state with the greatest immigrant population.

One may favor such a relationship between state and society as a higher form of representative government, directly exposed as Washington is to civic forces; or one may worry that a regime so easily dominated by civic society may be stalemated in its decisionmaking, the paralyzed victim of an overly participatory interest group society unable to agree on a common definition of the collective good; or one may simply marvel that whatever its apparent shortcomings in theory the system in practice works admirably well.[2] The argument is one which began between Alexander Hamilton and Thomas Jefferson and continues to this day. Regardless of the judgment, the important point for our deliberations is that it is not only because the United States is "a nation of immigrants" that ethnic groups have such influence on foreign policy in this country, but also because its pluralist politics facilitates the access of a wide gamut of interest groups to the exercise of public power. Among these groups, American ethnic groups are simply one subset—in fact, one that arrived rather late on the scene, long after states' rights, religious, and economic interest groups had prepared the way.

The balance between state and society is dynamic, of course, history favoring the one side, then the other. In a time of national emergency such as war or economic depression, the role of the state may expand.

The Civil War marked a first important step in the expansion of the state's authority, and in the twentieth century the Progressive era, the Depression, two world wars, and the Cold War all gave rise, each in its distinctive way, to a stronger government, one better able to raise resources from the citizenry and to unify the public around common goals requiring political leadership.

In the process, not only did the power of the state expand with respect to society, but the role of the executive gained relative to that of the legislature, an evolution of power consonant with the global trend in favor of stronger central governments increasingly able to regulate society. Thus, as late as 1939, President Roosevelt had only four professional assistants (above the clerical level) in the White House, whereas for subsequent presidents the number expanded considerably, many of them in the foreign policy bureaucracies created at the beginning of the Cold War and directly responsible to the Chief Executive, including the National Security Council, the Central Intelligence Agency, the Atomic Energy Commission, and the Council of Economic Advisers.

By contrast, during times of international peace and economic prosperity, the ability of dominant social forces to insulate themselves from interference from the state may grow. So it was in the late nineteenth century, and one hears the argument today that with the end of the Cold War and the robustness of the American economy the Presidency is weakening relative to the Congress while the state is weakening relative to society.[3]

Thus, not only was the Republican-dominated 104th Congress elected in 1994 hostile to the Presidency, but the 103rd, although controlled by the Democrats, marked its distance from Clinton as well, making it difficult for the executive to deploy troops in Haiti, Bosnia, or Somalia; to keep up the U.S. commitment to the United Nations; or to bail out Mexico when the North American Free Trade Agreement (NAFTA) got into difficulty in 1994. Similarly, there were efforts to scale back the size of government and balance the budget, involving cuts in taxes, welfare, and regulatory agencies. The upshot has been a double reduction of what Arthur Schlesinger Jr. once dubbed "the imperial Presidency": the executive has weakened relative to the legislature and the entire government has weakened relative to civic forces.

One should not trust to overly simplistic readings of the balance of political forces in this country, however. For the current rise of society relative to the state—especially insofar as ethnic group activism is concerned—did not begin with the end of the Cold War so much as in the mid-1960s. Here was the critical moment from which social scientists have measured a strong and steady expansion of interest group activity in this country, a time when the nation was going through an unpopular war and was simultaneously facing a serious social challenge. The Civil Rights and Antiwar Movements were the vanguard of this change, which in short order emboldened women, Hispanics, homosexuals, and others, in turn engendering a rise of conservative movements determined to preserve their values and interests against this leftist upsurge. Nor were all the new lobbies ideological or "public interest," for economic forces were also active. "Washington law is lobbying law," Jeffrey Berry has said, noting that from 1972 to 1994 the Washington bar grew nearly six times in size, from 11,000 to 63,000 members. Meanwhile, the number of lobbyists in Washington continued to multiply: from 14,946 in mid-1997 to 20,512 in mid-1999 (making thirty-eight lobbyists for each member of Congress). As a group lobbyists received, from those who wanted influence, $1.42 billion in 1998 (up 13 percent over the preceding year), or about $2.7 million per member of Congress.[4]

The rise of social activism in the second half of the 1960s continued into the first half of the 1970s with critical changes in the political organization of the country. The Legislative Reorganization Act of 1970 weakened the congressional seniority system and mandated publicly recorded votes on all issues; and party discipline was further eroded by the generalized use of primaries after 1970. The War Powers Resolution in 1973, enhancing Congress's power, the forced resignation of President Richard Nixon in the summer of 1974, and the final defeat in Vietnam the following spring continued this decade of state decline.

In due course, the legitimacy of the state was largely restored—but under Presidents Jimmy Carter and Ronald Reagan, both of whom came to power on platforms that in part explicitly criticized Washington as overly distant from the people. The Reagan administration was especially noteworthy for embracing the tenets of a populism which called for "getting government off the back of the American people," thereby validating for conservatives the kind of social activism that had been largely liberal in the 1960s and 1970s and preparing the country for the demobilization of the state that accelerated with the end of the Cold War.

As public opinion polls compiled by Robert Putnam and confirmed by others indicate, popular mistrust of government began to grow in the 1960s and continued into the 1990s,[5] so that governmental legitimacy was achieved in part, ironically enough, by attacks on government. "The era of big government is over," President Clinton twice announced during his 1996 State of the Union address, and the tax and welfare cuts, the failure to expand difficult environmental protection laws, the abandonment of efforts to secure national health insurance, and the failure to pass effective gun control legislation were all indications of the meaning of his declaration.

Thus, despite the growth of government's power as measured in the percentage of the Gross Domestic Product it controls or the spheres of life in which it plays a part, society has grown in strength as well, retaining a great deal of autonomy and finding new ways of gaining access to political decisionmaking. The Supreme Court has led the way in a rebirth of states' rights. Economic forces have been substantially tamed domestically, but certainly not captured, by the state, which by sponsoring an era of economic globalization should become increasingly unable to control capitalism in the future. Religious freedom continues to be jealously guarded, while religious activism with respect to world affairs has expanded notably in recent years. And a host of independent forces including the media, the universities, private foundations, gender, ethnic, and racial communities, and citizens' action groups have proliferated, giving new form and strength to society relative to the state. One should therefore not conclude from arguments that the state in general became stronger in the twentieth century that society necessarily became weaker or American democracy less pluralist.[6]

Some social groups favor a weaker state. But others—and this includes most ethnic communities—favor an activist state. Hence the paradox for these constituencies is that their access to political power may be increasing at the very moment when the amount of power the state possesses is decreasing, in part thanks to their efforts. The result may be surprising. Despite struggles against fascism and communism that endured for two generations, the United States retains strong isolationist and antistatist currents within it. If the state is weakened too much by the revival of these sentiments (as the 104th Congress appeared to be trying to weaken it), then the internationalist ambitions of many of these ethnic groups may correspondingly be without means to achieve their goals. For example, in the absence of a strategic threat, the question may be raised of why we should mobilize to promote stable government in Africa or to ensure the security of Israel. In sum, while on balance the end of the Cold War has facilitated ethnic groups' objectives in American foreign policy, the event is a two-edged sword and certainly has its liabilities so far as the ambitions of ethnic internationalism are concerned.

With respect to the role of ethnic groups in U.S. foreign policy, this brief review of the character of the American political system suggests four general propositions. First, ethnic interests should be studied as a subset of interest groups in general and thus related to a broader field of study.[7] Economic and religious interests have been especially important in shaping the character of American democracy, and ethnoracial groups should be seen as following in their footsteps.

Second, because of the decentralized nature of American politics, "playing the game" or "working the system" initially requires surprisingly little political capital. While the President is undoubtedly the most important decisionmaker in the land and ethnic groups are fortunate to have his direct support, the surest (or easiest) means of access for citizens to the political system is through those positions most exposed to direct public pressure—especially to candidates for office during primaries, to the House over the Senate, and to the Senate over the presidency (especially when the executive and legislative branches are controlled by different parties).

Third, although some groups are closely related to particular parties (Armenian Americans to the Republicans, African Americans to the Democrats, for example) ethnic group influence is likely to be greater when it appeals to both parties, when the Congress and the President belong to different parties, when the country is in a crisis that weakens the state as a whole (as in the late 1960s), or when the country is in a time of peace so far as threats to its vital interests are concerned, so that a bipartisan consensus on foreign policy is difficult to establish.

Fourth, the nature of American democracy is such that interest lobbies at times determine national policy, even on matters of critical importance to the entire citizenry, indeed at times in ways that may contradict what may reasonably be construed to be the common good. When benefits are concentrated among the few and costs are diffused over a large population, when special interests are focused and the public is inattentive, then the structure of American politics allows a determined, self-interested minority to speak for America in world affairs, especially at historical moments such as that following the end of the Cold War when the unity and purpose of the state has weakened and social activists stand ready with their demands. For when no threat to the national security can be cited, American politics is typically the politics of organized interests—not only of the "power elite" in the sense of the rich and the possessors of the commanding heights of the economy, but of virtually any civic action group that can marshal a relatively small cohort of voters, raise a relatively small amount of cash, and use these resources in a concentrated, focused manner in the absence of a determined opposition. Who speaks for America? In the absence of a clear and present danger to the nation, special interests do.[8]

Ethnic Groups and Foreign Policy

As we saw in Chapter 2, the record of ethnic group politicking is a rich one involving large segments of the American public in foreign policy decisions of great national importance. Attention can now be turned away from a review of what American ethnic groups wanted to achieve to the question of how some of them went about securing their ambitions.

For the sake of analytical clarity, it may be said that there are three general ways in which interest groups (and not only those which are ethnic) bring pressure to bear on the political establishment: through the vote; by campaign finance contributions; and by an organizational body (something more formidable than the word "lobby" usually connotes) that formulates the strategy for getting precise pieces of legislation passed, provides unity to the ethnic community, builds alliances with other social forces toward common political goals, and monitors decisionmaking to ensure that friends are rewarded, opponents punished, and feedback accumulated so that the organization can become ever more effective.

Voting

How important is ethnic voting to giving these constituencies influence over American foreign policy? At first glance, one may doubt that it is of much importance at all. Jews are scarcely 3 percent of the American population; Greeks barely 1 percent; Cubans and Armenians at most one-half of 1 percent. All have real clout in Washington, but to what extent is it due to their voting power?

Or consider Irish Americans. While it is common to read reference to the "44 million Americans of Irish ancestry" as an indication of the political power of this ethnicity, I have not been able to find a single quantitative study that demonstrates the impact of this community on foreign policy through voting since World War II. The way the census is compiled, anyone with any Irish ancestry may identify as such, meaning that the identity is not necessarily held strongly. Moreover, many of these "Irish" (perhaps half), if religious at all, are Protestants, and the great majority of those who are Catholic are far more concerned in their voting with class or religious issues than by the position Washington is taking on Ireland, which has been independent since 1937.[9]

Yet voting is, in fact, an important way in which ethnic communities make their voices heard in Washington. For example, in the 1992 Connecticut Democratic primary, Bill Clinton lost narrowly to Jerry Brown and interpreted his defeat as due to the preference of Irish Catholics in that state for Brown (who had once been a Jesuit seminarian and was of Irish descent). Senators Edward Kennedy and Daniel Patrick Moynihan also suggested to Clinton that to secure what might be the critical support of "Reagan Democrats" (blue-collar Catholics who traditionally voted Democratic but who had supported Reagan and then Bush) in New York City, Boston, and Chicago, Clinton should take more of an interest in the events in Northern Ireland. The result was Clinton's pledge to become personally involved in the Ulster peace process, a commitment which eventually brought Sinn Fein leader Gerry Adams to the White House, made former Senate majority leader George Mitchell the head of a special commission comprising Irish, British, and Northern Irish members, and took the President himself to Northern Ireland for a triumphal visit in November 1995.[10]

Did Irish American Catholics vote for Clinton because of his promises with regard to Ireland? One should perhaps be skeptical. Still, election estimates put Clinton's Catholic vote well ahead of the Republicans in 1992 and 1996, reversing the trend of the three previous presidential elections in which Catholics voted for the Republican over the Democratic candidate. Quite possibly his position on Northern Ireland made a real difference (along with his pledge to expand NATO, which appealed to Polish and Czech American Catholics as well).[11]

Certainly Clinton's foreign policy decisions rallied black voters. My assumption is that blacks do not vote primarily on such considerations. Nevertheless, TransAfrica and the Congressional Black Caucus had made issues such as Haiti an indicator of how hard they would push for Clinton; and this elite had ultimately been satisfied with his reaction, so helping to turn out the vote. Once again, then, even if indirectly, an important bloc of ethnic voters acted because of a foreign policy consideration.

The most dramatic evidence of ethnoracial voting power comes from the roles blacks and Hispanics played in Clinton's 1992 and 1996 general election victories. In 1996 Clinton received only 43 percent of the white vote while Robert Dole got 46 percent (the remainder going to other candidates). In these circumstances, Clinton's margin of victory came from receiving 84 percent of the black and 72 percent of the Hispanic vote. Given that Clinton got 78 percent of the Jewish vote and a majority of the white Catholic vote (much of it probably self-consciously ethnic, like the Irish and the Poles), Clinton's victory convincingly demonstrates the power of the ethnic vote in American politics— to such a degree that he might be called the ethnic groups' president.[12]

The mid-term elections in November 1998 showed much the same pattern. In voting for seats in the House of Representatives, the Democrats received 49 percent of the vote to 51 percent for the Republicans. Republicans won the white vote by 57 percent to 43 percent (and especially the white Protestant vote at 65 percent), while the Democrats took what could justifiably be termed the multicultural vote, backing from blacks (89 percent), Jews (79 percent), Hispanics (63 percent), Asians (53 percent), white Catholics (53 percent), women (53 percent), and homosexuals (67 percent). The Republicans' failure to court the black vote cost them especially dearly in dramatic Democratic victories in Georgia, Alabama, and South Carolina, thanks directly to unprecedented black turnout. Observers explained the success of Republicans

George and Jeb Bush in winning the governorships of Texas and Florida with the help of minority voters as a clear sign that Republicans must try to appeal to these important constituencies.[13]

For the Democrats, the most critical new factor in the last two national elections was the Hispanic vote. The foreign policy dimension of their current political activism lies in U.S. immigration policy. By the 1996 election Latinos constituted only 5 percent of the total vote, but that should rise by about 2 percent in each of the next presidential elections. And in 1996 they made up some 10 percent of the total vote in Arizona, 12 percent in Texas, and 15 percent in California. One report puts Hispanics at 30 percent of the population eligible to vote in California by the elections of 2000 and estimates that while Pete Wilson garnered 44 percent of their vote in his race for governor in 1990, after the anti-immigrant furor in 1994 related to Proposition 187 (which passed by a 59–41 percent total vote), Bob Dole won less than 10 percent of their vote in 1996.[14] Presumably one reason Clinton endorsed statehood for Puerto Rico when the island voted on a referendum in the fall of 1998 was that he assumed its population of 3.8 million was likely to vote Democratic if the measure passed.

Republicans have tried to cut their losses in these circumstances— for example, by changing their position on welfare benefits for legal immigrants resident in the United States prior to April 1997. Yet their primary effort still is to rally support against Latin immigration. Hence when the Republicans charged that the Immigration and Naturalization Service (INS) had improperly naturalized hundreds of thousands of foreigners in the months before the 1996 election—well over half of them Hispanics, and most of them likely to vote for Clinton—they were pointing their finger at attempts by Vice President Gore to speed up the process. In February 1996 a Latino group in southern California warned the White House that INS "inaction will prevent 300,000 Latinos from participating in the 1996 presidential election [and may] create the impression that the Clinton administration is anti-Latino." Gore took up the matter and had a senior adviser write INS that "the President is sick of this and wants action." In fact, the INS did resist suggestions that it farm out interviews for naturalization to private companies and also refused the President's request for a list of those naturalized so that he could send each of them personal greetings. Nevertheless, naturalization was expedited in a way that allowed tens of thousands to become citizens without proper background checks, meaning that perhaps as many as 71,000 persons who had had problems with the law nonetheless became American citizens.[15]

Subsequently, Republicans called for measures to verify citizenship when casting ballots. "They want to create unwarranted fear of the Hispanic community in the eyes of our fellow Americans," declared Representative Luis Gutierrez (D-Ill.). "I am not in the business of giving advice to Newt Gingrich, but let me say this: Latino voters are American voters. When we vote, we remember who stood with us and who stood against us." As a GOP member named Linda Chavez commented, "The Republican party sometimes shoots itself in the foot, as conservatives generally do when they talk about racial or ethnic issues." One indication that the GOP began to listen came with the passage of the Haitian Refugee Immigration Fairness Act of 1998, when Republicans from Florida (including gubernatorial candidate Jeb Bush, Senator Connie Mack, and Representatives Lincoln Diaz-Balart and Illeana Ros-Lehtinen) joined with Democrats like Edward Kennedy and the Congressional Black Caucus to extend to Haitian refugees the same right to stay in this country that applied to Cubans or Nicaraguans who had fled to the United States prior to 1995.[16]

Given the potential power of ethnic voting blocs, both the Republican and the Democratic national parties since the 1880s have both had what may be called "nationalities sections" (their exact titles have changed over time) designed to capture ethnic votes by staying in touch with ethnic group leadership. To be sure, at times presidents or presidential candidates have ignored these ethnic constituencies or (more often) tried to manipulate them. But since the 1940s, when Samuel Lubell published the first work powerfully demonstrating the potential power of these communities, candidates and their staffs have taken such voting power seriously. Today there is an "ethnic outreach" section in the White House with liaisons to every organized ethnicity in the country.

Ethnic voters do not have to make a decisive difference in national elections for their voice to be heard in Washington. It may be enough for ethnic lobbies to achieve their goals to be represented by well-placed members of Congress, preferably by senior senators or representatives in charge of committees whose duties give them a role in determining matters of significance to the ethnic community.

Thus Jewish Americans may be only 3 percent of the national population, but in 1992 they were over 9 percent of the population of New York (down from 14 percent twenty years earlier).[17] Since they are overwhelmingly Democrats, Jewish New Yorkers probably constitute something like 15 percent of the state's Democratic voters; and since they tend to vote at twice the levels of the state average, they may perhaps account for 30 percent of all of the votes cast in a Democratic primary in that state. Through their vote in New York state alone, then, Jews rather automatically have a place at the table in foreign policy deliberations in Washington. (Other states where Jewish populations exceed 5 percent of the total population, and where they may constitute at least 15 percent of the Democratic vote, are Florida and New Jersey, while they also have electoral weight in Democratic primaries in Massachusetts, Maryland, California, and Pennsylvania.) Of course, not all American Jews take their ethnic identities with them into the voting booth, and even when they do their opinions may vary greatly. Still, American Jewish concern with the Middle East is real, and politicians—especially in the Democratic party—act accordingly.

Because of the role of primaries in congressional elections, the decentralized character of the Congress itself, and the absence of strong mechanisms of national party discipline, voting pressure on Congress (especially on the House of Representatives) is a more likely source of access to decisionmaking for ethnic lobbies. Thus the number of Albanian Americans may be small, but they constitute about 17 percent of one congressional district in upstate New York, whose congressional representative is keenly attentive to their concerns (while their financial support to the Kosovo Liberation Army was apparently vital to that force in 1998/99).[18] Or again, Cuban and Armenian Americans, who make up only a tiny proportion of the population, can tell you where their demographic centers are (Dade County, Florida, and Union City, New Jersey, for the Cubans; Fresno, California, and Watertown, Massachusetts, for the Armenians). Deeply concerned about foreign relations as these groups are, they insist that their representatives in Washington take up their cases.

But to present voters as the active element, Washington as the reactive one, is to miss what is often the case. On occasion, officials in Washington, wanting to round up support for a foreign policy measure, rouse ethnic constituencies to pressure their representatives for policies whose authorship is in the government. It was Woodrow Wilson who first proposed to Polish American leaders that they set themselves up to influence foreign policy; it appears that it was John Foster Dulles's State Department that first mooted the idea of uniting American Jews to speak with one voice on world affairs; it was Richard Allen, on Ronald Reagan's election team, who first made a similar suggestion to the men who would soon found CANF (although some Cuban Americans claim the initiative was theirs); and it was with the support of the Clinton administration that Americans of East European ancestry pushed for the enlargement of NATO. (To assert, as Canadian Prime Minister Chrétien did, that NATO expansion was based on the administration's selling out to a lobby, is to miss the exchange of influence.) Or consider Haiti: was it really the African American community that brought about the occupation late in 1994, or was it (as some cynics say) that the United States did not want any more Haitian refugees and so put the onus for the undertaking, which was opposed by nearly 80 percent of the public, onto an ethnic group for reasons of political expediency?

Seen from this perspective, ethnic communities may offer grassroots support for policies adopted by political elites for the elites' own reasons, which they then phrase in the protective camouflage of ethnic argument in order to gain popular support in a political contest in Washington. So Steven Spiegel concludes that decisionmakers work in relative autonomy from interest groups and that ethnic lobbies "are relegated to the role of supplicants—hiding their weakness behind a facade of bravado and public activity."[19] As A. F. K. Organski suggests with regard to the Israel lobby, "it is misleading . . . to think that pressure from below is responsible for the policy and, that were such pressure to disappear, the policy itself would change at all significantly":

> Strategic considerations, rightly or wrongly, dictate what countries receive substantial American support. In the end, the real contribution of the pro-Israeli forces on the domestic scene is to lessen the political cost the government must pay in giving resources to a recipient whose enemies, the Arab states, are also friends of the United States . . . Were the American Jewish community to disappear, the aid the United States gives Israel would not decrease to any measurable extent. All that would happen is

that the leaders responsible for foreign-aid decisions would find the choice more costly in political terms.[20]

In my opinion, both Spiegel and Organski substantially underestimate the role of interest groups in shaping American foreign policy. But they make a valid point when they argue that political officials actively solicit such support and are not simply passively reacting to social pressures. The American political system not only permits, rather it actively promotes, ethnic group activism. In a word, to understand the impact ethnic groups can have on American foreign policy is to understand the character of the democratic system in which they operate.

Campaign Financing

Through contributing money to the campaigns of candidates for the presidency and the Congress, ethnic activists have another valuable source of access to decisionmakers. The key characteristic of campaign financing regulations that offers these groups influence is that individuals from *outside* a congressional district may make contributions for races in which they are not themselves eligible to vote. With their contributions, small ethnic communities, some almost utterly lacking in voting strength, may nonetheless find politicians willing to represent their interests.

If pride of place in buying influence in Washington goes to the business community, and if the activities of foreign governments may also be of concern, contributions based on ethnic lobbying are also a critical part of the process. For example, in a front-page article in the *Washington Post* on March 24, 1997, Dan Morgan and Kevin Merida reported how, in the unlikely place of South Dakota, Indian American and Pakistani American money had come to play an important role in the 1996 senatorial contest. The Republican Larry Pressler, a long-time friend of India and opponent of military aid to Pakistan, was defeated by the Democrat Tim Johnson, who had substantial Pakistani American backing. Johnson was not the only person running that year with such support. *The Hill* (a newspaper devoted to coverage of Capitol Hill) reported on April 16, 1997, that Representative Dan Burton (R-Ind.) had long received support from Pakistani and Sikh sources. Recently he had run into problems, however, and was under investigation by the

FBI for allegedly pressuring a lobbyist for the government of Pakistan for a $5,000 campaign contribution and for having received many tens of thousands more from American Sikhs in contributions illegally raised in their temples.

What the Indian/Pakistani/Sikh story illustrates is the way in which money can create ethnic group influence and conflicts in congressional districts where virtually no one of the ethnicities involved actually resides. Indeed, some in Congress have gone out of their way to solicit such money. For example, former representative Stephen J. Solarz began actively soliciting such money in the 1980s, using his position as head of the House Foreign Affairs Subcommittee on Asian and Pacific Affairs, the ethnic press, and specialized mailing lists to recruit contributions from Indian, Philippine, Vietnamese, Korean, and Cambodian Americans. According to Solarz: "My experience in fund-raising with various ethnic communities was that what was involved here was Americanism at its best. These people were, by and large, interested in contributing to the development of an American foreign policy that reflected the view of what our country was all about—namely a commitment to democracy and human rights."[21] In the 1987–88 fundraising season, Solarz may have raised $770,000 from these sources.

A part of the problem with funds raised from ethnic sources is that they may be illegal. On April 30, 1997, *The Hill* reported charges that the Indian embassy had contributed money illegally during the 1996 campaign, and in July of 1997 virtually every day's news carried more information on alleged illegal contributions from the Chinese government to the Democratic party preceding the 1996 election—the intention being to loosen U.S. export restrictions on military-related technology.

According to a report in the *New York Times* on December 29, 1996, it was an effort to make the Asian American community feel more "integrated" into the political system that prompted Vice President Gore in April 1996 to accept $80,000 in illegal contributions (since returned, but only when it became public knowledge) from Asian Americans (most of them penniless nuns) gathered at a Buddhist temple in California. The Democrats' overall strategy was to raise an unprecedented $7 million from Asian Americans and to create an "Asian Pacific American Leadership Council" (later called simply Pacific Leadership Council) from the ranks of those who gave at least $10,000.

It turned out that the money illegally raised from Asian American sources could not easily be separated in the public mind from money the Democrats illegally received from Chinese sources. Perhaps the two cannot be separated in reality either. In February 1998 the Republicans alleged that the Chinese-Indonesian Riady family and their American representative John Huang, working with Maria Hsia, had long-standing separate financial ties to Gore and to Clinton. In the 1996 campaign cycle these sources had contributed over $1.5 million to the Democratic party as well as given $100,000 to the President's former associate Webster Hubbell shortly before his indictment. Allegedly as a result of these payments, Huang had had dozens of classified briefings on matters unrelated to his position at the Commerce department but of concern to the Chinese intelligence service and the Riadys.[22]

The ever-growing need for money reached new heights in the 1996 election, when fundraising for both parties increased by more than a third over what it had been in 1992, which in turn was perhaps a fifth over what spending had been in 1988. Ronald Dworkin reported that in 1996 a presidential race cost $600 million to $1 billion; a Senate seat $5–$30 million (the *New York Times* put the median cost at $3.5 million, up from $2.7 million four years earlier); and a House seat perhaps $2 million (the *Times* put the median cost at $560,000, up from $348,000 four years earlier).[23]

Federal Election Commission (FEC) figures can be misleading, however, for certain types of spending may not appear while other types may be double-counted, so that it is difficult to be confident of final amounts. I was told by an analyst at the FEC, speaking off the record in July 1997, that total expenditures for *national* offices in 1995–96 were probably around $2.7 billion (the *New York Times* estimated $2.2 billion); in 1991–92 about $2 billion; and in 1987–88 perhaps $1.6 billion. February 1998 FEC reports indicated that the pursuit of financial support had intensified even more since the 1996 election, the collection of money increasing in the first quarter of 1997 by nearly 30 percent over what it had been in the first quarter of 1995. By the time of the November 1998 election, more money had been spent than in any mid-term election in U.S. history. And money talked. According to the Center for Responsive Politics, the candidate who spent most in a House contest won 95 percent of the time, in a Senate race 94 percent of the time.

Given the evident payoff, the pressure of collecting increasing sums of money has put tremendous stress on the political system. Days after the 1996 election, Clinton declared that the scandals he had been hearing about had "shown us once again that our campaigns cost too much, they take too much time, they raise too many questions, and now is the time for bipartisan campaign finance reform legislation." It may be true, as Herbert Alexander and Anthony Corrado point out, that in relative terms campaign spending is a trivial sum of money (their comparison is with the annual advertising budgets of Proctor and Gamble and Philip Morris, more than $3.2 billion in 1991–92). By comparison with the defense budget, the entire cost of all campaigns for national office is only 1 percent. Still, most politicians agree that the amount of time devoted to raising money is far too great and that the access to power the money buys is far too influential for the public good.[24]

Probably the most obvious payoffs for campaign contributions come from business groups, many of which are concerned with world affairs. In 1997 Common Cause published an analysis entitled "Return on Investment" detailing how millions of dollars in corporate contributions reaped billions of dollars for the donors in tax, subsidy, or regulation advantages. In 1998 Charles Lewis of the Center for Public Integrity published *The Buying of the Congress*, a far more extensive analysis of what money can buy in Washington.[25] On September 28 and 29, 1998, the *New York Times* published extensive articles by Jill Abramson detailing other aspects of lobbying, with special attention to the role of former public officials later representing a wide variety of organized social interests.

Foreign governments and companies also lobby aggressively in Washington. For example, the September 8, 1997, *U.S. News and World Report* listed Canada, Mexico, and Japan as each spending about $5 million a year on lobbying; Britain, Taiwan, and Israel each as spending $3–$4 million; and Haiti, Angola, Hong Kong, and Indonesia each as spending about $2 million. Here again, American foreign policy decisions were obviously of the utmost importance. But our concern must properly be restricted to domestic ethnic group calculations, and we should not be surprised to find abundant evidence of their participation in raising money for candidates for office as well.

On May 18, 1997, the *Washington Post* published an article based on Senator Robert Torricelli's disclosures of the financing of his 1996 campaign. For a year, the senator reported, he had spent some three hours a day fundraising on the phone and gone to some three hundred fundraising events to secure the $9.2 million he raised for his election (another $3.2 million was provided by others on his behalf). "A lot of House members duck Foreign Affairs because it doesn't bring lots of money to your district," Torricelli remarked, "but I never felt disadvantaged," for in raising money from ethnic constituencies, "nobody does it better than me." While his contributions from these communities could not be exactly ascertained, he reported $399,000 from Florida Cubans, $28,000 from pro-Israel PACs, and a single Greek event at which he netted $25,000. By his own account, he also received money from Iranian, Pakistani, Portuguese, and Chinese Americans. A 1996 publication of the Formosan Association for Public Affairs names him as their primary sponsor in Washington. "Hang in there. You're smarter and tougher than they think you are," Torricelli wrote to Israeli Prime Minister Netanyahu shortly before Netanyahu's visit to Washington in January 1998, presumably helping to secure thereby the support of the American Israel Public Affairs Committee (AIPAC) during his initial days in the Senate.[26]

In later remarks cited in the *New York Times* on August 9, 1997, Torricelli lamented not only the time he had to spend raising money for his campaign but also its effect on decisionmaking in Washington: "Our system of campaign finance is an invitation to any interest with a desire to compromise the policy of the United States to use money as a lever of power." The remark was perhaps heartfelt: in March 1997 I had asked a CANF official, who wished to remain anonymous, how it had happened that a man like Torricelli, known to be quite liberal on Latin American affairs (he had opposed the Contras and exposed CIA crimes in Guatemala) could be so close to CANF. "Money and votes in Union City," was the unhesitant reply delivered in a cynical tone.

Only a few days after his words on the Senate floor, Torricelli was at the Nantucket mansion of Senator John Kerry for a private weekend described by the *Boston Globe* on August 13, 1997, as "access-peddling" to Democratic contributors who gave at least $20,000 each (netting the party $4 million). Asked how he squared his plans for the weekend with his words in the Senate only a few days earlier, Torricelli invoked necessity, pleading that he also wanted "to change the tax code to help working families and students." The host of the party, Senator Kerry, was more candid in his comments about what money got, saying from the steps of his Nantucket estate to a surprised reporter: "I think it is sick. Do people get access? Yes, and I think it is wrong."

Republicans have expressed their concern over campaign finance reform as well. In June 1999 Governor George W. Bush announced that he had raised over $35 million in his bid to be the Republican presidential contender, a record for contributions so far ahead of primaries. Immediately thereafter, Senator John McCain, at the time Bush's leading rival for the position, challenged Bush to pledge to put campaign finance reform at the top of his political agenda. On July 1, 1999, the *New York Times* reported McCain declaring that the current system is "nothing less than an elaborate influence-peddling scheme in which both parties conspire to stay in office by selling the country to the highest bidder."

In my investigations into ethnic group financing of various campaigns, I found that it was often impossible to establish who contributed what or why. I was repeatedly told, for example, that Armenian Americans are generous contributors—how else, I kept hearing, could they get thirty-three representatives in the 105th Congress to sign up to be on the Congressional Caucus on Armenian Issues (co-chaired by Frank Pallone, D-N.J., and John Porter, R-Ill.)?—but that it would be counterproductive to let it be known how much, to whom, or why they gave as they did. (The *Boston Globe*, on April 23, 1995, listed representative Joseph Kennedy, D-Mass., as having received $120,000 from Armenians to date.) I was also told by staff members at the Center for Responsive Politics that PACs are a misleading estimate of what an ethnic community is giving: pro-Israel PACs, for example, represent only a small part of the money the Jewish community gives out of concern for Israel. And it should be obvious that the fact that contributors are, say, of Greek descent does not mean that funds they provide have necessarily to do with their feelings about Greek-Turkish relations or other matters in the Balkans. Finally, I was warned by congressional staffers that far from all funds turn up as campaign contributions. Foundations or businesses connected to an official or to his or her immediate family may be the preferred conduit by which persons using money to gain access make their presence known (for example, the fundraising of the Jesse Helms Center among the Taiwanese became a preoccupation of Democrats looking for irregular practices for the sake of influencing foreign policy). In short, money talks, no one doubts it; but it gains access in such a variety of guises that only the most patient of analysts working with the best of records can hope to track this "honest graft."

Hence it is of little more than anecdotal interest that when Michael Dukakis ran for the presidency perhaps a quarter of his financial backing came from Greek Americans. In alarm, the *Wall Street Journal* reported on July 26, 1988, that the Turkish government and the Turkish American community had mobilized; the lobby they created is slowly growing in importance. Or again, as the *New York Times* reported on April 4, 1997, a convicted drug runner, Jorge Cabrera, gave $20,000 out of a bank account that laundered his drug profits to the Democratic campaign at the time of a dinner he attended in Miami for Al Gore—all at the behest of Cuban Americans who hoped to "normalize" relations with Cuba. We may thus conclude that those with an ethnic agenda do give money: this much is clear. But just how decisive these sums are in determining an outcome appears to depend on specific cases.

One striking public example came in the 1992 primary when Bill Clinton visited Victor's Cafe in Miami's Little Havana section and received as much as $300,000 on the spot (and at least another $160,000 by the election) after he uttered words that would be widely cited in the Cuban American community: "I think the administration has missed a big opportunity to put the hammer down on Fidel Castro and Cuba . . . I have read the Torricelli-Graham Bill [the Cuban Democracy Act that later was greatly amended to become Helms-Burton] and I like it." To protect his strong Republican base in the Miami Cuban community, President Bush signed the measure weeks before the election.[27]

By all accounts, Jewish Americans are the largest ethnic contributors, probably contributing half or more of the funds the Democratic party receives for the national (not state and local) elections. (The several contacts I established who were in a position to evaluate this estimate confirmed it, adding that in his 1992 primary race perhaps 60 percent of Clinton's financing was from Jewish groups and individuals.)[28]

Of course, the question is open as to the extent to which Jewish money is tied to support for Israel. Like other donors, Jewish contributors are presumably motivated by a variety of concerns of which a commitment to Israel is only one. Yet surely David Schoenbaum and A. F. K. Organski seriously understate Jewish concern for Israel when they report only money coming from pro-Israel PACs (surely no more than a small percentage of contributions from Jewish donors for political reasons) as indicative of the role Jewish money plays with respect to foreign policy in elections.[29] Seymour Martin Lipset is probably closer to the truth when he writes that American Jews have many concerns (he lists six that are principal) that interweave with one another in ways that cannot be disaggregated easily. Still, he ranks as their number-one preoccupation "commitment to and activities in support of Israel" and writes that these concerns "have determined the nature of American Jewry since the formation of the state. Israel is the center of Jewish life, the cause to which more Jews are deeply dedicated than any other." Lipset's conclusion finds support in polls conducted by the American Jewish Committee (AJC).[30]

Finally, it is not simply that ethnic money buys political influence; it is also that political influence solicits ethnic money. Which is the active, which the reactive partner cannot be assumed without investigation. And it may well be that political leaders come to the policy conclusions they do for reasons independent of money. Bob Dole came to understand the Armenian point of view while recovering from wounds in the care of an Armenian American doctor after World War II. Organski maintains that public officials with a general conviction that the United States should play a leading role in world affairs are likely to be supportive of a strong relationship with Israel irrespective of financial concerns, pointing out that it was under Richard Nixon, who was little beholden to Jewish money or votes, that the United States made its decisive decision to back Israel come what may. In these instances money does not buy votes but simply supports leaders who have adopted positions on their merits alone.

Measuring the extent to which money buys policy is, of course, an impossible task. "I don't think you can find any evidence that I changed government policy solely because of a contribution," Clinton told reporters in March 1997. Although the operative word in the sentence for most who heard it was the word "solely," the question of measurement nonetheless remains.

Can the system be changed? Perhaps on the margins, for despite the defeat of the McCain-Feingold campaign finance reform in the Senate in February 1998, new reforms have been proposed. It would be naive to expect wholesale change in the system, however. The organized social interests that wield such power through the system are obviously far more mobilized than the public at large to defend an order that has served them well. What we saw in the February 1998 Senate vote was the ability of particularistic social forces to defend their policies not only with respect to specific legislation but more importantly with regard to the preservation of the system that gives them access to power in the first place.[31]

It was quite a performance. "Where's the outrage?" Bob Dole repeatedly asked in the 1996 election when the question of campaign financing surfaced. Given the degree of control of the political system by organized social interests working through financial contributions and the hefty benefits these investments reap, Dole might easily have answered his own question. Those citizens most likely to vote and to give money are those best represented by the political system. Why should they work to change an order that has done so much for them?

Organizational Leadership

Votes and money are far from enough to guarantee an interest group access to power. These popular forms of influence must be channeled in specific directions targeted at distinct issues, which sophisticated national organizations alone can manage. Of course, individual officials may spontaneously back a course of action favored by a domestic electorate without any sustained contact with that constituency. Yet, like any interest group, an ethnic community becomes a seriously viable political force only when it has an organization whose chief purpose is to influence decisionmakers to adopt policies favorable to the group's interests.

To be more specific, successful ethnic communities need specialized institutions whose major tasks can be broken into three broad categories: (1) ensuring the organizational unity of the ethnic community itself (a job that involves a variety of different functions); (2) forming or supervising alliances with other social forces to call in unison for government action; and (3) advocating policy positions and monitoring the behavior of government officials responsible for formulating and implementing policy.

In reviewing each of these functions, it would be impossible to consider the entire range of ethnic group experience in the United States. Instead, my effort is to suggest what a "model" ethnic organization is like. As a result, while I shall try to refer at least in passing to all the communities under discussion in this book, I have selected the Jewish community for special emphasis as the model form of organization, although many other constituencies with far less institutional clout also meet the requirements to achieve genuine political influence in Washington.

ORGANIZATIONAL UNITY

The first ambition of any organization should be its self-organization: to bring itself into existence as an effective part of the political process. Funds must be raised and voters mobilized if policy is to be affected, but the prerequisite for maintaining equilibrium and direction in the political fray is to gain and maintain institutional strength from which to try to influence decisionmakers. One challenge is to promote a harmony of personalities and ensure an ideological consensus within the organization. For the first step, this task may be largely accomplished by a single person—Eugene Rossides for the American Hellenic Institute, Jorge Mas Canosa for CANF, Randall Robinson for TransAfrica, or Edward Kennedy for the Irish Americans. But an institution becomes more "institutionalized" when it has regularized procedures for selecting its leadership and reaching a consensus that is more broadbased than one person can provide. Indeed, a single leader who created an institution may actually be hostile to later efforts to develop its capacities, convinced that he or she alone can guide it properly. The crisis that CANF underwent after the death of Mas Canosa in November 1997 is a case in point.

Surely one reason that AIPAC is universally recognized to be exactly what it calls itself—"the most powerful, best-run, and effective foreign policy interest group in Washington"—is that whatever its internal rivalries or the differences of opinion, they have usually been contained by a greater sense of purpose and weight of accumulated experience than the institutions leading any other ethnic community possess. Not surprisingly, a *Fortune* report of December 8, 1997, ranks AIPAC as the second most powerful pressure group in Washington—after the American Association of Retired Persons—and as the only foreign policy lobby in the top twenty-five lobbying groups in the country. A study commissioned by the Aspen Institute came to much the same conclusion. This achievement was not realized overnight. Samuel Halperin underscores the substantial differences among American Jews based on class, religious observance, country of emigration, and generation. All of these differences could only be overcome by the tragedy of the Holocaust and the miracle of the birth of Israel.[32]

Like other ethnic groups, the American Jewish community has a long history of institution building. The first truly national organization appeared in 1859, but the beginning of modern national Jewish organizations is usually thought to have been the American Jewish Committee, founded in 1906, soon to be followed by B'nai B'rith in 1913 and the American Jewish Congress in 1917.

While the American Jewish community made its voice heard in foreign policy circles before World War II, the creation of the state of Israel united its efforts to influence foreign policy to a much greater degree than ever in the past. In 1953, wanting to unify Jewish voices on foreign affairs, the State Department asked Nahum Goldmann, president of the World Jewish Conference, to oversee the founding of a single representative institution. The result was the creation of the Conference of Presidents of Major Jewish Organizations, expected to articulate general policy and to be in contact with the President, and the upgrading of AIPAC, which had been founded (under a different name) in 1951, to operationalize policy and deal with the Congress.

The institutional diversity of Jewish life in America and its democratic mode of operation mean that there has never been monolithic unity for this community. Still, in the early 1980s, in the struggle pitting Israel and the Israel lobby against Reagan's efforts to sell sophisticated aircraft to Saudi Arabia, AIPAC became the most important of the various Jewish organizations in terms of general foreign policy concerns, although a range of leading institutions in the community enjoyed a series of interlocking directorates that facilitated consensus.[33]

In the process of becoming the leading organization in the Jewish community to speak on U.S. foreign policy, AIPAC was aided by the Israeli government, which saw that unity was clearly essential to its own influence in Washington and which actually proposed the creation of such an organization. As early as the Suez invasion of 1956, the Eisenhower administration found that in its search for critics of the Israeli government it could not divide the Jewish community. (Instead, ironically and tellingly, it was the American government that divided when the Senate majority leader, Lyndon Johnson, began to attack Eisenhower for his insistence that Israel leave Sinai. Johnson said to Israeli

Ambassador Abba Eban about the Eisenhower administration, "They're not going to get a goddam thing here [from Congress] until they [treat you fairly].") The same bipartisan competition was evident forty-two years later, when the Republican Speaker of the House, Newt Gingrich, denounced the Clinton administration for suggesting that the Israeli government of Benjamin Netanyahu might do more to respect the Oslo Peace Accords: "It's become the Clinton Administration and Arafat against Israel. The Clinton Administration says: 'Happy Birthday. Let us blackmail you on behalf of Arafat.'"[34]

Thereafter, the Israeli government repeatedly acted to assure itself not only of the unity of American Jewish organizations but also of their recognition that policy would be established by Jerusalem. Disputes might be inevitable within American Jewry and between this community and Israel, but they should be handled privately. In the event of unresolved disagreements, the argument prevailed that the position of the Israeli government superseded all others: that government was democratically constituted, and ultimately it was the entity that bore responsibility for the consequences of policy. With the Six Day War in June 1967, which galvanized American Jewry like no other event in the defense of Israel, the conviction was widespread that Jewish strength lay in unity. As Edward Tivnan puts it: "Total support of Israel had become a requirement of leadership in local Jewish communities throughout America. An American Jewish leader could be married to a gentile, he could be a stranger to the synagogue, but if he became a public critic of Israel, he would soon become a former Jewish leader."[35]

Yet however united the American Jewish community was persuaded it should be, and however much Israel approved these efforts, there were sure to be differences. The greatest challenge was between rival conceptions of what was good for Israel and how American Jewry should behave if it disagreed with specific policies adopted by the Israeli government.

The crux of the matter lay not so much in organizational or personal rivalries—although both existed in plenty—as in the fact that the American Jewish community has typically been far more liberal than mainstream Israeli society, particularly as a demographic shift reduced the hold of Jews of European ancestry on Israeli politics beginning in the late 1970s. Hence the right-wing Likud governments of Menachem Begin, Yitzhak Shamir, and Benjamin Netanyahu were unlikely to receive the degree of support that Labor governments might expect from American Jews.[36]

Not surprisingly, with the election of Begin as prime minister in May 1977, troubles soon began with Washington. Since many American Jews believed that U.N. Resolution 242, the "land for peace" formula, was essentially correct as the basis for negotiations with the Arabs, trouble with a rightist Israeli government was an ever-present possibility for them too. To be sure, AIPAC and other leading Jewish organizations made their commitment to Israel clear, and the Camp David meetings held between Begin and Sadat in September 1978 at President Carter's invitation for a time relieved the pressure of disagreement. However, subsequently it became apparent that Begin did not mean to abandon the territories he called Judea and Samaria; to make the point, he approved the invasion of Lebanon in 1982. Reflecting the differences between the liberal Jewish American community and the Begin government, a 1983 poll revealed that 48 percent of the American Jewish community found itself "often troubled by the policies of the current Israeli government," a proposition agreed to by an astonishing 70 percent of the board members of leaders of major Jewish organizations. Yet in public, ranks remained relatively closed. As the Presidents' Conference had put it in its 1977 annual report, "Dissent ought not and should not be made public because . . . the result is to give aid and comfort to the enemy and to weaken that Jewish unity which is essential for the security of Israel."[37]

More than a decade later, related splits appeared. In August 1995 the American Jewish Committee conducted the third in a series of polls among American Jews with respect to Arab-Israeli relations. It found that 66 percent of the community continued to support the peace process (down from 84 percent in September 1993) launched by Yitzhak Rabin (who had become prime minister in June 1992). Similarly, while 78 percent of the respondents agreed that "caring about Israel is a very important part of my being a Jew," 71 percent disagreed with the proposition that "American Jews should not publicly criticize the policies of the government of Israel." Given that AJC polls in 1993 and 1994 had found that 57 percent, then 53 percent of American Jews favored the eventual creation of a Palestinian state (while 30 percent, then 34 percent opposed it), one can appreciate the tensions within this community, and between it and AIPAC in the late 1990s, when to many in the

community the Netanyahu government appeared unwilling to continue the peace process, while AIPAC endorsed Netanyahu's position
in Washington.[38]

The split in popular opinion and AIPAC's position was underscored
by a January 1996 American Jewish Committee survey of American
Jews on the subject, in which 85 percent gave a favorable rating to
Shimon Peres, as opposed to 8 percent unfavorable, whereas Netanyahu got only a 37 percent favorable rating and a 37 percent unfavorable. In 1997–1999 there was additional controversy between Orthodox Jews (who constitute about 10 percent of American Jewry) allied
with elements of the religious right in Israel and the bulk of American
Jews over the normative status of Conservative and Reformed Jewry—
those who had, in the words of Israel's Chief Rabbinate, "brought
about disastrous results of assimilation among Diaspora Jewry—the
Sages of Israel have forbidden any cooperation with them and their
methods." In such circumstances, AIPAC leadership may have found in
the late 1990s that its most serious organizational problems did not lie
in its relations with the Israeli government, nor did they stem from rival organizations in the United States, but instead they arose from
within its own ranks.[39] (Indeed, on February 28, 1999, the *New York
Times* reported that if Hillary Rodham Clinton ran for the Senate from
New York in 2000, her statement in 1998 that a Palestinian state was
"very important" for peace in the Middle East would not significantly
diminish her chances of winning strong support from Jewish voters.
On August 8, 1999, the same paper reported that a poll found Ms.
Clinton had a favorable image among 72 percent of New York Jews
surveyed, even before she called Jerusalem the "eternal and indivisible
capital of Israel." Her potential Republican rival for the post, New
York City Mayor Rudolph Giuliani, nonetheless insisted that her
remarks were "a very big mistake," but for our purposes, the finding
suggested once again the potential distance between Jewish American
opinion and positions taken by AIPAC.)

In one way, however, the late 1990s differed significantly from the
early 1980s. Begin's problems reflected the liberality of both the American Jewish community and its leadership. But by the time Yitzhak
Rabin became prime minister in 1992, AIPAC's leadership had moved
so far to the right that Rabin reprimanded it as a tool of the Likud opposition and announced he would deal with the United States on a

state-to-state basis, without the help of such intermediaries.[40] Apparently, the Likud leadership in 1998–99 benefited from stronger support among leaders of American Jewish organizations than Begin ever possessed. Perhaps that explains why AIPAC's publication *Near East Report* could state on January 26, 1998, that 60 percent of American Jews had come to have a "favorable opinion" of Netanyahu, while only 13 percent found him "unfavorable." Presumably, however, the American Jewish community was substantially more comfortable with the inauguration of Ehud Barak as prime minister of Israel in July 1999.

Whatever its internal differences, no other American ethnicity has the organizational strength that the Jewish community enjoys. One advantage of this group is that in many respects it may be considered a "single issue" constituency; that is, its primary concerns focus on Israel, even if it is actively involved in a variety of domestic causes as well. Another is that the community has large revenues: approximately $3.5 billion were collected in 1996, $4.5 billion in 1997.[41] Still another is that the state of Israel and concerns about its security linked to the Holocaust act to impose a consensus—"my country, right or wrong"—that might otherwise be lacking.

Yet there are some reasonably close parallels between the Jewish American experience and other ethnic lobbies. Greek and Armenian Americans also enjoy a solidarity based on having distinctive religious bases in their Orthodox churches, foreign governments to which they can relate (although Greek American relations with the government of Andreas Panpandreou were often tense between 1981 and 1989), and a powerful foreign enemy that stirs deep emotional fears: Turkey. In addition, each of these groups has assimilated smoothly into American life and is relatively affluent, allowing them to focus most of their political attention on foreign affairs.

Americans of East European ancestry have a similar profile: although they have moved easily into mainstream American life in class and cultural terms, they have languages, religious affiliations, and cultural practices that continue to tie them to their ancestral homelands. The newly independent governments of those homelands are now asking for their support against the menace of the potential revival of power of their traditional enemy: Russia.

Perhaps the most striking of these groups is the Cuban Americans. Although they have been in the United States in large numbers for scarcely a generation, they quickly became economically successful and converted their wealth into political power. Yet they have remained culturally distinctive, and foremost in the minds of many of them has been the fate of their former homeland under communist rule.

None of these communities—Greek, Armenian, East European, or Cuban—has the strength of the American Jewish community, but the parallels are readily apparent. The contrast with Mexican Americans and African Americans is much greater. To be sure, Mexican Americans have come to wield real political power through the vote, and have two effective national organizations in the National Council of La Raza and the Mexican American Legal Defense and Education Fund. In the debates over immigration legislation in the 1980s and 1990s, they successfully formed coalitions with business, civil libertarians, and the Catholic church to block substantive reforms.[42] So too, African Americans have institutional power through TransAfrica and the Congressional Black Caucus.

Still, by comparison with the Euro American ethnicities I have just mentioned, both Mexican American and African American leaders are preoccupied most by domestic economic and political concerns, for assimilation is not assured. Funds are short (and often derived from sources outside the community). There is no strong external state or clear foreign enemy to encourage ethnic cohesion with respect to foreign affairs. Their membership rolls involve smaller proportions of the community. And their organizations lack interlocking directorships and depend instead on strong (and therefore often competitive) personalities. Their roles in the formulation of foreign policy are accordingly more problematic.

Thus, for example, whatever the momentary excitement of La Marcha on Washington in October 1996, when perhaps 30,000 Latinos protested before the Capitol, its lack of institutional backbone was readily apparent in the unreality of its demands, the absence of important Latino officials at its head, and the fact that a year later it was largely forgotten. Or again, the Million Man March organized by Louis Farrakhan in the fall of 1995 suggested a gap between much of the mainstream black leadership and the community it claims to represent. Similarly, there are evidently splits within the black leadership, as illustrated by disagreements over U.S. trade with and aid to Africa. The Congressional Black Caucus evidently supported a measure that gained

House support in March 1998, only to have the measure denounced by Jessie Jackson and Randall Robinson shortly thereafter as, in Robinson's words, "a very bad piece of legislation that will undermine Africa's independence, undermine Africa's development and serve only American private-sector entities."[43]

Nevertheless, future developments may make Mexican American and African American lobbies much more potent forces in U.S. foreign policy than they are at present. The intensity of domestic concerns ensures that they will stay united, and their large numbers suggest their potential clout. Other groups, by contrast, appear to be losing momentum. My investigation of Irish American organizations indicates that one should not confuse their numbers with their strength: personalities, not institutions, determine agendas; disagreements among these groups are deep (only the Irish have two congressional caucuses, for example, but this is more a sign of disagreement than of strength); and actual ethnic support is shallow (being Catholic or working class appears to be far more critical than being of Irish descent when it comes to voting). Whatever the concerns for the Catholics in Ulster, Irish assimilation is far too complete, and the situation in the old country far too settled in terms of what it was prior to 1937, for this community to have much clout in Washington apart from what individual legislators like Edward Kennedy or Daniel Patrick Moynihan might decide to use (and they are a dying breed, as several Irish activists regretted to me). Should the situation in Northern Ireland finally be normalized in the wake of the Good Friday accord of 1998, Irish American activism with respect to foreign policy will become a subject for the history books, to join the stories of Italian American and German American ethnic activism. In the case of these communities, there are no conceivable foreign issues that might trigger an ethnic awakening, and assimilation into mainstream society has progressively removed many of the cultural particularities that once set these peoples apart.

What then of Asian Americans? For them, assimilation remains a primary objective (and more than 50 percent of Japanese Americans are now marrying outside their communities), and foreign affairs do not yet much concern them (although incidents such as the assassination of Benigno Aquino in the Philippines in 1983 did mobilize Filipino Americans in a way that helped turn Washington against the Ferdinand Marcos regime and supported the democratic transition thereafter).

Moreover, the word "Asian" camouflages the enormous differences within these communities. The rise of China may eventually clarify this situation, as Americans of Korean, Japanese, Indochinese, Taiwanese, and Thai ancestry confront those descendant from mainland China (much as around the time of World War I German, Irish, and Scandinavian Americans feuded with those of British or East European descent). Polls taken prior to 1997 indicate a mild Asian American preference for the Republican party, a commitment that will perhaps grow in the aftermath of the scandals surrounding Democratic efforts to raise funds in this community in 1996 (even if many of the Republican charges of espionage can themselves be read as smears on the Chinese American community).[44]

COALITION BUILDING AND AGENDA SETTING

Organizational unity may be an end in itself, but it is not an exclusive end. A political agenda must be established, allies sought, and actual political pressure brought to bear—all matters that involve action outside the ethnic community itself.

The political goals sought by American ethnic groups come in several forms. One set of demands is that values such as human rights (in American parlance usually meaning something like the Bill of Rights that protects the citizenry from the state) and democratic government be respected abroad. These demands have been primary for a host of American ethnic communities—most notably those of African, Irish, Cuban, Armenian, and East European origin—and have contributed to the strength and character of nationalist movements abroad as a consequence.

A second set of demands is economic. Development requires an infrastructure, and foreign aid is requested. Virtually all ethnic groups therefore ask for ever more generous appropriations for their kinfolk abroad. Israel receives over $3 billion annually, while subsidies to its Arab neighbors willing to live in peace account for billions more. Ukraine, Armenia, and Greek Cyprus receive far more than one might expect were ethnic lobbying not so active. The $20 million paid annually to the International Fund for Ireland is generally called "a farewell tribute" to House Speaker Tip O'Neill. Or again, efforts by African Americans in the summer of 1997 to secure $750 million in new trade funds for Africa for several years running fall into the same category:

appropriations whose logic is difficult to understand but for ethnic pressures.

In recent years economic embargoes against enemies of ancestral homelands have become increasingly prevalent. In the late 1990s the United States not only had an embargo on aid to Azerbaijan authored by the Armenian Caucus, but had developed the novel, and contentious, idea of applying penalties to third parties who deal with countries the United States is seeking to isolate. Thus in 1996 the Cuban embargo called for by CANF was greatly expanded by the Helms-Burton bill (although the Clinton administration announced repeated delays in its implementation) and the Iran embargo, apparently initiated by AIPAC, was signed. (Greek willingness to challenge the U.S.-led embargo on Serbia because of differences with Macedonia raised still other issues, but a new government in Athens ended the stand-off in 1997.) The European Union has strongly criticized third-party provisions of the U.S. embargo on Iran and has been joined by Mexico and Canada in denouncing Helms-Burton, in each case apparently tempering Washington's behavior.[45]

However, demands related to security are the most critical ones made by ethnic lobbies, for they involve the possibility of armed confrontation for the sake of the survival of a foreign state. Hence the prize for an ethnic lobby is greatest when the U.S. government endorses the enlargement of NATO, pledges to defend the security of Israel, or announces its intention to support a "balance" in the Eastern Mediterranean that in practice favors Greece.

In order to gain leverage for the passage of legislation they favor, ethnic lobbies will do as other interest groups do and look for allies from other communities. Thus, speaking very generally, the Mexican lobby works closely with the Catholic church, some business organizations, and the Ford Foundation; the Israel lobby promotes ties with some unions and the Christian right as well as public opinion at large; African Americans cooperate with Arab Americans and Christian liberals; Greeks act with Armenian and Kurdish Americans; and East European Americans work with one another and with business interests anticipating the privatization of regional economies.

Let us again focus on the Israel lobby as the model ethnic interest group with respect to foreign affairs. The range of Jewish allies among American social forces is one of the greatest strengths of the lobby. For while American Jews are predominantly liberal and typically vote for Democrats (some 78 percent for Clinton in both the 1992 and 1996 elections), probably the strongest proponents of Zionism outside the Jewish community are conservative Christians who typically vote Republican.

Thus, in a full-page statement in the *New York Times* on April 18, 1997, Pat Robertson, Oral Roberts, Ralph Reed, Jerry Falwell, and several other prominent conservative Christian clerics announced a Christian "Call for a United Jerusalem." Little wonder, then, that on his visit to the United States in January 1998, even before he was received at the White House, Prime Minister Netanyahu met with Jerry Falwell (as Menachem Begin had before him) and leaders of the Southern Baptist Convention, who reported to him that some 200,000 evangelical pastors in America would "go to their pulpits and use their influence in support of the state of Israel and the Prime Minister." The *New York Times* reported on January 21, 1998, that the executive director of the Anti-Defamation League called the meeting "crude" and "curious," while the executive director of the American Jewish Committee called it "tricky, very tricky." But in fact conservative Christian Zionism is far from a recent creation and draws support from chiliastic Christian beliefs in Armageddon and the Second Coming of Jesus, prophecies that can only be realized following the return of the Jewish people to Israel.

Not only does this right-wing Christian-Jewish agreement lead to the support of certain of the maximum Likud demands on the Palestinians, but it is also in general accord that much of the Muslim world is implicitly antagonistic to the West. Since early 1996, groups like the National Association of Evangelicals (over 10 million strong in some fifty denominations) and the World Evangelical Congress have become increasingly assertive in calling for the United States to stop the persecution of Christians abroad. They point not only to specific Muslim countries like the Sudan but also to Russia and China, yet their preoccupation with restraints on the freedom of religion in much of the Islamic world potentially makes them allies of Israelis like former Prime Minister Benjamin Netanyahu, who insisted in 1995 that "the West had better wake up to the new terrorism" and pointed to a number of Muslim groups as the objects of his concern. According to reports in the *New York Times*, many Christians engaged in the struggle against religious persecution see Islam itself as the essential problem (as opposed to movements within Islam) while failing to see that ethnic or economic rivalries may explain some conflicts even better than religious affiliation.[46]

If allies must be gained, enemies must be countered. For example, Arab, and increasingly Muslim, Americans may argue (in different ways) against aid to Israel or Armenia. In the past most Arab Americans were Christians. But in the last twenty years the Muslim population of the United States has greatly expanded, and by the year 2000 it should be about 6 million, roughly the same size as the Jewish population. It is unlikely, then, that Arab money will be returned, as it was by Walter Mondale in 1984, or that candidates for office will refuse even to meet with Arab Americans, as Michael Dukakis did in 1988.[47] Muslims may be joined by African Americans as well as the oil industry, which is likewise involved with Turkey and Azerbaijan in the exploitation of the 50–200 billion barrels of oil in the Caspian Sea as well as the oil wealth of the Arab world. To the extent that Turkey's role in the region and its cooperation with Israel are more appreciated in Washington, Greek Americans are also sure to be concerned.

AIPAC pulls no punches on its opponents. In 1982 Jewish voters reportedly donated 90 percent of the funds raised to defeat Representative Paul Findlay (R-Ill.) and in 1984 AIPAC targeted Senators Roger Jepsen (R-Ia.) and Charles Percy (R-Ill.) (opposing the latter by financing his opponent in the Republican primary as well as in the general election), in each case because of the candidate's supposed "anti-Israel" positions in Congress. As Hedrick Smith reports:

> [AIPAC director] Tom Dine claimed after the election that Jewish efforts and money had beaten Percy and helped tip other races. "Like an Indian elephant, we don't forget," Dine boasted to a Jewish audience . . . In 1986, another AIPAC executive told me that the "Percy factor" and the "Jepsen factor"—that is, memories of AIPAC's opposition to them in 1984—had swayed senators against the Jordan and Saudi arms sales, especially among Republicans facing reelection in 1986.[48]

Perhaps no alliance is more important than that with the media: news and documentary television, talk radio, and the national press are indispensable means of communication. Through the media both elite and popular opinions are formed. Here again, Jewish influence is greatest in reaching American opinion at large, and on the specific choice between sympathy for Israel or the Arab states, Israel emerges considerably more popular, although some Jewish groups claim that the media is actually biased toward the Arab position.[49] And finally, lobbyists need to feel they have supporters on both sides of the aisle in Congress. American Jews may vote overwhelmingly for the Democratic party, but AIPAC is concerned to see that Republican legislators who support Israel gain their backing as well.[50]

MONITORING POLICY

A final hallmark of a successful ethnic lobby is its ability closely to monitor, and if possible actually define, the policymaking process. It is not at all enough for successful lobbyists to have access to policymakers and to make their preferences known. Specific policy expectations have to be generated and the reactions of public officials must be monitored and evaluated (often with mathematical scoring, the composite sums published on easily accessible web sites). Here the task requires building up a strong network of information providers so that one can influence a process of decisionmaking that is inherently dynamic. Having contacts in the White House, on congressional staffs as well as with legislators, and with the media guarantees that a lobby can help orchestrate the actions of its supporters and anticipate the moves of its opponents.[51]

The President is the most important decisionmaker, of course, and for that reason ethnic lobbies do what they can to secure his support for their preferred policies. But ethnic activists understand that it is far more difficult to gain access to the President and effectively influence his policies than it is to lobby members of Congress, where the threshold of entry is far lower and a much closer working relationship can be established. Hence, while not for a moment forgetting the paramount importance of the White House, ethnic lobbies invariably focus most of their energy on the Congress, especially on the House, while their members at the grassroots anxiously await primaries.

For ethnic groups the surest way to have a voice is to have members of their community as lawmakers. A Paul Sarbanes or John Brademas for the Greeks, an Edward Kennedy or Daniel Patrick Moynihan for the Irish, a Maxine Waters or Charles Rangel for the blacks—these are leaders who have been counted on to keep ethnic issues alive in Washington. Still, as the examples of Senators Alfonse D'Amato representing Jewish concerns, Robert Dole articulating Armenian issues, and Robert Torricelli reminding his colleagues of Cuban affairs all illustrate, effective spokespersons for ethnic interests need not be members of these communities.

Congressional caucuses may also be critical actors in proposed legislation. In the first months of the 105th Congress that opened in January 1997, the Armenian Caucus reported thirty-three members, the Hellenic Caucus sixty-three, and the Congressional Black Caucus forty. J. J. Goldberg talks about Jewish Congressional members as the "core of the pro-Israel activity in Washington . . . a sort of legislature in the legislature."[52] There were also caucuses for the Hispanics, Portuguese, Albanians, and Indians, as well as two for the Irish, and one for House Republicans on Israel (not to be confused with the bipartisan House Congressional Task Force to End the Arab Boycott on Israel). The purpose, quite simply, is to have significant political players in Congress committed to the agenda of an ethnic community, for the critical concern is to "become part of the system" by having "a place at the table" where decisions are made.

If the Devil is in the details, then it is here that lobbyists must be as well. "Early money" for new candidates is one form of attention to detail; another is constant contact with congressional staffers, whose leaks and initiatives are often underappreciated by those not in political life; still another is regular meetings with contacts in the various bureaucracies, especially State, the National Security Council, and Defense. Long before public attention is focused on an issue, effective ethnic lobbies have identified possible problems and begun to deal with them, following the admonition that an ounce of prevention is worth a pound of cure.

Presumably, the closer the contacts to decisionmakers, the greater the influence. For example, it surely mattered that all four of George Bush's top advisers on the Middle East were reportedly Jewish.[53] Thanks to its American supporters, Camille Mansour notes, Israel may often know more than the Pentagon about the thinking at the Defense Department. Mansour also cites an AIPAC staffer's comment: "It is common for members of Congress and their staffs to turn to AIPAC first when they need information, before calling the Library of Congress, the Congressional Research Service, committee staff or administration experts. We are often called upon to draft speeches, work on legislation, advise on tactics, perform research, collect co-sponsors and marshal votes."[54] Money and votes alone cannot buy this kind of access, which is gained instead by patience, intelligence, determination, and the time to build up an infrastructure of influence—attributes that neither single individuals nor an ethnic community alone can provide but which are hallmarks of an institutionally effective lobby.

At this point in the discussion, a careful reader might legitimately ask what the foregoing information has established. To take the example of U.S.-Israeli relations, is it only because of domestic ethnic lobbying that Washington has the policy it does? Surely that would be an exaggeration. Israel has the strongest military force in the Middle East, and the steadfastness of its commitment to work with the United States on matters of common interest cannot be doubted. Here is the reason that Richard Nixon decided to underscore America's strategic commitment to Israel. Moreover, the strength of Israel's appeal domestically in the United States is not restricted to the Israel lobby. The convictions of the Christian right, as well as the feelings of many other Americans impressed by the courage of Israel and the character of its democratic institutions, mean that concern for Israel's security has a high degree of popular support in the United States. To assert that the activities of the Israel lobby alone explain America's commitment to Israel's security is to simplify by a large measure the thinking in Washington.[55]

The problem, then, is the particularly bedeviling one of measurement. In discussions with experts on interest groups, I have been repeatedly told that this is the unsolved—nay, the insolvable—problem: how to establish the importance of one factor when a complicated set of factors are working together to a similar outcome. If U.S.-Israeli relations depend on objective security considerations, popular political support, and the activities of an ethnic lobby, how do we measure the strength of the last of these relative to the others?

One way to appreciate the relative strength of interest group organization is to look at instances when a lobby is essentially on its own countering a myriad of other forces in Washington. In this respect, the most dramatic examples of the power of ethnic lobbying within the government have come in the public showdowns between AIPAC and presidents over arms for Arab states or over the possibility that the United States might "reassess" its policy in the Middle East in such a way that Israel did not have American support for whatever solution Israel itself deemed finally appropriate for peace.

Under Presidents Nixon, Ford, Carter, Reagan, and Bush there were public clashes of this kind, which the Israel lobby usually won and never clearly lost. During the Nixon years a difference surfaced between Israel and the United States over the so-called Rogers Plan, a proposal the American Secretary of State made (without securing the prior support of either Nixon or Henry Kissinger) late in 1969 to implement U.N. Resolution 242, exchanging Arab land held by the Israelis for recognition and peace. Prime Minister Golda Meir immediately denounced the plan as a threat to the very survival of Israel, and Jewish American leaders closely followed suit. Nixon also faced serious challenge to his policy of détente with the Soviet Union from an American Jewish community mobilized to tie U.S.-Soviet trade relations to the right of Soviet Jews to emigrate (through the so-called Jackson-Vanik amendment). In each case, the lobby won.[56]

Nixon's setbacks were not isolated events. Concerned over Israeli refusal to enter into negotiations with its Arab neighbors, Henry Kissinger persuaded President Gerald Ford to call for a "reassessment" of American policy in the Middle East early in 1975.[57] Interpreting this effort to pressure Israel as a threat to abandon that country, AIPAC managed in only three weeks to get seventy-six senators to sign a letter to the President protesting his intentions and warning that good relations between the executive and the legislature on a host of issues were tied to his policy. In the words of Maryland Senator Charles Mathias, who reluctantly signed the letter:

> Seventy-six of us promptly affixed our signatures although no hearings had been held, no debate conducted, nor had the administration been invited to present its view. One senator was reported to have candidly expressed a feeling that in fact was widespread: "The pressure was just too great. I caved" . . . As a result of the activities of the lobby, congressional conviction has been measurably reinforced by the knowledge that political sanctions will be applied to any who fail to deliver.[58]

Democrats fared similarly. President Jimmy Carter's proposal in March 1977 that a Palestinian "entity" be created prompted AIPAC's circulation of a list of twenty-one grievances against his administration.

To compound matters, the White House issued a joint communiqué with the Soviet Union in October 1977 calling for the convening of a meeting to establish a comprehensive settlement including the Palestinians. The proposal contravened the basic principle of the Israel lobby that Jerusalem alone would decide the terms and the timing of any such negotiations. Within a week, responding to a furor of opposition from Israel and the American Jewish community, Carter abandoned his plans. Despite the Camp David Agreements between Israel and Egypt a year later, Carter never recovered his credibility with the American Jewish community.[59]

Relations between the Israel lobby and the Reagan administration were generally quite positive. Yet the most celebrated of the confrontations between AIPAC and Washington occurred in 1981 over sales of advanced aircraft (the AWACs) to Saudi Arabia which Reagan endorsed. The Israel lobby, strongly backed by Begin, managed at first to line up 54 senators in opposition and to organize the House so that the sale was initially defeated 301–11. A combination of corporate lobbying, the assassination of Anwar el-Sadat, and the fact that Ronald Reagan put his prestige on the line and rallied behind him an impressive set of past presidents and secretaries of state and defense meant the Senate finally approved the sale 52–48.

AIPAC's defeat on the AWACs sale turned out to be momentary. In short order the Israel lobby increased its budget eightfold, its staff over threefold, and its membership over sixfold. Within months the United States concluded a Memorandum of Understanding with Israel that guaranteed $200 million in annual military purchases by the Pentagon of Israeli munitions and conveyed an understanding of closer security arrangements between the two countries with respect to countering Soviet expansionism. American aid to Israel then rose in 1985, 1986, and 1987, and AIPAC succeeded in blocking arms sales to Jordan and Saudi Arabia. Hedrick Smith writes that ultimately "Secretary of State George Shultz had to sit down with AIPAC's executive director—not congressional leaders—to find out what level of arms sales to the Saudis AIPAC would tolerate."[60] Such influence did not end when Reagan left office in 1989. In 1998–99 I was told by different knowledgeable observers that Turkey and Jordan considered the body with which they must first negotiate their relations with the United States to be not the State Department or some congressional body but AIPAC.

For President George Bush a significant joust with AIPAC came when, in order to pressure the Israeli government to commit itself to stop settlements in the occupied territories, he suspended for four months a $10 billion loan guarantee for housing for Soviet Jews arriving in Israel. Given that the government of Yitzhak Shamir was not interested in a land-for-peace resolution of the confrontation between Israel and the Arabs but instead was increasing Jewish settlements in the disputed territories, the stage was set for a confrontation between Israel and Washington, one all the more anguish-ridden because most American Jews were themselves critical of the expansion of these settlements.

In the event, the Bush administration had its way, but not without incurring the wrath of AIPAC and perhaps at the cost of losing a Senate seat in Pennsylvania a few weeks later. With the election of Yitzhak Rabin as prime minister of Israel in June 1992, the way was open to reaching an accord. Israel ordered a stop to housing construction in the occupied territories and Bush agreed to allow the loan guarantees to be extended. But the furor set off a movement of Jewish votes and money in the 1992 election year that benefited Clinton and the Democrats.[61]

There was no public division between the Clinton administration and AIPAC on the scale of these earlier administrations. But it was common knowledge that Clinton strongly preferred Shimon Peres to Netanyahu in the 1996 Israeli election, and that on both the settlement issue and that of relations with Iran the possibility of a public confrontation was ever present. Thus Secretary of State Madeleine Albright repeatedly indicated that she viewed Jewish settlements in the occupied territories as contradictory to American policy and a violation of U.S. expectations of Israeli obligations in the peace process with the Palestinians. Or again, in June 1998 President Clinton vetoed the Iran Missile Proliferation Act, authored by the pro-Israel Representative Benjamin Gilman, which mandated sanctions automatically to be imposed on any government or corporation supplying ballistic missile technology to Iran. An Aspen Institute report suggests the magnitude of Clinton's opposition, noting that by a vote of 418–8 the House had passed a resolution asking that the White House impose sanctions on Russian firms that might be helping Iran to develop missiles capable of reaching Israel. "We were sending an alert to all our members every day telling them that time was running out," an AIPAC representative declared. "Everybody was engaged through our regional offices. Literally, within a matter of weeks, we got close to 200 cosponsors in the House and 82 cosponsors in the Senate."[62]

OBVIOUSLY such a brief survey cannot do justice to the enormous complexity of how civic society gains access to the policymaking process. My intention instead has been to highlight its most important features. Two related points call out for special emphasis: the need for any successful interest group to have a primary concern for its own institutional structure, and the need in analyzing any interest group to understand the character of the American political system, and particularly the relatively low threshold of access that one must cross to become a player with influence.

A major problem for an ethnic group (as for any interest group) is to speak with a single voice. To be successful, the group must mobilize funds and votes, propose policies, and closely monitor the behavior of public officials. Yet in the pursuit of these tasks, personalities and ideologies may war with one another, which may quickly lead to fragmentation and ineffectiveness. As an antidote, groups may seek to find unity through a single leader, but this decision in turn leads to problems with institution building—dilemmas that a group may solve by deciding to follow the preferences of a foreign government. Only the Israel lobby has found a way to handle all these difficulties, but here too one sees serious problems facing an organization built on voluntary membership and consensual decisionmaking.

Still, the character of American democracy is such that ethnic groups with far less influence than the Israel lobby can have a significant impact on U.S. foreign policy. Votes and financial contributions ensure access to decisionmakers. It is then the responsibility of the lobbies to define the policies they favor, to find allies among other social forces, and to see that in the policymaking process the representatives of their viewpoints act effectively. The logic of American democracy ensures those who learn its rules a place in the councils of government.

It is not simply because this country is a nation of immigrants that ethnic groups have the influence they do, but because the structure of parties, the Congress, and executive-legislative relations are as they are. One may disagree with the particular policy outcomes or call for reforms in this or that aspect of the structure itself, but it is unrealistic to believe that the essential nature of the open American state will be more than marginally altered by any of the criticisms we hear on every side today. The structure of the party system, the government itself, and a society jealous of its power have been evolving in a rather consistent way for over two centuries now and should not be expected to change in any fundamental fashion. Economic interests, religious confessions, and the philosophic concerns of Americans opposed to governmental tyranny long ago set the traces in which ethnic groups act today.

Who speaks for America in world affairs? Often, special interests do. But these pressure groups, as we have seen, comprise a wide cross-section of the American people. The problem in democratic theory arises, then, not so much from the malfunctioning of a particular aspect of the American political system—although clearly certain reforms may be in order, especially on campaign financing—as from the character of the system itself. Nor is the problem a new one. Since James Madison wrote in the *Federalist Papers* about the "mischiefs of faction" in American life, theorists have worried about not only the tyranny of the majority but also the tyranny of the minority. Here is one of democracy's irresolvable tensions, as select social interests are empowered by right to make their interests and values known.

Our task at this point is to examine the theoretical basis of the legitimacy of interest group lobbying and to propose from this investigation certain limits on such activities. What we need is not only a justification of ethnic and other interest groups' right to act politically but also an understanding of their obligation to respect the values and interests of the national community. In the process we may be able to outline the terms of debate in multicultural America as fellow citizens from different ethnic backgrounds—or who recognize no special background at all aside from their Americanness—gather to debate the foreign policy of the Republic.

FOUR

E Pluribus Unum or
Ex Plures Uno?

E pluribus unum: one out of many. The United States had a brilliant
solution for the inherent fragility, the inherent combustibility, of a
multiethnic society: the creation of a brand-new identity, carried forward by individuals who, in forsaking old loyalties and joining to
make new lives, melted away ethnic differences—a national identity
that absorbs and transcends the diverse ethnicities that come to our
shore, ethnicities that enrich and reshape the common culture in the
very act of entering into it.

—*Arthur Schlesinger Jr.*

Thus far I have tried to establish two key points: that ethnic groups
have had far more effect on the formulation of American foreign policy
in the past century than is generally realized; and that at this stage in
the discourse on democratic citizenship in the United States, the right
of ethnic communities to organize themselves politically and to make
demands on the government is widely accepted. Put succinctly, ethnic
groups have power to influence American foreign policy, and they have
an acknowledged right to exercise this power.

But to recognize the empowerment of ethnic communities morally
and practically is not enough. Any theory of democratic citizenship
must also be able to specify the limits, obligations, and responsibilities
of politically active citizens so far as the greater national community is
concerned. In a democracy, the state is ultimately subordinate to the
society, and political stability therefore requires a certain consensus
among the citizenry on the bounds of acceptable political behavior.
Over time, for example, Americans have come to see business and labor
organizations as legitimately involved intimately in the nation's political life, and to believe that religious organizations should stand somewhat apart from daily politics, ministering to their members in the

130

social realm, venturing into affairs of state (or being interfered with by the state) only in extreme cases. What, then, are the limits in democratic theory to ethnic politicking in multicultural America?

The reasons for taking this matter seriously should be abundantly clear at the dawn of the twenty-first century, for ethnic conflict was a terrible scourge in the century that just closed. On some occasions ethnic hatred set nation against nation; on others it sparked furious internal conflicts as tribal passions were released in ways that led to race murder. Democratic states, with their ingrained tolerance of social diversity, were considerably better than other types of political regimes at containing, indeed at overcoming in a way that strengthened their cosmopolitan character, the fear and loathing that ethnic difference can inspire. Yet there were also serious challenges within the democracies themselves from those who would exploit these primordial feelings to destructive ends. And who can pretend that we are now past the worst, that somehow we have figured out how to deal with the deep-set tensions of making one people out of many in a way that respects difference, in fact that prizes the benefits of diversity?

We should avoid forecasting Armageddon: the United States has made enormous strides in trying to deal equitably with its heavy legacy of ethnoracial discrimination.[1] Nevertheless, class differences remain in American life and are a serious source of tension that cannot be divorced from ethnoracial concerns. Moreover, the task of what is known in many countries as "truth and reconciliation" based on a confrontation with our history is far from completed in the United States, while today's unprecedentedly great wave of immigrants from Latin America and Asia raises new issues of diversity at the same time that the end of the Cold War has removed an important source of a sense of national unity. Without exaggerating America's problem of national cohesion in an era of heightened ethnic awareness, we would be foolhardy not to take the challenges seriously and so inquire into the sources of national identity, purpose, and unity in an era of multicultural empowerment.

These various questions resolve themselves into a single issue: the character of the obligations of citizenship in a multiethnic society. In the face of intense ethnic feelings, what holds a nation together? How can we be confident that the affirmation of a right to be different, and the recognition that to suppress this right would be dangerous, will lead to measures that necessarily result in a political environment conducive to the public good? A cause for concern is that the ethnic groups that are most politically active seem least likely to ask such a question. And a reason to expect that this problem may be difficult to rectify is that most multiculturalists today—individuals who salute ethnic empowerment—do not propose any theory of national citizenship worth the name.

Multiculturalists have poured much effort into making the case for the right of individuals to organize along ethnoracial lines, but they have given comparatively little thought to qualifying this right. Understandably, then, multiculturalism's critics have pointed to the fragmentation of many peoples around the globe, cases in which national identity and the civic virtue it reflected have been lost in flood tides of ethnic demagoguery, hatred, and murder that have shattered the legitimacy of the nation state. These critics have wondered to what extent a democracy can tolerate a social order increasingly given to dissention and disrespectful of the moral dignity and practical utility of national union without this democracy becoming a victim of its own permissive logic.[2] But to date the majority of multicultural thinkers have answered the critics with platitudes, silence, or in some cases outright vilification.

Nowhere is the specification of limits on ethnic activism in democratic theory more appropriate than in foreign affairs, for here more than elsewhere we might suppose we are united as Americans, with enough of a "national identity" and "national interests" that "politics stops at the water's edge." Of course, the concept of a national identity or interest is legendary for its ambiguity, and assertions that the country is united when it acts abroad have never fully reflected reality. Still, the notion that Americans share a minimum set of values as a people, enough to give them a workable national identity with a degree of purpose in world affairs, and thus with some recognizable interests as a community, needs to be defended. Even if we recognize that in practice democracy itself empowers organized social interests so that "the tyranny of the minority" is an ever present possibility, even if we recognize that the final meaning of a term like "national interests" will always be in dispute, nonetheless, we need a sense of national history and purpose adequate for political unity. It is ironic that many multiculturalists posit a theoretical unity to ethnic communities—groups that themselves are never monolithic but always divided internally so that their common interests can never be determined without dispute—yet fail to accord the same theoretical unity to the democratic nation that makes their enjoyment of ethnic solidarity possible.

Who speaks for America in world affairs? The answer should be "those who think of themselves first and foremost as Americans"—an obvious response that many multiculturalists today appear, regrettably, to be reluctant to give.

Dual Loyalties vs. Conflicted Loyalties

Domestically, debates over what multiculturalism means in actual practice have come in different forms. In the schools, there have been arguments over bilingual education, the "cultural canon," and "political correctness." In the workplace, controversies have surrounded affirmative action and the concept of set-asides for women and minorities in public contracting. In politics, multiculturalists have called for new forms of democratic governance, including proportional representation and "consociational" arrangements involving electoral districts created to ensure the election of minority leaders.

In foreign affairs, too, multiculturalism has expressed itself in a variety of forms, all of which promote the rights of ethnic groups to participate in the formation of public policy on the basis of their distinct identities, which give them values and interests that may not be shared by the greater population. Thus, as we saw in earlier chapters, Greek and Armenian Americans are attentive to American policy toward Turkey; Muslim and Jewish Americans have special concerns about Israeli-Arab relations; African Americans have particular interests in Africa and the Caribbean; Cuban Americans keep a close eye on developments in Havana; Irish Americans focus on developments in Northern Ireland; Mexican Americans are especially vigilant with respect to immigration reform; and East European Americans are mobilizing to ensure the future expansion of NATO.

Nonetheless, we should *not* conclude that America's ethnic groups should have free rein to define Washington's policy toward the areas of the globe that matter to them most. I would argue that while ethnic constituencies have every right to organize and make themselves heard in the formulation of this country's foreign policy, they do not have exclusive and unlimited license to determine that policy.

Yet, as we have seen, something approaching this outcome has often occurred in Washington as the result of lobbying by American ethnic groups. To be sure, there is nothing unique about this practice; ethnic lobbying is only a variation on a leading theme of American democracy, in which a wide variety of interest groups (of which economic actors are the most critical) work the corridors of power in Washington to secure legislation whose intention is to benefit the few rather than the many. But the American public is understandably bothered. A *USA Today* poll taken in August 1990 found that 69 percent of Americans agreed "somewhat" or "strongly" that "special interests" have too much influence in Washington. Two months later a *CBS News/New York Times* poll found that 71 percent thought Congress more committed to serving "special interest" groups (a term the public despises compared to "public interest" groups) than to serving its own constituents. Again, in a national poll conducted by the Foreign Policy Association in 1998, 56 percent of respondents felt that "ethnic lobbies have too much influence on U.S. foreign policy" (while 92 percent felt campaign finance reform to be necessary).[3]

Perhaps different wording in these polls would have produced different results. "Special interests" are never liked, whereas ethnic groups may be respected or at least tolerated as a more legitimate expression of popular sentiment. Yet given the ability of ethnic activists to concentrate money, votes, and behind-the-scenes pressure on policymakers to promote courses of action that favor the few over the many, popular opinion might be aroused if the public knew the nature and extent of ethnic group efforts to influence foreign policy.

A "tyranny of the minority" is a special problem for American democracy because of the particular openness of our political system (see Chapter 3). But the special problem when ethnic groups are concerned is that the agenda they are promoting often derives from the perceived needs or expressed ambitions of foreign movements or governments.

It is, after all, a striking peculiarity of American political life that foreign leaders—be they Polish, Czech, Irish, Israeli, Greek, or Armenian—feel they have a right to address their American kinfolk directly, over the head of the U.S. government, encouraging these ethnic citizens to take positions that promote the interests of the ancestral homeland as defined by these foreigners. It is equally striking that many with strong ethnic identities rally to these foreign leaders' views of what U.S. foreign policy should be.

The question is how a dialogue may be entered into that assumes a reasoned patriotism on the part of ethnic minorities as a counterpart to their "right to be different." Following in the pluralist tradition, multiculturalists can be excellent at laying out the historical and normative basis for citizens to have "dual loyalties," but far fewer are engaged in determining what should occur in instances where loyalties instead are "conflicted."

As I indicated in earlier chapters, we must be careful using a term like *divided loyalty*. The experiences of Japanese Americans during World War II and of leftists generally during the McCarthy period of the early 1950s give this term a bad name. Nevertheless, "division" is a normal part of democratic life and may be expressed by business or labor groups, religious or environmental activists every bit as much as by ethnic communities. If an ethnic group demands a particular foreign policy, how is that different from a business or labor demand, a religious or environmentalist effort to promote a particular role for Washington in world affairs?

Yet, as the parallels with these other groups suggest, the demands of groups with a variety of agendas often may plausibly be criticized as narrow, self-interested, or even detrimental to the greater community. Hence, the problem of conflicted loyalties for Americans with strong ethnic loyalties is far from a merely abstract and theoretical question. Before World War I, both President Woodrow Wilson and former President Theodore Roosevelt decried the opposition of German and Irish (and to a lesser extent Scandinavian) Americans to U.S. entrance into the war in Europe. These ethnic communities vigorously supported neutrality as a way to oppose American support for London, and Washington reacted by pointing out to these communities—dubbed "hyphenated Americans" to suggest their divided loyalties—that for the sake of "the national interest" this country might go to war with their homeland (in the case of Germany) or become allied with a government exercising unjustifiable imperial control over their homeland (in the case of Ireland) or work with Russia, feared by the Scandinavians for its past expansionism and by Jews for its treatment of their kinfolk.

Today there are similar issues of conflicted loyalties even if the stakes are arguably not as high as they were in the period 1914–1941. More than eighty years have elapsed and still we do not know how in theory to address this issue. And we never will; no solution will ever be perfect. Democracy's irresolvable tension lies in the question of how to make one out of many. But at least we can make an effort to understand our internal contradictions with respect to ethnic loyalties.

Consider our relative success in discussing economic interests that may be criticized when they pollute abroad, export jobs, sell foreigners technological know-how with security implications, avoid taxes or exploit workers across national boundaries, or make a consistent or coherent U.S. foreign policy hard to fashion because of narrow, short-term, or mutually contradictory demands. Agreement on policy may be difficult to achieve, but at least the terms of discussion are established and hence familiar, allowing for reasoned civic debate.

The equivalent for ethnic groups is when, for the sake of foreign governments or peoples, they lobby for aid, demand diplomatic initiatives, or try to commit this country to security guarantees that it might be wise to avoid. For example, when it was discovered during the 1996 election campaign that the Chinese government had apparently tried to gain influence by committing some two million dollars to various races, a great uproar ensued in Washington.[4] That far greater sums are spent legally by foreign governments, and that much greater amounts again come from domestic ethnic groups apparently seeking to serve the self-defined interests of foreign governments, seemed to bother no one.

To illustrate the failure of the multiculturalists to provide a satisfactory account of ethnic obligations to the greater democratic national community, let us look at three forms the multicultural discourse has taken: the argument for hyphenation, the case made for "dual" or "post-national" citizenship, and the literature on the role of "diasporas" in world affairs.

Hyphenation

Around the time of World War I, both Woodrow Wilson and Theodore Roosevelt gave "hyphenation" a bad name, insisting that citizens should consider themselves to be Americans, first, last, and always. To be "hyphenated" suggested a loyalty to some country other than the United States, an allegiance that could enormously complicate America's role in the world by undermining the national unity needed for resolute action in foreign affairs.

Today, thanks to the rise of multiculturalism, hyphenation has made a comeback. A good example of the issues involved can be seen in the writings of Michael Walzer, a leading American political theorist. In *What It Means to Be an American* (1992), Walzer tries to reconcile ethnic loyalties and American citizenship. "Engaged men and women tend to be multiply engaged," he writes of the virtues of a citizenship inspired by multiple loyalties. As he sees it, by far the greater danger than that one's communitarian allegiance will come into conflict with one's loyalty to the nation is that one will be a passive, not an active, citizen.[5]

Walzer's point is a fair one: there is abundant empirical confirmation of his thesis that the most engaged citizens are those with multiple commitments, that those who act locally are also more likely to think globally.[6] But can it be left at that? Is there not a possibility that multiple loyalties create multiple contradictions? Walzer does see a tension in the "peculiarly American alternation" among identities: "American patriotism is always strained and nervous because hyphenation makes indeed for dual loyalty but seems, at the same time, entirely American." Despite this recognition, "in the case of hyphenated Americans, it doesn't matter whether the first or the second name is dominant . . . an ethnic American is someone who in principle, lives his spiritual life as he chooses, *on either side of the hyphen.* In this sense, American citizenship is indeed anonymous, for it doesn't require a full commitment to American (or any other) nationality." In the case of Irish Americans, for example, Walzer denies that they are "culturally Irish and politically American . . . Rather, they are culturally Irish American and politically Irish American . . . their politics is still, both in style and substance, significantly ethnic."[7]

Should we be satisfied with such an open-ended finding? If there are moments when, indeed, one may have dual or triple allegiances and find them mutually enriching, surely there are other moments when no such happy synergy is possible. Is it then for individuals to determine their loyalties as they will without some guidance as to how they might make difficult choices? And how might a national discourse be conducted that allows those who disagree with the choices made by a group of "hyphenates" to enter into constructive dialogue with them, avoiding the danger that terms like "racist" and "un-American" will be hurled back and forth?

It is worth underscoring that Walzer implicitly sanctions a choice to give preeminence to one's ethnic identity over loyalty to the nation in determining one's political position. Like many multiculturalists, he does not come to terms with the practical difficulties of his position in the real world of civic life and policymaking. On occasion he admits the possibility of establishing "the common good." Yet the weight of his argument falls on the dangers of trying to set up such an overarching togetherness, which might stifle pluralism and indeed liberal democracy itself: "*E pluribus unum* is an alchemist's promise; out of liberal pluralism no oneness can come." Hence one's more essential emotional and spiritual life is likely to be led in one's ethnic community, for that is where one's personal and group values are apparently born. In the wider world of citizenship, meanwhile, one stands alone as an individual, equal to others in the rational evaluation of what is good for the nation, but not engaged in as vital a way as through the particularistic ties to one's ethnic cohort. "For support and comfort and a sense of belonging, men and women look to their groups," Walzer writes in one typical passage; "for freedom and mobility they look to the state."[8]

This position is not unique to Walzer but is contained within the contradictions of liberalism. If the government is to be a "night watchman," if it cannot itself cultivate virtue (for that might be a recipe for totalitarianism), then, as the political theorist Michael Sandel puts it, "a just society seeks not to promote any particular end, but enables its citizens to pursue their own ends, consistent with a similar liberty for all."[9] To those who believe, as many liberal theorists do, that the complexity of American society precludes the kind of communality that can create the obligations that give the individual character, while ethnic, especially ethnoreligious or ethnoracial, communities are better able to foster such communality, hyphenation seems not simply a possible but a desirable form of moral existence, perhaps even superior to that of those who have only a national identity and allegiance. As for the concept of "the national interest" or "national interests," it becomes synonymous with whatever policy is finally decided upon through a Madisonian struggle of faction against faction, devoid of any necessarily higher ethical meaning.

Accordingly, Walzer repeatedly finds that the public inter-ethnic life of general American citizenship has a rational, instrumental, individualistic, ultimately utilitarian cast to it, wherein individuals find "a peculiar anonymity," a term he often uses, in which there is no "natural or organic loyalty that we (rightly or wrongly) recognize in families." The result: Walzer seems not to recognize that life as a non-ethnic American can be as rich in these dimensions, as worthy of spiritual respect and emotional attachment, as ethnic allegiance: "Politics offers neither self-realization nor communion. All intensity lies, or should lie, elsewhere," he writes, with "the primacy of ethnic and religious identity."[10]

Such thinking is characteristic of what Richard Rorty has called "the unpatriotic Academy":

> In the name of "the politics of difference," it refuses to rejoice in the country it inhabits. It repudiates the idea of a national identity and the emotion of national pride. This repudiation is the difference between traditional American pluralism and the new movement called multiculturalism. Pluralism is the attempt to make America . . . a community of communities, a nation with far more room for difference than most. Multiculturalism is turning into the attempt to keep these communities at odds with one another . . . Like every other country ours has a lot to be proud of and a lot to be ashamed of. But a nation cannot reform itself unless it takes pride in itself—unless it has an identity, rejoices in it, reflects upon it and tries to live up to it. Such pride sometimes takes the form of arrogant, bellicose nationalism. But it often takes the form of a yearning to live up to the nation's professed ideals.[11]

Rorty has put his finger on the essential problem of many multiculturalists. Why should we assume that national life cannot be the basis for an identity equally robust emotionally and ethically as that found in ethnic communities? Democratic national life concerns participation in the state—a form of political involvement ethnic attachments alone cannot provide—and hence involvement in debates of matters of substance where authoritative decisions will be made. National life also involves the association of class issues with those of race and ethnicity—another matter multiculturalists tend to ignore. In a democracy, national political life thus has the potential to offer a form of citizenship as rich as ethnic life can normally provide, perhaps richer. In an authoritarian state, to be sure, our conclusion might be different. But in a democratic society based on voluntary membership and universal citizenship, only groups that can demonstrate they have been marginalized by the greater society—African Americans or Native Americans, for example—should be entitled to claim a priority of ethnic rights over national obligations.

Grasping this point should not be difficult for most multiculturalists. Unlike traditional liberals, for whom reconciling a national identity with their cosmopolitan values is a difficult undertaking,[12] multiculturalists typically understand that a political community may be conceived of as having a collective identity and interest, even if the specific terms of that communal purpose may always be contested. If multiculturalists accept the notion of a collective identity, purpose, and interest for an ethnic community, then on what grounds can they deny an equivalent right to their compatriots in a democratic nation to talk in terms of a national identity, purpose, and interest?

What, for example, would a contemporary multiculturalist say that might have restrained a German or Irish American of the period of World War I when it came to defining America's national interest in the struggle in Europe? Nor do many multiculturalists have the concepts to restrain Americans with ties to Greece, Armenia, Israel, or Poland from deciding to use their American citizenship as a way of promoting an ethnic agenda set by a foreign government.

Of course, defining what a "national identity" is, or what "national interests" actually are, is a controversial problem in its own right. The latter term connotes the common good or the general will, something that benefits the entire citizenry and not only a portion of it. Yet as those familiar with debates over how to define the national interest in specific contexts will readily attest, defending one policy rather than another with the national interest in mind is seldom a simple task. For instance, according to Stephen Krasner, the national interest is whatever the state unconstrained by social forces determines it to be. Yet for Hans Morgenthau the national interest lies in indisputable security concerns that are common to the entire community. And for Peter Trubowitz the national interest is an arbitrary construction reflecting the wishes of that section of society which succeeds in getting Washington to act as these dominant social forces see fit. Clearly we have three rival concepts of what the idea itself means, even before we get to the far greater difficulty of translating theory into practice.[13]

However, in the abstract realm of this discussion, it is not necessary to define what the national interest is (or what community-wide national interests are) in order to take issue with, for instance, Walzer's posing of the choices open to a hyphenated individual. It appears that, for Walzer, "what it means to be an American" is that those who are hyphenates can concern themselves with the needs of another country or people before the needs of the United States. Paradoxically, what it means to be an American is that one does not necessarily have a strong sense of national identity at all, so that terms like the common good, the public interest, and the national interest are all somewhat suspect, the reifications of nationalists who would have us forget what is really more primary: ethnicity. Such multiculturalists seem to bite the hand of the very nation that gives them their democratic due, refusing necessarily to value their national as highly as their ethnic identity or to recognize obligations of national citizenship with priority over their ethnic attachments.

Are there no obligations that flow from citizenship in a democratic polity composed largely of voluntary immigrants and their descendants? Since an act of Congress of 1868, Americans have had the right to expatriate themselves. If one thinks of oneself primarily as African or Israeli, as Irish or Polish, nothing legal stands in the way of one's leaving the United States. And indeed many Americans have availed themselves of this opportunity, from the founding of Liberia in 1823 to making *aliyah* to Israel. Mona Harrington writes of the status of "sojourners" of the early twentieth century, immigrants who came to this country to seek their fortune and then returned home; she points out that they constituted the great majority of immigrants from Turkey and Hungary.[14] Still other groups have considered themselves "exiles" here, waiting temporarily in the United States, like the Irish in the nineteenth century or many Cubans today, for conditions to change in their homeland. "Fellow exiles in America," declared John O'Mahoney, president of the Fenian movement, in 1865, to his companions of the "Irish race," evoking their diaspora in Canada, Australia, England, France, and the United States, "you are strangers wherever else you may go," and "you owe to that dear land [Ireland] your first and warmest love."[15] How many other ethnic communities resident in the United States have surely felt the same emotions, considering themselves but momentary sojourners, or aggrieved exiles, in this land?

But with the exception of African and Native Americans, who have a special status because they were not voluntary immigrants here and whose ethnicity has often been their only protection against a national majority bent on denying them their rights of democratic citizenship (one might debate other exceptions, such as Chicanos), most Americans (and surely all Euro Americans), I believe, have an obligation to privilege their loyalty to the United States over that to an ancestral homeland. Thus I believe Walzer is quite mistaken to say that American citizenship is "anonymous," that "an ethnic American is someone who in principle, lives his spiritual life as he chooses, *on either side of the hyphen.*" In a case where loyalties are conflicted, the national, not the ethnic, allegiance should in most instances have the greater moral authority; and where it does not, special arguments need to be made (for example, that one's kinfolk abroad face genocide).

The error in Walzer's thinking seems to me to be related through an antinationalist affinity lodged in liberalism to a similar kind of reasoning displayed by Martha Nussbaum in her claims for the superiority of cosmopolitan allegiances over national ones. "I am a citizen of the world," Diogenes the Cynic declared, and Nussbaum takes his stand as hers, declaring herself a "person whose primary allegiance is to the community of human beings of the entire world . . . to no mere form of government, no temporal power, but to the moral community made up by the humanity of all human beings."[16] But the corrective to Nussbaum is the same as to Walzer: the history of the human experience and the logic of democratic discourse invalidate her, to my mind, extraordinary assertion that the democratic nation is a "morally arbitrary boundary." Democratic citizenship involves a form of participation with others in the civil realm and with the state that over time should yield enough of a "national identity," based on an historically constructed consensus of community membership, that members are morally bound to respect the essential rules of life that their association has engendered.

Just as I believe it is a mistake to privilege ethnic over democratic national loyalty, so too I think it wrong to privilege "world citizenship" over that to the democratic nation. For most people, narrow ethnic loyalties, like broader cosmopolitan allegiances, are emotionally and spiritually thinner for solid historical and normative reasons than is democratic national life. To make such an assertion is not to deny the importance of subnational or cosmopolitan allegiances, or the difficulty on occasion of choosing between church and state or ethnicity and nation. But it is to affirm that the arguments in favor of a national identity and a responsibility toward national obligations should usually (not always) take precedence over cosmopolitan or ethnic loyalties in the case of a conflict. Rather than assuming a happy coincidence of multiple loyalties, or the easy superiority of cosmopolitan or ethnic allegiances to national ones, the job of political philosophers today should be to lay out how difficult, indeed painful, moral choices may be made when subnational or cosmopolitan obligations clash with those of national democratic citizenship.

We confront here a stubborn problem for liberal theorists: they are better today at defining universal human rights or subnational ethnic rights than they are at delineating the obligations of citizenship in the very nation that respects these other loyalties and makes honoring them possible. During the Progressive era and the New Deal, liberals were different: they sided with "the public interest" and called on the national state to realize it. But to add irony to the current problem, most liberals now call for a more active national state—whose legitimacy they implicitly dispute—for the sake of subnational entitlements or cosmopolitan goals they pursue, without a thought of reconciling these agendas with the rights of the national community and state on whose power they depend.

Post-National Citizenship

Michael Walzer's privileging of ethnic over national allegiance and Martha Nussbaum's privileging of world over national citizenship are not isolated cases. They are congruent with positions taken by other multiculturalist theorists, such as that advanced on "post-national" citizenship by Yasemin N. Soysal. While Soysal's principal preoccupation is specifying the rights of migrants in foreign lands, her concern is not so much the traditional one of extending their rights in their adoptive country (those of Turks in Germany, for example) as it is to celebrate their unadulterated right to benefit from multiple loyalties: "A new and more universal concept of citizenship has unfolded in the postwar era, one whose organizing and legitimating principles are based on universal personhood rather than national belonging. To an increasing extent, rights and privileges once reserved for citizens of a nation are codified and expanded as personal rights, undermining the national order of citizenship."[17]

From Soysal's perspective, national citizenship came fully into itself only with the French Revolution and entered into decline with the increasing integration of the world economic system in the aftermath of World War II. As a result, "the state is no longer an autonomous and independent organization closed over a nationally defined population. Instead, we have a system of constitutionally interconnected states with a multiplicity of membership."[18]

Basing her analysis on the experience of the many millions of guestworkers who have in effect become immigrants throughout Western Europe, Soysal writes of a political practice and a normative discourse wherein "national citizenship is losing ground to a more universal model of membership, anchored in deterritorialized notions of persons' rights" in such a way that people acquire the rights of participation in the political life of wherever they happen to live even if they lack formal citizenship status: "This transformation requires a new understanding of citizenship and its foundation."[19]

Soysal's discussion is directly related to multiculturalism in the growing international reality of "dual citizenship." Unlike Walzer, who sees multiple identities and allegiances forming within a polity, she sees them as operating internationally. Yet neither is a cosmopolitan in Nussbaum's sense of the term, and both advance a claim for the right to have multiple loyalties without any recognition of the tensions this might cause with national citizenship.

It is interesting to see how American law has evolved on this question. In nationality statutes passed in 1907, 1940, and 1952, the Congress included provisions that mandated the loss of citizenship when American citizens demonstrated a primary loyalty to another country. As late as the 1952 act, voting in a foreign election, serving in a foreign army without explicit U.S. government authorization, or being employed by a foreign government in posts to which only nationals were assigned was taken as *prima facie* evidence of belonging to another nation and hence grounds for the loss of American citizenship. Indeed, the preface to my passport, issued in 1996, still declares:

Loss of Citizenship: Under certain circumstances you may lose your U.S. citizenship by performing any of the following acts: 1) naturalization in a foreign state; 2) taking an oath or making a declaration to a foreign state; 3) certain service in the armed forces of a foreign state; 4) accepting employment with a foreign government; or 5) formally renouncing U.S. citizenship before a U.S. consular official overseas.

In fact, over the last generation these provisions have eroded almost completely. Americans who serve under "compulsion" in foreign armies (defined as situations where there is universal conscription) are no longer considered to have lost their citizenship because the service is not voluntary; living long periods abroad similarly is no longer grounds for losing citizenship. It was especially after *Afroyim v. Rusk* (1967), when the Supreme Court determined that voting abroad was also permitted, that courts began to find that to lose U.S. citizenship one must explicitly and voluntarily give it up.[20] Since the end of the Cold War, Americans claiming dual citizenship (but sometimes with the permission of the U.S. government or after formally renouncing their U.S. citizenship) have served, among other capacities, as the foreign minister of Armenia (in 1996), as ambassadors to the United States and to Germany from Baltic republics (in 1996–1997), as a prime minister of Serbia (in 1992), and as president of Lithuania (in 1998).

In a world of increased technological and economic interconnection, in a world where the United States stands supreme, it may be easy to interpret the spread of dual citizenship as a normal, even desirable, turn of events. People with dual or triple nationality presumably may be more cosmopolitan than those with narrower nationalist interests, and accordingly they may spread the value of tolerance of diversity and promote human rights in general, so that multiculturalism may actually become an effective arm of American Wilsonianism and directly serve the national interest.

Yet many multiculturalists appear to see only the rosy side of postnational citizenship. Let us not forget that in 1938 and 1939 Nazi Germany justified the invasion of both Czechoslovakia and Poland under the pretext of defending German citizens resident in those countries.

Fortunately for world peace (but not necessarily for those Chinese who might have wanted the protection of dual citizenship), in 1955 China officially abrogated its right to interfere in the affairs of neighboring countries on behalf of Chinese communities resident there. Hence when large numbers of ethnic Chinese were killed, allegedly as communists, in Malaysia and Indonesia over the next years, Beijing refrained from coming to their defense.[21] With ethnic violence growing in Indonesia after the economic collapse of 1997–1998 and the wealthy Chinese minority there being a principal target, one may wonder if in similar situations an increasingly mighty China will continue to abide by its 1955 decision, and how multiculturalists will react if it does not.

In contrast to current Chinese practice, in 1993–1994 Russia made it a prime object of its policy toward the Commonwealth of Independent States to guarantee dual citizenship to the Russians resident in these lands (in especially large numbers in Kazakhstan, Ukraine, Belarus, and the Baltic countries). The dual aim was to protect its kinfolk and to have influence over the domestic affairs of these new countries. It is not surprising that all of these countries categorically refused the Russian proposal. Moscow subsequently dropped its demands.[22]

Could any of these complications of dual citizenship trouble the United States? Clearly, participating in an international regime promoting such rights could have destabilizing effects for others that they might ultimately depend on Washington to resolve. After embracing dual citizenship, how do we then react to what might be Chinese or Russian pretexts to protect their citizens resident abroad, used as a disguise for expansionism?

A different category of problems concerns the obligation of the United States to defend the rights its citizens have acquired as citizens of other countries. For example, to what extent is the United States government bound to aid Cuban Americans in the restitution of the property they lost as Cubans in Cuba after 1959? The Cuban American National Foundation (CANF) has a clear answer that depends on a notion of dual citizenship. It asserts that property rights once enjoyed by those who fled the island continue to be theirs—that *as Cubans* they are entitled to restitution. But it has also succeeded in getting American courts to defend the claims of these same people *as Americans* whose property has been seized abroad.

The Helms-Burton bill, signed into law in March 1996, was CANF's greatest triumph to date (except perhaps for this organization's control of publicly financed Radio and TV Martí, a position that at taxpayer expense gave it great power in the Cuban American community). Thus "aliens" coming into possession of "confiscated American property" in Cuba (including property taken from persons who were not yet Ameri-

can citizens but who retroactively claim that status) are subject to prosecution in American courts. The democratic government that succeeds
Castro will be held responsible for: "taking appropriate steps to return
to United States citizens and entities property taken by the Government of Cuba from such citizens and entities on or after January 1,
1959, or to provide equitable compensation to such citizens and entities for such property."[23]

A potentially far greater problem of the spread of dual citizenship
concerns the character of immigration into the United States. On
March 20, 1998, Mexico began to grant dual citizenship to those Mexicans who were permanent residents outside its borders. Previously,
Mexicans who had adopted American citizenship lost a number of legal
rights in their homeland. Now some 3 million Mexicans who are legal
residents in the United States may naturalize.[24]

By an act of the Mexican Congress, it appears there may be another
increase of immigration from that country to the United States as these
residents become citizens and bring in additional family members. A
Mexican American population already more than 15 million strong
stands to expand by several million (with perhaps an additional two to
three million, should undocumented aliens be given a general amnesty
as some are suggesting).

For the Mexicans involved in these reforms there can be little doubt
that dual citizenship is a positive gain. For fear of losing certain rights
in Mexico (such as that of inheritance), they refrained from demanding
certain rights in the United States. When they now ask for American
citizenship, it will not be either legally or ethically appropriate to deny
them.

Most multiculturalists presumably welcome this turn of events. If
ethnic diversity is to flourish in the United States, then it needs contin-
ual fresh infusions of immigrants from abroad to keep the wellsprings
of ancient affections properly nourished. Indeed, some multicultural
theorists maintain that the very balance between state and society
might be threatened over the long term were immigration severely
constrained—a national identity might develop that would constrain
ethnic space; the melting pot might actually be successful. Hence
Walzer's first rule on a "checklist of the principles" to undergird multiculturalism:

Don't shut the gates. This is not Europe; we are a society of immigrants, and the experience of leaving a homeland and coming to this new place is an almost universal "American" experience. It should be celebrated. But the celebration will be inauthentic and hypocritical if we are busy building walls around our country. Whatever regulation is necessary—we can argue about that—the flow of people, the material base of multiculturalism, should not be cut off.[25]

While the black/white divide that has plagued American society may well diminish as Latinos and Asians increase in relative numbers, we cannot stop with this observation. Is it really a secondary matter to worry about specific regulations, as Walzer maintains? Current immigration law sets a cap on the number of persons to be admitted to the United States as immigrants, but in the case of close family of citizens, the cap can be "pierced." The result will probably be a noticeable increase in the population of Mexican Americans, reaching perhaps 25 million early in the twenty-first century if another amnesty is granted and the law is not changed to make family immigration more difficult.

Debates are ferocious on the matter of whether the United States gains or loses from Mexican immigration. One need not endorse the extremist, indeed nativist-xenophobic, reactions of some in this country—such as Peter Brimelow's offensive assertion that "current immigration policy is Adolf Hitler's posthumous revenge on America [for it may] destroy the one unquestioned victor of World War II: the American nation . . . Today, U.S. government policy is literally dissolving the people and electing a new one"[26]—to recognize that there are at least three reasons to be skeptical that such a large number of Mexican immigrants is an unmixed blessing. First, most Mexican migrants are largely uneducated and unskilled. Their arrival may depress wages for other poor groups in the United States. Special sectors of the economy surely benefit from their labor, which is the reason some business groups want the immigration to continue. But from the perspective of the income distribution, which today is becoming increasingly polarized (or shaped like an hourglass as the middle class declines), and from the point of view of America as a "post-industrial" economy where decently paid manufacturing jobs are declining, there is an argument to be made that immigration of this kind of labor is socially regressive.[27] I believe it is thus a mistake to separate immigration policy from issues of general welfare as Walzer does:

> There are more important and harder questions that Americans have to answer, having to do with economic decline, growing in-equality, the condition of the underclass. Against that background, the debate over multiculturalism is almost a diversion. Still, we are in the midst of a second "great immigration," comparable to that of the years 1890–1910, multiplying American cultures and open-ing the way for new articulations of difference. So this is a good time to reassert the twinned American values of a singular citizen-ship and a radically pluralist civil society.[28]

Will the problem be eased by the fact that Mexican Americans often call for affirmative action treatment in employment? At its origin, affirmative action was designed to redress the historically based griev-ances of communities that had been deliberately marginalized by main-stream society: Native Americans, blacks, and Chicanos. But with the tide of Mexican and Central American immigration riding on the cur-rent legislation, literally millions of new immigrants who have not been the victims of this country's past discriminatory policies may find them-selves privileged over white Americans in considerations for jobs. Nei-ther morally nor practically is there much to be said in defense of these actions, supported as they may be by an ever more powerful Mexican American lobby.[29]

A second consideration is that a liberal immigration policy may often be bad for the Mexicans who come, given the inhospitality of the American wage and educational system to unskilled immigrants. Low wages mean that migrants frequently work two jobs; family structures may weaken; the second (or third) generation may join the American underclass. Some recent statistics show that Hispanic youth (and Mexi-cans especially) are much more likely than the general population not to complete high school. Even when adjustments are made to discount recent arrivals, the same figures show that U.S.-born Hispanics are suf-fering a real decline in their standard of living and now rank at the bot-tom of the American ethnic hierarchy in terms of income. High levels of teenage pregnancy and gang violence relative to other sectors of the population are inevitable results. I have heard people who oppose current levels of Mexican immigration called "racists," but there is an argument to be made that is quite the opposite—that those who promote this immigration are more truly insensitive to the genuine well-being of Mexicans.[30]

Finally, there is the political question. The great majority of Mexican Americans prefer to live in the Southwest—California, Arizona, New Mexico, and Texas. From the point of view of some of their historians, these lands could be considered Mexican, taken as they were from Mexico by Texas independence in 1836 and the war that was concluded on American terms in 1848. No matter that these territories had fewer than 80,000 Mexicans in them at the time they joined the Union. As names like Los Angeles and Santa Fe, San Antonio and Sacramento suggest, Mexican these lands were and Mexican they may once again become (unless the country of "Aztlan" is set up, as some hope). Even now, electoral redistricting strengthens the Mexican American political presence as illegal as well as legal immigration affects congressional representation. In a study completed late in 1998, the Center for Immigration Studies found that the censuses of 1990 and 2000 combined will lead to thirteen seats being lost by Louisiana, Michigan, Montana, and Ohio (after 1990) and by Michigan, Mississippi, Ohio, Pennsylvania, and Wisconsin (after 2000) thanks to illegal as well as legal immigration.[31]

It is of real importance to underscore the national identity and loyalties of Americans of Mexican descent. I do not agree with those who foresee a time when Mexican Americans will come to consider themselves as the Québecois consider themselves in Canada: a conquered people with rights to self-government that will rectify their second-class economic status.[32] Yet some of their intellectuals clearly want to persuade them to think in these terms. For example, Rodolfo Acuña entitled a book *Occupied America* (1981) and implied that all the Mexican Americans now living in the lands taken by the United States in 1848 are descendant from those who lived there then (whereas surely fewer than 5 percent of them are). Accordingly, he entitled his first chapter "Legacy of Hate," declaring in his opening:

> The tragedy of the Mexican cession is that most Anglo-Americans have not accepted the fact that the United States committed an act of violence against the Mexican people when it took Mexico's

northwestern territory. Violence was not limited to taking the land. Mexico's territory was invaded, her people murdered, her land raped, and her possession plundered. Memory of this destruction generated a distrust and dislike that is still vivid in the minds of many Mexicans, for the violence of the United States left deep scars. And for Chicanos—Mexicans remaining within the boundaries of the new United States territories—aggression was even more insidious, for the outcome of the Texas and the Mexican-American wars made them a conquered people.[33]

Acuña's is not an isolated voice. A four-part KCET–Los Angeles TV documentary entitled *Chicanos!* produced in 1996 and narrated by Henry Cisneros, opens with scenes making charges against the legitimacy of U.S. sovereignty over the region from Texas to California that sound borrowed from Acuña's book. Peter Skerry opens his book on Mexican Americans with other examples of these contentious claims.[34]

Organized Mexican American interest groups are not united in the position they take on the questions of immigration and dual citizenship—nor is the Mexican American citizenry of one mind. Most Mexican Americans today identify with many core American values (indeed they may well exceed their fellow Americans in terms of commitment to the work ethic and family values), and even if they think of themselves as an ethnicity, are also confident of their identity as Americans.[35] Many of them may also recognize a need to limit immigration in their own economic interest. But in October 1996 the first Hispanic March on Washington occurred, when perhaps 30,000 demonstrators made a list of demands on the government. Among these were amnesty for undocumented aliens currently here, demands for control of the border police that can easily be read as loosening restraints on immigration, and calls for affirmative action consideration for new arrivals.[36] In arguing against employer verification schemes and national identity cards designed to restrict illegal immigration, and in supporting generous family reunification plans for legal immigrants, some Hispanic organizations—supported by the Catholic church, some business interests, libertarian groups like the Cato Institute, and the Ford Foundation—were calling for measures that erode the country's ability to control its borders.

It is difficult to stake out a reasoned, moderate multiculturalist position given the nativists on one side prophesying doom in the face of the current wave of immigration and the immigrants-rights groups on the other side acting as deeply offended parties, their cultural identities under siege. Nevertheless, Peter H. Schuck makes such an attempt, stating as his credo: "Immigration, including the post-1965 wave, has served America well. If properly regulated, there is every reason to expect that it will continue to do so." The trick comes, of course, in laws that "properly regulate" immigration, and Schuck apparently has some sympathy for those he calls "pragmatic restrictionists," people who believe that "immigration's actual effects on population, the environment, national unity, cultural consensus, and so forth are empirical questions whose answers depend on a variety of factors . . . [people who] are open to argument and evidence about what those levels should be and about what immigration's actual effects are."[37]

In line with Schuck's suggestion, it is possible to identify several concerns raised by immigration since 1965 that are open to empirical investigation, in addition to the problems of dual citizenship discussed above:

> The educational and skill levels of many immigrants, especially from Mexico and Central America, which may put them in direct competition with the poor in U.S. society while sentencing them to a future in the underclass.
>
> The high school dropout rates and teenage pregnancy rates suggesting how well second- and third-generation immigrant families of Mexican and Central American descent are faring in the United States today.
>
> The existence of a sustained effort to reinforce ethnic at the expense of national thinking as group-centered rights replace those conferred on individuals, as ethnic entrepreneurs promote bilingualism and measures favoring political redistricting and try to extend affirmative action protection to Latino newcomers.
>
> The practical problems posed by high crime rate among illegal aliens and the difficulties set in the way of controlling these influxes of foreigners by the political activism of their ethnic kinfolk already here.[38]

The point of this discussion is not to come to a final decision as to what American immigration law should be—although the debates are serious and bear comparisons with what is going on in Western Europe as well—but instead to ask how to formulate the law in a way that respects the dignity of immigrant cultures while recognizing that there may be a national interest in controlling our borders much more tightly than we do at present. Even those who declare themselves in favor of continued high rates of immigration may object strongly to many aspects of the process as it is currently structured, and so may resemble Schuck's "pragmatic restrictionists." To date, multiculturalist thinkers have not aided this important and sensitive debate. To the contrary, by celebrating hyphenation and dual and post-national citizenship, multiculturalists have encouraged the indignation of Latinos who feel their culture is being unfairly stigmatized, and have validated the all-too-easy belief that those who feel immigration is a critical issue for the future social and political culture of this nation are simply racists.

Diasporas

Yet a third stream of multiculturalist thinkers has emerged in recent years to comment on the role of "diasporas" as a subgroup of "transnational actors" in world affairs. A good deal of the literature is devoted to establishing the existence of these communities and documenting their impact. However, much of this literature also reveals that many of these writers are sympathetic to notions of hyphenation and post-national citizenship.

Thus, in the new literature on the world's diasporas, writers may point to the importance of Jews, Greeks, Chinese, Africans, and Russians (among others) playing a role in world affairs. Yet, to my mind, serious conceptual problems are suggested by aspects of diasporic terminology, as when the term *homeland* or *home country*, rather than *ancestral homeland* (or "the old country," as many in the Irish diaspora put it), is adopted for the land where the diaspora has its ethnic allegiance, to be distinguished from the *host country* where members of the diaspora are now living.

For example, Gabriel Sheffer explicitly singles out American Jews and Hispanics as being part of "diasporas," where the United States is the "host country" and Israel and various parts of Latin America are the "homelands." Indeed, he writes of triadic attachments American Jews may have to the United States, to the Jewish diaspora as something of a corporate body, and to Israel, implying that the obligations of U.S. citizenship stand as the third and least important of these loyalties.[39] Michael Walzer makes much the same point, apparently purporting to speak for all Americans:

> The United States isn't a "homeland" (where a national family might dwell), not, at least, as other countries are, in casual conversation and unreflective feeling. It is a country of immigrants who, however grateful they are for this new place, still remember the old places . . . their children . . . no doubt are native born, but some awkward sense of newness here, or of distant oldness, keeps the tongue from calling this land "home."[40]

Sheffer's nomenclature is used not only by others in the book he edited, *Modern Diasporas in International Politics* (1986), but in a follow-up volume that appeared in 1995, *Diasporas in World Politics*, edited by Dimitri Constas and Athanassios Platias.[41] It is noteworthy that all three writers, as well as the contributors to these two books and the journal *Diaspora*, assume the rights of multiple citizenship with only cursory examination of the potential for ethical conflicts given what at times must be not only dual but also conflicted loyalties.

To his credit, Sheffer does note that multiethnicity may "evoke loyalties and solidarities inconsistent with and sometimes even contradicting the traditional allegiances to territorial states." And in *Diasporas in World Politics* Sheffer has an essay on Israel's attempts to bend the will of the Jewish diaspora to the policies of whatever regime is in power in Jerusalem, while Nikolaos Stavrou writes on the vicissitudes of the Greek American community's relations with Athens. But the analyses are too brief and too anecdotal to constitute more than passing references to the serious practical and moral problems that dual loyalties may raise when they become divided. What is needed is some guidance on how to prioritize national, ethnic, and diasporic loyalties and obligations from a theoretical point of view.

It should be clear that my objection to this literature is not that it takes diasporas seriously as actors in world affairs. To the contrary, a sense of the importance of the Chinese, Armenian, Jewish, and Greek diasporas (among others) is all too absent in debates over international relations. My objection instead is to the implicit assumption of much of this literature that ethnic identity is somehow emotionally and morally privileged over national allegiance—a spirit best captured by labeling the land of citizenship the "host country" and the country of ethnic descent the "homeland." For example, in 1999 Cambridge University Press published a book by Yossi Shain unselfconsciously entitled *Marketing the American Creed Abroad: Diasporas in the U.S. and Their Homelands.*

We encounter, then, the familiar problem in the diaspora literature that we saw earlier in the literature on hyphenation and post-national citizenship: it celebrates the rights and powers of the diasporic communities while omitting any corresponding discussion of their obligations as citizens of democratic states. By the same token, it fails to deal at all adequately with problems not of dual but of conflicted loyalties. The ethical problem is summed up in the responsibilities incurred at the moment of naturalization in the United States:

> I hereby declare, on oath, that I absolutely and entirely renounce and abjure all allegiance and fidelity to any foreign prince, potentate, state or sovereignty, to whom or which I have heretofore been a subject or citizen; that I will support and defend the Constitution and laws of the United States of America against all enemies, foreign and domestic; that I will bear arms on behalf of the United States when required by the law . . . and that I take this obligation freely without any mental reservation or purpose; so help me God.

Under the terms of this oath, the national interest of the United States becomes a primary loyalty—certainly not exclusive, but one that only in extreme cases needing special justification may be treated as secondary to the citizen's religious or ethnic allegiances. Hence the use of American citizenship by members of a diaspora as a tool in the service of a foreign government or people would be a practice that, I think, these ethnics' fellow Americans could reasonably deplore.

Nevertheless, foreign governments have been quick to realize the advantages they might gain in Washington from rousing their kinfolk in the United States to their defense. Israel, Greece, Armenia, and Poland have all done so with notable success, as have movements like the

Irish Republican Army (and Sinn Fein with Gerry Adams) and the African National Congress party (under Nelson Mandela). For example, Athens is unabashed in reminding the estimated 5.6 million members of the Greek "Diaspora" that it is the "center of Hellenism" to which all owe a special allegiance. Even Mexico, which until recently derided its kinfolk north of the border for abandoning the national territory, has come to realize that, given the perhaps $3 billion in annual remittances from Mexican Americans to relatives in the ancestral homeland, as well as the influence they might bring to bear on a host of U.S.-Mexican issues, it should be concerned about the foreign policy thinking of the millions of U.S. citizens of Mexican descent. Accordingly, the Mexican government has created new transnational organizations (such as the Program for Mexican Communities Living in Foreign Countries) and has begun to cultivate Mexican American leaders as a way of increasing its own voice in what happens in Washington.[42]

Trading on what Woodrow Wilson called these "ancient affections" is thus a widespread feature of American political life. As evidence of how natural such feelings are, note the use of "we" in the statement by the Hungarian-born Democratic Representative Tom Lantos as cited in the *New York Times* on March 12, 1999, on the accession of his native country to NATO:

> After a thousand years of desperate craving to be part of the West, today it's official—we're in, we get the imprimatur of NATO. A pagan Hungarian King, St. Stephen, embraced Western civilization in 1001 by accepting a crown from Rome. But it has taken a millennium to complete the process. In the interim, we missed the Renaissance because we were occupied by the Turks. We spent centuries as an appendage of Vienna, clinging to the West through the hyphen that connected us, humiliatingly, to Austria. We stumbled through the 20th century cut off from the mainstream.

To cite still another contemporary example (many more could be produced), as America and its NATO allies attacked Serbian forces in and around Kosovo in the spring of 1999, newspapers and television carried stories of American citizens of Serbian or Albanian ancestry fiercely taking sides as combat raged in the Balkans, referring to themselves as Serbs or Albanians still, their American identities evident only in their American accents. Indeed, within two weeks matters appeared even more serious as Orthodox churches (with at least 4 million members in the United States), including Greek and Russian American congregations, came out with only some nuance on the side of Serbia.[43]

There should be no denying that on occasion transnational ethnic networks have worked in a way favorable to American interests, either by involving America in world affairs in a forward fashion that its isolationist impulses might otherwise regrettably have precluded, or by providing means to influence foreign capitals. Still, only to celebrate the existence of these ties, as if they almost never raised serious practical problems for American foreign policy and posed no ethical dilemmas for theories of democratic citizenship, is all too common among multiculturalist writers today. There is a growing literature on the international spread of ethnic conflicts due in part to the ways diasporas carry the contagion of struggle in one part of the world to another by way of their "diasporal" loyalties. Such developments underscore the seriousness of the question of how a pluralist democracy might protect itself from self-interested minority groups which use their rights as citizens to push agendas for American foreign policy that can plausibly be argued to make America's role in world affairs inconsistent and incoherent on the one hand, if not fixed and self-destructive on the other.[44]

A "Community of Communities"?

How should a national conversation on a reasoned patriotism be founded in an era of multiculturalism? This issue is difficult and contentious, and often treated as taboo. Ethnic organizations themselves typically insist that what they want for Greece, Armenia, Israel, or wherever else is exactly in line with American national interests. Often they may be right. I have no quarrel, for example, with the arguments that the search for Nazi plunder and the Oslo peace accords, the end of apartheid in South Africa and the restoration of Aristide in Haiti, and the peace process in Northern Ireland all depended in their unfolding on the determination of certain American ethnic groups to bring Washington into line behind policies that might otherwise never have existed, policies that served the entire country. Yet these cases by no means exhaust the matters concerning which ethnic lobbies work long and hard to influence U.S. foreign policy. As I argued in earlier chapters, ethnic demands in some cases compromised American influence in world affairs during the twentieth century, and still do so today. How, then, are we to phrase our objections when ethnic lobbies seem to be using American power to help kinfolk or foreign governments in ways difficult to reconcile with what we believe are general U.S. interests?

Neither the leadership of ethnic organizations nor their rank-and-file membership is likely to welcome such a discussion. The best evidence I have been able to find on the psychological difficulties of debating U.S. foreign policy concerns American Jewry. Five different Jewish American authors remark that while institutionalized anti-Semitism virtually vanished in the United States some time ago (and was never as bad here as in most European countries), American Jews are nonetheless convinced that it is a growing danger to them. J. J. Goldberg reports: "The percentage of Jews who tell pollsters that anti-Semitism is a 'serious problem' in America nearly doubled during the course of the 1980s, from 45 percent in 1983 to nearly 85 percent in 1990." Charles Liebman and Steven Cohen, analyzing "the unwillingness of many American Jews to come to terms with their own acceptance in American society," cite Abba Eban's comment that American Jewry "can't take yes for an answer." And Seymour Martin Lipset writes:

> The United States has been open to Jews and the evidence clearly points to a sharp falloff in social and economic restrictions on, and prejudice toward, them since World War II. Still Jews remain fearful of anti-Semitism. Only one out of seven of those responding to [the] questionnaires agreed that "Anti-semitism in America is currently not a serious problem for American Jews." An overwhelming majority, over three quarters (76%) replied that it is a serious problem; two-thirds disagreed with the statement: "Virtually all positions of influence in America are open to Jews" . . . Among contributors to the San Francisco Jewish Community Federation . . . one third agree[d] that a Jew cannot be elected to Congress from San Francisco . . . in 1985 when all three members of contiguous districts in or adjacent to the city were Jewish, as were the two state senators, the mayor, and a considerable part of the city council.

Peter Novick explains this increased sense of anti-Semitism here as a reaction to the 1967 War between Israel and the Arab states and to the growth of the Holocaust as the dominant symbol of Jewish unity. Prior to the late 1960s, he writes:

> Jewish organizations had had an outward orientation, had emphasized building bridges between Jews and gentiles, had stressed what Jews had in common with other Americans. Now there was an inward turn, an insistence on the defense of separate Jewish interests, a stress on what made Jews unlike other Americans. Previously, the history of Jews in America was seen as a success story. Now, increasingly, American Jews came to see themselves as an endangered species, and searched for themes and programs that could promote Jewish solidarity.[45]

Accordingly, while Jews score the highest among white ethnics on measures of group self-confidence, they score the lowest in terms of trusting other groups. The result is a marked intolerance of non-Jewish criticism of Israel, as revealed in surveys by the American Jewish Committee, which on two separate occasions found that while most American Jews feel they have a right to criticize Israel publicly, almost as many feel that when others do so it is because they are anti-Semitic:[46]

"American Jews should not publicly criticize the politics of the government of Israel." Agree: 29%. Disagree: 68%. Not sure: 2%.
    "The criticism that we hear of Israel derives mainly from anti-Semitism." Agree: 59%. Disagree: 36%. Not sure: 5%.

To illustrate the point, consider the position of Elie Wiesel: "I support Israel—period. I identify with Israel—period. I never attack, never criticize Israel when I am not in Israel." As Wiesel put it in rebuking the actor Richard Dreyfuss for referring to the sometimes "inappropriate defensiveness" of American Jews in reaction to criticism of Israel: "The role of a Jew is to be with our people. *Ahavat Israel* [love of Israel] means when Israel needs us, we must be there. When Israel is attacked, we must defend her."[47]

It is well to remember that over the centuries and throughout the world Jews have been accused by anti-Semites of possessing far more power than they ever have had, power which Jews allegedly used in a self-interested way destructive to the societies in which they lived. This is an important Jewish historical memory. Hence simply to call attention to the existence of Jewish political power, much less to suggest that its preferences are debatable, is to raise understandable concerns that once again Jews are endangered by racists who would turn nationalist sentiment against them. Critics of the American Israel Public Affairs Committee (AIPAC) should thus recognize that the American Jewish community has cause for anxiety when its power is questioned.

Yet the sensitivities of many American Jews notwithstanding, non-Jewish Americans have a right to make their position on U.S. policy in the Middle East well known. Every year the American treasury dispenses billions in grants to Israel (and billions more in subsidies to Arab states based in good measure on their conduct toward Israel), which also enjoys preferential trading and military procurement relations with the United States. The entire country (and not just Jewish Americans) is thus practically and morally implicated in the Arab-Israeli confrontation. Moreover, the energy reserves of the region are of fundamental importance not only to our own economy but even more to those of our closest allies in Western Europe and the Pacific. Particular critics of Israel may be anti-Semitic, to be sure, but there should be no automatic assumption that such is the case, or that non-Jewish Americans have no business being concerned about Jerusalem's policies toward its Arab neighbors.

In a word, when right-wing Israeli governments—like those of Menachem Begin, Yitzhak Shamir, and Benjamin Netanyahu—contradict long-established American positions on the terms of a peaceful resolution of differences in the area (most obviously by backing the expansion of Jewish settlements in areas long under Arab control), Americans of all stripes may have a right to feel concerned. But to AIPAC, to be a "friend of Israel" or "pro-Israel" apparently means something quite simple: that Israel alone should decide the terms of its relations with its Arab neighbors, and that the United States should endorse these terms, whatever they may be. One need only look at any issue of AIPAC's publication *Near East Report* to see clear evidence that organization allows for no divergence whatever between what America and Israel should do in the Middle East—as decided by the Israeli government.

The result of these considerations is that neither American Jews nor their fellow Americans are often at ease deliberating American policy toward the Middle East. As we saw in Chapter 3, despite the many differences between the relatively liberal Jewish American community and Israel, it has been generally understood among leading Jewish American organizations since the 1950s that it is for the democratically elected government of Israel to decide what it is good for that country to do; and it is for American Jewry, which bears none of the consequences of that policy, to be loyal in its support even when it disagrees with positions taken by the Israeli government. Given the moral authority the Israeli government seems to have over American Jewry (although one should not underestimate splits among American Jews any more than efforts by this community to influence developments in Israel), and, in turn, the influence of American Jewry on American policy in the Middle East, it thus appears that a foreign state with the active help of a powerful domestic lobby is trying to determine American policy in a critical region of the world.

Those who have studied the Greek and Armenian American lobbies report similar stories of the unwillingness of the organized leadership of an ethnic community to concede that any voice but theirs should be authoritative with respect to the area of the world that concerns them—and similar discoveries that these groups are being strongly influenced by foreign governments to take positions that may contradict American policy or interests in the region. With the states of Eastern Europe consolidating their independence and questions of the enlargement of NATO appearing, we may expect to see increased communication between the governments in Prague, Budapest, and Warsaw and their kinfolk in the United States as well. And even now some groups in Taipei are working with Taiwanese Americans to get U.S. support to make the island independent of China, a position that if taken would be sure to embroil Washington in a direct confrontation with Beijing.

The vocabulary and the rules of engagement for public discussion of interest group demands on foreign policy are constantly undergoing alteration. Thus oil companies, agribusiness, or big business and finance in general may work for the adoption of foreign policies that can create problems for large sectors of the population or vulnerabilities for the country at large (for example, the export of jobs or technology, the evasion of taxes or pollution controls). No amount of invocation by these self-interested economic actors of the common good and the laws of the market can often persuade many of the rest of us that their policy preferences are other than measures pursued for special interests at public expense. Or again, since the 1930s, when the Roman Catholic church asked the Roosevelt administration to intervene in Mexico to prevent the seizure of church properties by the Mexican government, there has been a general understanding that the American state will not back religious demands abroad (an understanding that today may be changing as Christian denominations make religious persecution a human rights issue and ask Washington to take action).

As these analogies suggest, the problem with cultural pluralism comes not in its abstract description—most might agree that it is a worthy ambition in line with the promise of American democracy that ethnic groups be validated and empowered in society—but in its actual implementation. For if we are indeed to be, in Amitai Etzioni's useful term, a "community of communities," trying to reconcile subnational loyalties with loyalty to the nation, the hard job is not so much determining what the "communities" are about internally—that is their business for the most part—as determining how the "community" that holds us all together might be structured in a multicultural setting.[48]

Etzioni shares his concerns with his fellow "communitarians." These are public philosophers committed to multiculturalism who have nonetheless tried to deal with the contradictions between respecting the rights of ethnic communities and insisting that they, in turn, respect the obligations of national citizenship. For example, the communitarian William Galston writes of the widespread "tendency to assert rights without accepting responsibilities . . . to gain the benefits of social cooperation without accepting the burdens of the shared activities that are needed to produce those benefits." Similarly, he worries about "the loss of confidence in the definition, acceptance, or enforceability of a shared national identity." One telling example of the problems that arise came in 1995, when Etzioni was president of the American Sociological Association. He decided to organize a forum on "the community of communities," inviting social scientists representative of the African, Asian, and Hispanic American ethnicities to say how they saw a "shared framework of values" emerging by the year 2020. He reports that all three of his speakers dwelt on past abuses their ethnicities had suffered in this country; two foresaw civil war; and none addressed the assigned topic, the shared framework of values.[49]

THE REASON for the extreme sensitivity of many intercultural dialogues should be apparent. Ethnoracial minorities in the United States recall outrages they have suffered at the hands of white America. Small wonder that their positive associations are with their ethnic kinfolk; their experiences of nationalist solidarity with the rest of America have often been conspicuous by their absence or actually used to exploit them (as in the disproportionate loss of life by black American and Hispanic servicemen in Vietnam). Accordingly, racial minorities may feel that to negotiate or compromise with the white majority on various policy matters is to replay historic patterns of subordination.

Other groups who have found America a land of promise may nonetheless be haunted by ethnic traumas—the Greeks or Armenians with Turkey, Poles with Russia, or Jews with the memory of the Holocaust and understandable fears about Arab extremist opposition to the existence of Israel. Accordingly, the stakes for their kinfolk abroad may seem so commandingly important, and the price to the United States so marginal, that they may perceive no conflict between foreign commitments and national ones. They may see themselves, not as prioritizing foreign interests above American ones, but as simply respecting one allegiance that is not in contradiction with another.

But if the sensitivity of ethnic groups to world affairs is understandable, the idea that they might determine the policy of the entire country with respect to issues important to them cannot stand close scrutiny. For the country has a right—and its leaders an obligation—to determine as a national community appropriate foreign policy. Its leaders must not abdicate this right at any time to self-concerned interest groups for the sake of interests and values remote from, or contrary to, the interests and values of the greater American community.

To assert the rights and interests of the national community against ethnic demands should not be seen as an effort to silence these voices. Who can doubt that the ability of democratic society to respect difference and disagreement, and to grow stronger in the process, has been one of its greatest achievements, permitting a degree of social freedom and political power unrivalled in world history? Nor should we forget that the opponents of racial and gender equality, the right of labor to organize and to bargain collectively, and religious tolerance all maintained that expanded notions of social freedom would undermine the Republic—and all were mistaken.

American nationalists should therefore recognize that pluralism is basic to this country's democratic life and is intrinsic to the many benefits the United States celebrates. They might also recall the price of the denial of civil liberties in the name of the national solidarity. For their part, ethnic groups must recognize the legitimacy of American concerns that differ from those of their ancestral homelands. The dilemma of pluralism lies in the irresolvable tension of how the community as a whole speaks of a shared framework of values and interests yet respects the right of distinct subnational communities to organize freely. By failing to address this problem frankly, much of contemporary multiculturalist thinking is both practically and philosophically flawed.

The most important single argument modern pluralists or moderate multiculturalists must make concerning foreign affairs is that except in circumstances where their kinfolk are in clear and present danger through no fault of their own, ethnic communities have the responsibility to think of themselves as Americans first and to ask what is good for the country at large. Given the essential patriotism of most ethnic communities, this task should not be unduly difficult, for it does not mean that American ethnics should cease to care about their kinfolk abroad and do what they can to ensure their well-being—so long as their actions are without prejudice to their primary loyalty to the United States and to a reasonable construction of its national interests in world affairs.

Such a conclusion leads to several recommendations for multiculturalists today so far as their activism with respect to foreign policy is concerned. For a start, their vocabulary needs to be amended. The use of "homeland" to refer to their ancestral land and "host country" to refer to the United States is an obviously unacceptable usage of these terms. Their homeland is unambiguously the United States; to say that America is their host country is to imply a transitory, tentative citizenship at odds with the obligations a democratic nation rightly presupposes. It also implies a willingness to use their American citizenship as agents of foreign governments or movements, a willingness that must be firmly rejected as a right of citizenship.

Similarly, in order to foster constructive discussion and debate, ethnic groups need to respond to fair criticisms of their demands in ways that deal with the merit of the charges, rather than simply reacting, calling their critics "racists" engaged in "ethnic smears."[50] Ethnic groups should recognize that all Americans have a legitimate right to be concerned about matters that involve these groups' kinfolk when the power of this country is committed in world affairs. The assumption of many ethnic group lobbies that they alone should determine U.S. policy toward a particular region of the world is manifestly indefensible.

Again, multiculturalist thinkers should recognize that ethnic groups are often led by individuals who have an organizational incentive to exaggerate what America can or should do abroad. A principal obstacle to open discussion lies with certain ethnic organizations that seem to develop something of a stake in promoting fear and mistrust so as to gain members, funds, and political influence. The Cuban American National Foundation and the Anti-Defamation League of B'nai B'rith (ADL) have been repeatedly cited as examples of such undertakings. Under the leadership of Jorge Mas Canosa, CANF acquired the reputation of committing widespread acts of community terrorism, including physical assaults on many individuals.[51] By contrast, the ADL's critics allege that it has engaged in blackballing and public harassment that often infringe on its opponents' right to free speech, combined with appeals to the Jewish community that some feel are deliberately exaggerated to fan fears of anti-Semitism.[52] Quite apart from these groups, ethnic politics is often typified by an intensity of emotion and a rigidity of behavior that may make agreement on what constitutes obligations to some concept of the American *unum* far more problematic than recognition of the rights of the ethnic *pluribus*. Ethnic politics is sometimes demagogic, and the inability to say this self-evident truth given the strictures of multicultural thought often impedes the democratic discourse.

Finally, it needs to be acknowledged that ethnic leaders sometimes work to further the agendas of foreign groups or governments regardless of the thinking in Washington or in America at large. The unexamined assumption that American ethnics are "goodwill ambassadors" advancing U.S. interests abroad through the dissemination of American values may at times be a self-serving disguise donned by Americans who are effectively (although not legally) agents of foreign powers. That their fellow Americans may be critical of ethnic organizations on these grounds should come as less of a rude surprise than it often does.

Multiculturalism involves a welcome expansion of what it means to be an American citizen. It is a politics of identity and of difference creating links of solidarity in values and interests among peoples defined ethnically and racially, reflecting this country's history as formed by slaves and immigrants as well as by Native Americans and Chicanos, and as responding to world affairs that legitimately involve peoples here in events concerning their kinfolk abroad.

But it is not enough for multiculturalists to insist on the respect and rights of ethnic groups without a corresponding sense of pride and purpose in the country's national democratic traditions even if critically expressed. Their task today is to use responsibly the power and the rights they have under democratic government to work to reconcile ethnic and national identity and interests. They should learn to respect what Irving Howe called the "limits of ethnicity" and the "grandeur of the American idea: . . . The province, the ethnic nest, remains the point from which everything begins and without which, probably, it could not begin; but the province, the ethnic nest, is not enough, it must be transcended." And they might consider the meaning of Linda Chavez's experience: "When I recently told a university audience that American blacks, Hispanics, Asians, and whites have more in common with one another than they do with their contemporaries in any of their ancestral homelands, the students literally gasped in disbelief." Harold Isaacs made the point some years earlier:

> One can catch dramatic glimpses of [the melting pot] in the experience of Americans who go, out of some feeling of lostness, in search of their remoter roots—the many black Americans who have made pilgrimages to Africa in recent years, American Jews who have gone to Israel to try to become Israelis, Japanese Americans who have gone to Japan, Italian Americans who have gone to Italy. Whatever new view they acquire of their ancestral cultures

> . . . there is a remarkably uniform experience that turns up during these quests. The seekers find out that they are not African, not Japanese, not Italian, or whatever, but something quite else, something quite distinctive: they are Afro American, Japanese American, Italian American.[53]

I believe President Clinton was correct when he said, in his 1997 State of the Union address, "We must never believe that diversity is a weakness—it is our greatest strength." Or at least I believe we have no other option but to make this assertion true. Perhaps Clinton should have been more temperate, recognizing that our diversity should become (rather than already is) our greatest strength. Certainly if we think of our multicultural champions of hyphenation, post-national citizenship, and diasporas, much remains to be done.

Clinton was also correct, I think, to talk about the relevance of events in this country to other democracies: "All over the world, people are being torn asunder by racial, ethnic, and religious conflicts that fuel fanaticism and terrors. We are the world's most diverse democracy. And the world looks to us to show that it is possible to live and advance together across those kinds of differences." What he might have added is that we too can learn from others, from the efforts of the Canadians, the Australians, the Israelis, the Indians, the South Africans, and the various peoples of Europe as they deal with problems often painfully similar to our own.[54]

THE QUESTION remains: Who speaks for America in world affairs? Those who think of themselves foremost as Americans do—or should. What does it mean to be an American? The answer undergoes constant change, always revolving around the question of citizenship—its rights and its obligations and the character of those who possess it—a topic at the heart of the democratic process.

Today the answer lies in the debate over the meaning of multiculturalism for the character of the American union, a debate I have analyzed in terms of the making of this country's foreign policy. My core argument is that while ethnic groups undoubtedly have the right to seek to influence Washington, they also have the obligation to recognize that national interests may conflict with their ethnic preferences. Resolving this contradiction between particular and general interests and values will never be easy, for it is inscribed in the logic of democratic government. But frankly recognizing that pluralism has its contradictions is a major step toward dealing with them more fruitfully, and nowhere is this observation more relevant today than in our efforts to determine the role the United States should play in world affairs.

Notes

Index

Notes

Introduction

1. Alexis de Tocqueville, *Democracy in America* (New York: Harper and Row, 1966), 228ff.

2. George Kennan, *The Cloud of Danger: Current Realities of American Foreign Policy* (Boston: Little, Brown, 1977), 4ff.

3. Isaiah Berlin, "Two Concepts of Liberty," in *The Proper Study of Mankind* (New York: Farrar, Straus, Giroux, 1998), 4.

4. Robert A. Dahl, *Dilemmas of Pluralist Democracy: Autonomy vs. Control* (New Haven: Yale University Press, 1982), 1. See also Jeffrey M. Berry, *The New Liberalism: The Rising Power of Citizen Groups* (Washington: Brookings Institution, 1999).

5. Samuel P. Huntington, "The Erosion of American National Interests," *Foreign Affairs*, 76, 5, 1997, 42.

6. Randall Robinson, *Defending the Spirit: A Black Life in America* (New York: Dutton, 1998).

7. Pacific Council on International Policy, "Advancing the International Interests of African-Americans, Asian-Americans, and Latinos" (Los Angeles, 1998), 10.

8. Citation downloaded from the Southwest Voter Registration Institute website on 12/15/97. In 1998 the SVRI became the William C. Velasquez Institute. Yossi Shain cites a statement from the chairman of the League of United Latin American Citizens in 1978 after a meeting with the President of Mexico, Lopez Portillo: Mexican Americans "are ready to help Mexico in the United States . . . We feel that in the future Mexico can use us as Israel uses American Jews." Cited in Shain, *Marketing the American Creed Abroad: Diasporas in the U.S. and Their Homelands* (New York: Cambridge University Press, 1999), 184.

9. David J. Vidal, "Defining the National Interest: Minorities and U.S. Foreign Policy in the 21st Century" (New York: Council on Foreign Relations, 1997).

10. Alexander DeConde, *Ethnicity, Race, and American Foreign Policy: A History* (Boston: Northeastern University Press, 1992). In fact, dislike of Great Britain began during the Revolutionary War and was carried forward by Thomas Jefferson thereafter and in the War of 1812, ignited again during the Civil War, and was evident in the Venezuelan Boundary dispute at the end of the nineteenth century. For one perspective on the evolution of Anglo-American relations, see John M. Owen IV, *Liberal Peace, Liberal War* (Ithaca: Cornell University Press, 1997); and on the twentieth century, see John E. Moser, *Twisting the Lion's Tail: American Anglophobia between the World Wars* (New York: New York University Press, 1999).

11. Nadav Safran, *The United States and Israel* (Cambridge, MA: Harvard University Press, 1963), 276f. See also the way Yossi Shain speaks of the "Anglo-Saxon establishment" as if its great strength and very existence were self-evident facts, in Shain, 12f, 207.

12. Charles McC. Mathias Jr., "Ethnic Groups and Foreign Policy," *Foreign Affairs*, 59, 5, 1981, 981.

13. *House Congressional Record*, 105th Cong., 2nd sess., 144, 124, 9/17/98. See also Albright's statement before the House Appropriations Committee, 3/4/98; and on the oil industry, *Journal of Commerce*, 12/15/97.

14. Full-page ad in the *New York Times*, 5/2/99, paid for by Orthodox Christian groups; Council of Hellenes Abroad for the North and South America (SAE), letter to Jewish organizations and press release of 11/12/98, www.saeamerica.org, downloaded 4/12/99; letter to President Clinton, members of Congress and other high officials, from Eugene T. Rossides, President of the American Hellenic Institute Public Affairs Committee, 4/2/99, www.ahiworld.com, downloaded 4/12/99.

15. I would cite as examples of "pluralist" thinking on this matter Amitai Etzioni, *The New Golden Rule* (New York: Basic Books, 1996); William A. Galston, "A Public Philosophy for the 21st Century," *The Responsive Community*, 8, 3, 1998; Nathan Glazer, *We Are All Multiculturalists Now* (Cambridge, MA: Harvard University Press, 1997); and Arthur M. Schlesinger Jr., *The Disuniting of America: Reflections on a Multicultural Society* (New York: Norton, 2nd ed., 1998).

1. Multiculturalism and U.S. Foreign Policy

1. See, e.g., Nathan Glazer, *We Are All Multiculturalists Now* (Cambridge, MA: Harvard University Press, 1997); Philip Gleason, "American Identity and Americanization," in Stephan Thernstrom, ed., *Harvard Encyclopedia of American Ethnic Groups* (Cambridge, MA: Harvard University Press, 1980); Susan D. Greenbaum, "Multiculturalism," in Susan Auerbach, ed., *Encyclopedia of Multiculturalism* (New York: Marshall Cavendish, 1994), vol. 4; Charles Taylor, "The Politics of Recognition," in Amy Gutmann ed., *Multiculturalism: Examining the Politics of Recognition* (Princeton: Princeton University Press, 1995); Will Kymlicka, *Multicultural Citizenship* (Oxford: Oxford University Press, 1995); Yael Tamir, *Liberal Nationalism* (Princeton: Princeton University Press, 1993); Stephan and Abigail Thernstrom, *America in Black and White: One Nation, Indivisible* (New York: Simon and Schuster, 1997); Michael Walzer, *What It Means to Be an American* (New York: Marsilio, 1992).

2. Ted Robert Gurr, "Peoples against States: Ethnopolitical Conflict and the Changing World System," *International Studies Quarterly*, 38, 3, 1994; Donald L. Horowitz, *Ethnic Groups in Conflict* (Berkeley: University of California Press, 1985); Michael Ignatieff, *Blood and Belonging: Journeys to the New Nationalisms* (New York: Farrar, Straus, and Giroux, 1994).

3. Census figures reported in the *New York Times*, 11/8/97. Seymour Martin Lipset, *American Exceptionalism: A Double-Edged Sword* (New York: Norton, 1996), ch. 1, 51f, 288ff; Michael Lind, "The Beige and the Black," *New York Times Magazine*, 8/16/98. Thernstrom and Thernstrom, *American in Black and White*, 179, report a 1994 poll that asked "'do you think America is the very best place in the world to live?' Both whites (82 percent) and blacks (74 percent) said it was."

4. Robert J. McMahon, "The Study of American Foreign Relations: National History or International History?" and Emily S. Rosenberg, "Walking the Border," in Michael J. Hogan and Thomas G. Paterson, eds., *Explaining the History of American Foreign Relations* (Cambridge: Cambridge University Press, 1991); Charles Maier, "Marking Time: The Historiography of International Relations," in Michale Kammen, ed., *The Past before Us: Contemporary Historical Writing in the United States* (Ithaca: Cornell University Press, 1980).

5. Benedict Anderson, *Imagined Communities: Reflections on the Origin and Spread of Nationalism* (New York: Verso, rev. ed., 1991); Liah Greenfeld, *Nationalism: Five Roads to Modernity* (Cambridge, MA: Harvard University Press, 1992); Joseph Rothschild, *Ethnopolitics: A Conceptual Framework* (New York: Columbia University Press, 1981); Anthony Smith, "The Ethnic Sources of Nationalism," in Michael G. Brown, ed., *Ethnic Conflict and International Security* (Princeton: Princeton University Press, 1993).

6. Tony Smith, *America's Mission: The United States and the Worldwide Struggle for Democracy in the Twentieth Century* (Princeton: Princeton University Press, 1994), 333ff.

7. Hélène Carrere d'Encausse, *The End of the Soviet Empire: The Triumph of the Nations* (New York: Basic Books, 1993).

8. K. Anthony Appiah, "The Multiculturalist Misunderstanding," *New York Review of Books*, 10/9/97; John A. Hall and Charles Lindholm, *Is America Breaking Apart?* (Princeton: Princeton University Press, 1999), esp. ch. 10.

9. Alexander DeConde, *Ethnicity, Race, and American Foreign Policy: A History* (Boston: Northeastern University Press, 1992), 11f.

10. Thomas Jefferson, *Notes on the State of Virginia* (Chapel Hill: University of North Carolina Press, 1955), 84f.

11. Michael Lind, *The Next American Nation: The New Nationalism and the Fourth American Revolution* (New York: Free Press, 1995), 48; Felix Gilbert, *To the Farewell Address: Ideas of Early American Foreign Policy* (Princeton: Princeton University Press, 1961), 138.

12. John Higham, *Strangers in the Land: Patterns of American Nativism, 1860–1925* (New York: Atheneum, new ed., 1963).

13. Louis L. Gerson, *The Hyphenate in Recent American Politics and Diplomacy* (Lawrence: University of Kansas Press, 1964), chs. 3–6; Samuel Lubell, *The Future of American Politics* (New York: Doubleday, 2nd rev. ed., 1955); William S. Bernard, "Immigration: History of U.S. Policy," in Thernstrom, ed., *Harvard Encyclopedia of American Ethnic Groups*.

14. Peter H. Schuck, *Citizens, Strangers, and In-Between: Essays on Immigration and Citizenship* (Boulder, CO: Westview Press, 1998), 76ff.

15. Arthur Link, ed., *Papers of Woodrow Wilson*, vol. 30: *1914* (Princeton: Princeton University Press, 1979), 35.

16. John Higham, *Send These to Me: Immigrants in Urban America* (Baltimore: Johns Hopkins University Press, 1984), chs. 9–10; Mona Harrington, "Loyalties: Dual and Divided," in Thernstrom, ed., *Harvard Encyclopedia of American Ethnic Groups*; Glazer, ch. 6.

17. Glazer, 7f, ch. 6; Lipset, ch. 4. Jeffrey Berry, *The New Liberalism: The Rising Power of Citizen Groups* (Washington: Brookings Institution, 1999), ch. 2.

18. Ernest W. Lefever, *America's Imperial Burden: Is the Past Prologue?* (Boulder, CO: Westview Press, 1999), 158.

19. James Kurth, "The *Real* Clash," *National Interest*, 37, Fall 1994.

20. Linda Chavez, "Divided We Stand," *Commentary*, May 1997.

21. Thomas Sowell, "Surrendering to the Multiculturalists," *Forbes*, 6/16/97.

22. Samuel P. Huntington, *The Clash of Civilizations and the Remaking of World Order* (New York: Simon and Schuster, 1996), 21f.

23. Ibid., 198ff; and Huntington, "The Erosion of American National Interests," *Foreign Affairs*, 76, 5, 1997.

24. Nadav Safran, *The United States and Israel* (Cambridge, MA: Harvard University Press, 1963), 276ff; David J. Vidal, "Defining the National Interest: Minorities and U.S. Foreign Policy in the 21st Century" (New York: Council on Foreign Relations, 1997).

25. Ole Holsti, *Public Opinion and American Foreign Policy* (Ann Arbor: University of Michigan Press, 1996).

26. Randall Robinson, *Defending the Spirit: A Black Life in America* (New York: Dutton, 1998).

27. Huntington, 1997, 33.

28. James Schlesinger, "Fragmentation and Hubris: A Shaky Basis for American Leadership," *National Interest*, 49, Fall 1997.

2. Three Historical Stages of Ethnic Group Influence

1. See Andrew J. Wilson, *Irish America and the Ulster Conflict, 1868–1995* (Washington: Catholic University of America Press, 1995); Mabel Gregory Walker, *The Fenian Movement* (Colorado Springs: Ralph Myles, 1969); Jack Holland, *The American Connection: U.S. Guns, Money and Influence in Northern Ireland* (New York: Viking, 1987).

2. Frederick C. Luebke, *Bonds of Loyalty: German-Americans and World War I* (De Kalb: Northern Illinois University Press, 1974), 142ff; Alexander DeConde, *Ethnicity, Race, and American Foreign Policy: A History* (Boston: Northeastern University Press, 1992), 82ff; Louis L. Gerson, *The Hyphenate in Recent American Politics and Diplomacy* (Lawrence: University of Kansas Press, 1964), chs. 3–4.

3. U.S. Department of Commerce, Bureau of the Census, *Historical Statistics of the United States: Colonial Times to 1970*, pt. 1, 116f.

4. Melvin Small, *Democracy and Diplomacy: The Impact of Domestic Politics on U.S. Foreign Policy, 1789–1994* (Baltimore: Johns Hopkins University Press, 1996), 43; see also Robert W. Tucker, "Immigration and Foreign Policy: General Consid-

erations," in Tucker et al., *Immigration and U.S. Foreign Policy* (Boulder, CO: Westview Press, 1990).

5. Arthur Link, ed., *Papers of Woodrow Wilson*, vol. 31: *1914* (Princeton: Princeton University Press, 1979).

6. DeConde, 97f; Gerson, ch. 6.

7. Penny M. Von Eschen, *Race against Empire: Black Americans and Anticolonialism, 1937–1957* (Ithaca: Cornell University Press, 1997), chs. 2–3; Brenda Plummer, *Rising Wind: Black Americans and U.S. Foreign Affairs, 1935–1960* (Chapel Hill: University of North Carolina Press, 1996), chs. 2–3.

8. Citation from Tucker, 8; see also Samuel Lubell, *The Future of American Politics* (New York: Doubleday, 2nd rev. ed., 1955); Gerson, ch. 7; Luebke, 325ff; and for a contrary opinion, Manfred Jonas, "Immigration and U.S. Foreign Policy: The Interwar Period," in Tucker.

9. For a discussion of Polish Americans, see Martin Weil, "Can the Blacks Do for Africa What the Jews Did for Israel?" *Foreign Policy* 15, Summer 1974; also Gerson.

10. Bennett Kovrig, *Of Walls and Bridges: The United States and Eastern Europe* (New York: New York University Press, 1991).

11. Laurence Halley, *Ancient Affections, Ethnic Groups and Foreign Policy* (New York: Praeger, 1979), ch. 15; Z. A. Kruszewski, "The Polish American Congress, East-West Issues, and the Formulation of American Foreign Policy," in Mohammed E. Ahrari, *Ethnic Groups and U.S. Foreign Policy* (Westport, CT: Greenwood Press, 1987).

12. Yossi Shain, *Marketing the Democratic Creed Abroad: Diasporas in the U.S. and Their Homelands* (New York: Cambridge University Press, 1999), ch. 2.

13. Samuel Halperin, *The Political World of American Zionism* (Detroit: Wayne State University Press, 1961); Peter Novick, *The Holocaust in American Life* (Boston: Houghton Mifflin, 1999), ch. 8.

14. Uri Bialer, *Between East and West: Israel's Foreign Policy Orientation, 1948–1956* (New York: Cambridge University Press, 1990).

15. Henry Kissinger, "Between the Old Left and the New Right," *Foreign Affairs*, 78, 3, 1999; David Remnick, "Letter from Jerusalem," *New Yorker*, 8/11/97; Edward Tivnan, *The Lobby: Jewish Political Power and American Foreign Policy* (New York: Simon and Schuster, 1987), ch. 4; J. J. Goldberg, *Jewish Power: Inside the American Jewish Establishment* (Reading, MA: Addison Wesley, 1996), ch. 7.

16. King cited in Von Eschen, 189; see also Plummer, chs. 1–2; Elliott P. Skinner, *African Americans and U.S. Policy toward Africa, 1850–1924* (Washington: Howard University Press, 1992); Skinner, "Ethnicity and Race as Factors in the Formation of United States Foreign Policy: Theoretical and Practical Considerations," in Michael P. Hamilton, ed., *American Character and Foreign Policy* (Grand Rapids, MI: Eerdmans, 1986); Sudarshan Kapur, *Raising Up a Prophet: The African-American Encounter with Gandhi* (Boston: Beacon Press, 1992); Ronald Walters, *Pan Africanism in the African Diaspora: An Analysis of Modern Afrocentric Political Movements* (Detroit: Wayne State University Press, 1993); Alusine Jalloh and Stephen E. Maizlish, *The African Diaspora* (Austin: University of Texas Press, 1996).

17. Plummer, 178ff.

18. Malcolm X, *Malcolm X Speaks: Selected Speeches and Statements* (Westmin-

ster, CA: Grove Press, 1966), 5; Michael I. Krenn, ed., *Race and U.S. Foreign Policy: From the Colonial Period to the Present*, vol. 4: *Race and U.S. Foreign Policy during the Cold War;* vol. 5: *The African American Voice in U.S. Foreign Policy since World War II* (New York: Garland, 1998).

19. Robert Singh, *The Congressional Black Caucus: Racial Politics in the U.S. Congress* (Thousand Oaks, CA: Sage, 1998).

20. Cited in Tony Smith, *America's Mission: The United States and the Worldwide Struggle for Democracy in the Twentieth Century* (Princeton: Princeton University Press, 1994), 246.

21. Elizabeth S. Rogers, "The Conflicting Role of American Ethnic and Business Interests in the U.S. Economic Sanctions Policy: The Case of South Africa," in David Skidmore and Valerie M. Hudson, eds., *The Limits of State Autonomy* (Boulder, CO: Westview Press, 1993); Michael Clough, *Free at Last? U.S. Policy toward Africa and the End of the Cold War* (New York: Council on Foreign Relations Press, 1992); Shain, 84ff.

22. Monteagle Stearns, *Entangled Allies: U.S. Policy toward Greece, Turkey, and Cyprus* (New York: Council on Foreign Relations Press, 1992); see also Paul Watanabe, "Ethnicity and Foreign Policy: Greek American Activism and the Turkish Arms Ban," in Dimitri C. Constas and Athanassios G. Platias, *Diasporas in World Politics: The Greeks in Comparative Perspective* (London: Macmillan, 1995); Paul Watanabe, *Ethnic Groups, Congress, and American Foreign Policy: The Politics of the Turkish Arms Embargo* (Westport, CT: Greenwood Press, 1984).

23. Jack Citrin et al., "Is American Nationalism Changing? Implications for Foreign Policy," *International Studies Quarterly*, 38, 1, 1994; John E. Rielly, ed., "American Public Opinion and U.S. Foreign Policy, 1999" (Chicago Council on Foreign Relations, 1999), 4, finds support for an active role at 61 percent among the public at large, but at 96 percent among policy leaders.

24. Dick Kirschten, "Ethnic Resurging," *National Journal*, 2/25/95.

25. *Detroit News*, 11/23/96; *Chicago Tribune*, 1/28/97.

26. *New York Times*, 8/11/97.

27. Ibid., 6/6/97; on Albright's enthusiasm over the expansion of NATO, see ibid., 3/13/99.

28. Reports on the growing political solidarity of Orthodox Americans appeared in the *New York Times*, 3/25/99, 4/4/99; and on the *Lehrer NewsHour*, 3/26/99. But presumably undercutting this sentiment, on July 4, 1999, the *New York Times* reported that the Patriarch of the Serbian Orthodox church in Serbia was denouncing crimes of the Serbian army in Kosovo.

29. Shain, ch. 3.

30. *Wall Street Journal*, 6/18/96; *New York Times*, 5/1/96; 8/6/96; *Journal of Commerce*, 12/15/98.

31. Frontline, "Nazi Gold," 6/17/97; Gordon A. Craig, "How to Think about the Swiss," *New York Review of Books*, 6/11/98; *New York Times*, 7/23/97, 7/31/97, 10/10/97, 12/2/97. In December 1999 Germany announced a related settlement on the claims of Nazi forced laborers amounting to $5.1 billion.

32. Patrick J. Haney and Walt Vanderbush, "The Role of Ethnic Groups in U.S. Foreign Policy: The Case of the Cuban American National Foundation," *International Studies Quarterly*, 43, 2, 1999; Patrick J. Kiger, "Squeeze Play: The United States, Cuba, and the Helms-Burton Act" (Washington: Center for Public

Integrity, 1997); Peter H. Stone, "Cuban Clout," *National Journal*, 2/20/95; *International Herald Tribune*, 7/12/96; *New York Times*, 10/23/96.

33. Carroll J. Doherty, "Armenia's Special Relationship with U.S. Is Showing Strain," *Congressional Quarterly*, 5/31/97; *Washington Post*, 8/1/96.

34. ANCA web page, dated 11/1/96, retrieved 11/5/97.

35. *Boston Globe*, 11/13/97.

36. *New York Times*, 7/14/94; Thernstrom and Thernstrom, 304f; Peter J. Boyer, "The Rise of Kweisi Mfume," *New Yorker*, 8/1/94; Shain, 70ff. Georges A. Fauriol, ed., *Haitian Frustrations: Dilemmas for U.S. Policy* (Washington: Center for Strategic and International Studies, 1995).

37. *New York Times*, 2/21/96; *Washington Post*, 2/26/96; Karin L. Stanford, *Beyond the Boundaries: Reverend Jesse Jackson in International Affairs* (Albany: State University of New York Press, 1997); Robert Singh, *The Farrakhan Phenomenon: Race, Reaction, and the Paranoid Style in American Politics* (Washington: Georgetown University Press, 1997); Thernstrom and Thernstrom, 304f; Shain, 70ff.

38. Tim Pat Coogan, *The Troubles: Ireland's Ordeal 1966–1996 and the Search for Peace* (Niwot, CO: Roberts Rinehart, 1996).

39. Joseph O'Grady, "An Irish Policy Born in the U.S.A.," *Foreign Affairs*, 75, 3, 1996; Karen Donfried, "Northern Ireland: Fair Employment and the MacBride Principles," Congressional Research Service, Library of Congress, 4/18/96; Adrian Guelke, "The United States, Irish Americans and the Northern Ireland Peace Process," *International Affairs*, 72, 3, 1996; Ray O'Hanlon, *The New Irish Americans* (Niwot, CO: Roberts Rinehart, 1998).

40. Michael Jones-Correa, "New Directions for Latinos as an Ethnic Lobby in U.S. Foreign Policy," *Harvard Journal of Hispanic Policy*, 9, 1995–96; Shain, ch. 5.

41. Peter H. Schuck, *Citizens, Strangers, and In-Between: Essays on Immigration and Citizenship* (Boulder, CO: Westview Press, 1998), pt. 3; *New York Times*, 3/14/96; *Washington Post*, 6/14/97.

42. Schuck, 3; Joyce C. Vialet, "Immigration: Reasons for Growth, 1981–1995," Congressional Research Service, Library of Congress, 2/12/97.

43. Joel Millman, *The Other Americans: How Immigrants Renew Our Country, Our Economy and Our Values* (New York: Viking, 1997).

44. John J. Miller, *The Unmaking of Americans: How Multiculturalism Has Undermined America's Assimilation Ethic* (New York: Free Press, 1998). US INS, Statistical web page downloaded 2/16/99; David Kennedy, "Can We Still Afford to Be a Nation of Immigrants?" *Atlantic Monthly*, Nov. 1996.

45. Kitty Calavita, "U.S. Immigration and Policy Responses: The Limits of Legislation," in Wayne Cornelius et al., *Controlling Immigration: A Global Perspective* (Stanford: Stanford University Press, 1994); Peter Skerry, *Mexican Americans: The Ambivalent Minority* (Cambridge, MA: Harvard University Press, 1993), 300ff; Raoul Yzaguirre, "Statement before the Subcommittee on Immigration, Committee of the Judiciary, U.S. House of Representatives, 6/29/95," National Council of La Raza, Washington (also House of Representatives, 96–521–27, 6/29/95, 153ff, Hearing before the Subcommittee on Immigration and Claims to Consider H.R. 1915).

46. Daniel Patrick Moynihan and Nathan Glazer, eds., *Ethnicity: Theory and Experience* (Cambridge, MA: Harvard University Press, 1975), 23f.

47. Richard N. Haass, "Sanctioning Madness," *Foreign Affairs*, 76, 6, 1997;

Robert A. Pape, "Why Economic Sanctions Do Not Work," *International Security*, 22, 2, 1997.

48. Brannon P. Denning and Jack H. McCall, "States' Rights and Foreign Policy," *Foreign Affairs*, 78, 1, 2000.

49. *New York Times*, 11/11/99, 12/2/99; William Safire, "Israel's Shame," *New York Times*, 12/23/99.

50. Samuel P. Huntington, "The Erosion of American National Interests," *Foreign Affairs*, 76, 5, 1997. James Schlesinger, "Fragmentation and Hubris: A Shaky Basis for American Leadership," *National Interest*, 49, Fall 1997.

51. Huntington, 49; see also Huntington, "The Lonely Superpower," *Foreign Affairs*, 78, 2, 1999.

52. Lee H. Hamilton, "Statement before a Hearing on the Use and Effect of Unilateral Sanctions," House Subcommittee on Trade, Oct. 23, 1997, reported as H.R. 2708, 105th Congress, 1st sess.

53. *New York Times*, 7/31/98, 11/30/99.

3. Gaining Influence in Washington

1. Peter Katzenstein, ed., *Between Power and Plenty: Foreign Economic Policies of Advanced Industrial States* (Madison: University of Wisconsin Press, 1978); George F. Kennan, *The Cloud of Danger: Current Realities of American Foreign Policy* (Boston: Little, Brown, 1977); Joel S. Migdal et al., *State Power and Social Forces: Domination and Transformation in the Third World* (Cambridge: Cambridge University Press, 1994); Migdal, *Strong Societies and Weak States: State-Society Relations and State Capabilities in the Third World* (Princeton: Princeton University Press, 1988); Walker Connor, "Diasporas and the Formation of Foreign Policy: The US in Comparative Perspective," and Dimitri C. Constas and Athanassios G. Platias, "Introduction" in Constas and Platias, *Diasporas in World Politics: The Greeks in Comparative Perspective* (London: Macmillan, 1995); Samuel P. Huntington, *Political Order in Changing Societies* (New Haven: Yale University Press, 1968), ch. 2.

2. John J. Coleman, *Party Decline in America: Policy, Politics, and the Fiscal State* (Princeton: Princeton University Press, 1996); Jessica Korn, *The Power of Separation: American Constitutionalism and the Myth of the Legislative Veto* (Princeton: Princeton University Press, 1996); Daniel Lazare, *The Frozen Republic: How the Constitution is Paralyzing Democracy* (New York: Harcourt Brace, 1995); James M. Lindsay, *Congress and the Politics of U.S. Foreign Policy* (Baltimore: Johns Hopkins University Press, 1994); Robert Putnam, "Diplomacy and Domestic Politics: The Logic of Two Level Games," *International Organization*, 42, 3, 1988; David Skidmore and Valerie M. Hudson, eds., *The Limits of State Autonomy* (Boulder, CO: Westview Press, 1993).

3. Daniel Bell, "'American Exceptionalism' Revisited: The Role of Civil Society," *Public Interest*, 95, 1989; Samuel P. Huntington, *American Politics: The Promise of Disharmony* (New Haven: Yale University Press, 1984); G. John Ikenberry and Daniel Deudney, "America after the Long War," *Current History*, Nov. 1995; Ivo H. Daalder, "The United States and Military Intervention in Internal Conflict," in Michael E. Brown, ed., *The International Dimensions of Internal Conflict* (Cambridge, MA: MIT Press, 1996); Michael C. Desch, "War and Strong States; Peace and Weak States?" *International Organization*, 50, 2, 1996; Alan Brinkley et al., *New*

Federalist Papers: Essays in Defense of the Constitution (New York: Norton, 1997); Jeremy D. Rosner, *The New Tug-of-War: Congress, the Executive Branch, and National Security* (New York: Carnegie Endowment, 1995).

4. Jeffrey M. Berry, *The Interest Group Society* (Reading, MA: Addison Wesley Longman, 3rd ed., 1997); *New York Times*, 7/29/99, 11/16/99.

5. Joseph S. Nye, "In Government We Don't Trust," *Foreign Policy*, 108, 1997; Robert D. Putnam, "Bowling Alone," *Journal of Democracy*, 6, 1, 1996; Seymour Martin Lipset, *American Exceptionalism: A Double-Edged Sword* (New York: Norton, 1996), 267, 281ff. Garry Wills, *A Necessary Evil: A History of American Distrust of Government* (New York: Simon and Schuster, 1999).

6. See, e.g., Jeffrey M. Berry, *The New Liberalism: The Rising Power of Citizen Groups* (Washington: Brookings Institution, 1999).

7. John W. Spanier and Eric M. Uslaner, *American Foreign Policy and the Democratic Dilemmas* (London: Macmillan, 1994).

8. Eric Alterman, *Who Speaks for America?* (Ithaca: Cornell University Press, 1997); William Greider, *Who Will Tell the People? The Betrayal of American Democracy* (New York: Simon and Schuster, 1992).

9. Marc R. Levy and Michael S. Kramer, *The Ethnic Factor: How America's Minorities Decide Elections* (New York: Simon and Schuster, 1972), ch. 5.

10. Tim Pat Coogan, *The Troubles: Ireland's Ordeal 1966–1996 and the Search for Peace* (Boulder, CO: Roberts Rinehart, 1996), ch. 12; Conor O'Clery, *Daring Diplomacy: Clinton's Secret Search for Peace in Ireland* (Boulder, CO: Roberts Rinehart, 1997); Joseph O'Grady, "An Irish Policy Born in the U.S.A.," *Foreign Affairs*, 75, 3, 1996.

11. *New York Times*, 11/10/96.

12. *New York Times*, 11/16/96. But for a restrained evaluation of the impact of Latino voting, arguing that it was decisive only in New Mexico and Arizona, see Rodolfo O. de la Garza and Louis DeSipio, eds., *Awash in the Mainstream: Latino Politics in the 1996 Elections* (Boulder, CO: Westview Press, 1999).

13. *New York Times*, 11/5–9/98.

14. *New York Times*, 11/16/96, 12/9/97.

15. *Washington Post*, 3/4–5/97.

16. *New York Times*, 2/27/98; *Congressional Quarterly*, 1/10/98; *Miami Herald*, 10/16/98.

17. *American Almanac*, 89; Levy and Kramer.

18. *Washington Post*, 3/24/97; *New York Times*, 4/18/99; *Time*, 5/17/99.

19. Steven Spiegel, "Ethnic Politics and the Formulation of U.S. Policy toward the Arab-Israeli Dispute," in Mohammed E. Ahrari, *Ethnic Groups and U.S. Foreign Policy* (Westport, CT: Greenwood Press, 1987), 42.

20. A. F. K. Organski, *The $36 Billion Bargain: Strategy and Politics in U.S. Assistance to Israel* (New York: Columbia University Press, 1990), 6.

21. Solarz cited in *Washington Post*, 3/24/97; see also Chuck Alston, "Solarz Looks Abroad to Find Election Cash at Home," *Congressional Quarterly*, 3/11/89.

22. *New York Times*, 2/8/98, 2/15/98, 2/16/98, 2/22/98, 4/17/99. In 1999 Jeff Gerth received the Pulitzer Prize for journalism for his *New York Times* coverage of government-approved high-technology sales to China by U.S. corporations despite national security risks.

23. Ronald Dworkin, "The Curse of American Politics," *New York Review of*

Books, 10/17/96; Federal Election Commission, various reports on campaign contributions, March-June 1997; *Washington Post*, 2/9/97; *New York Times*, 11/25/97; interviews at the Center for Responsive Politics, July 1997; *Economist*, 11/7/98.

24. Clinton cited in Gil Troy, "Money and Politics: The Oldest Connection," *Wilson Quarterly*, Summer 1997, 32; Herbert E. Alexander and Anthony Corrado, *Financing the 1992 Elections* (Armonk, NY: M. E. Sharpe, 1995), ch. 1.

25. Charles Lewis, *The Buying of the Congress: How Special Interests Have Stolen Your Right to Life, Liberty, and the Pursuit of Happiness* (New York: Avon, 1998).

26. *Congressional Quarterly*, 1/10/98, 85.

27. *New York Times*, 4/23/92.

28. J. J. Goldberg, *Jewish Power: Inside the American Jewish Establishment* (Reading, MA: Addison Wesley, 1996), 276; George W. Ball and Douglas B. Ball, *The Passionate Attachment: America's Involvement with Israel, 1947 to the Present* (New York: Norton, 1992), 297; Camille Mansour, *Beyond Alliance: Israel in U.S. Foreign Policy* (New York: Columbia University Press, 1994), 244ff; *Christian Science Monitor*, 6/28/91.

29. David Schoenbaum, *The United States and the State of Israel* (Oxford: Oxford University Press, 1993), 3; Organski, 70ff.

30. Lipset, 168; Mansour 249; Renae Cohen, "The Palestinian Autonomy Agreement and Israel-PLO Recognition: A Survey of American Jewish Opinion," American Jewish Committee, 1994, 38; Charles S. Liebman and Steven M. Cohen, *Two Worlds of Judaism: The Israeli and American Experiences* (New Haven: Yale University Press, 1990), 84f.

31. *New York Times*, 2/27/98.

32. Susan Rees, "Effective Nonprofit Advocacy" (Aspen, CO: Aspen Institute [Nonprofit Sector Research Fund WP 98.031], 1998); Samuel Halperin, *The Political World of American Zionism* (Detroit: Wayne State University Press, 1961), epilogue.

33. Edward Tivnan, *The Lobby: Jewish Political Power and American Foreign Policy* (New York: Simon and Schuster, 1987), chs. 5–6; Goldberg, 199ff.

34. Tivnan, 34f, 40ff; *New York Times*, 5/7/98.

35. Tivnan, 60, 68, 94ff, 111; Goldberg, 206ff, 219; Gabriel Sheffer, "Jewry, Jews and Israeli Foreign Policy," in Constas and Platias, *Diasporas in World Politics.*

36. Liebman and Cohen, ch. 5; Schoenbaum, 322ff; Lipset, 170ff.

37. Tivnan, 119, 124; Goldberg, 216; Marla Brettschneider, *Cornerstones of Peace: Jewish Identity Politics and Democratic Theory* (New Brunswick, NJ: Rutgers University Press, 1996).

38. Cohen; American Jewish Committee, "American Jewish Attitudes toward Israel and the Peace Process," 1995, 5, 26f; Renae Cohen and Jennifer Golub, "The Israeli Peace Initiative and the Israel-PLO Accord," American Jewish Committee, 1995; Goldberg, ch. 3; Abraham Ben-Zvi, *The United States and Israel: The Limits of the Special Relationship* (New York: Columbia University Press, 1993), 183f.

39. American Jewish Committee, "In the Aftermath of the Rabin Assassination: A Survey of American Jewish Opinion about Israel and the Peace Process," Feb. 1996; *Washington Post*, 4/2/97; *New York Times*, 5/1/97, 2/10/98, 7/19/99.

40. *New York Times*, 9/30/95; Goldberg, 210ff, 347; Sidney Blumenthal, "The Western Front," *New Yorker*, 6/5/95.

41. Figures for 1996, Lipset, 168; for 1997, *New York Times*, 11/17/97.

42. Christian Joppke, "Why Liberal States Accept Unwanted Immigration," *World Politics*, 50, Jan. 1998.

43. *Public Citizen News*, 9–10, 1998.

44. *National Journal*, 11/29/97; Myron Wiener, "Asian Immigrants and U.S. Foreign Policy," in Robert W. Tucker et al., *Immigration and U.S. Foreign Policy* (Boulder, CO: Westview Press, 1990).

45. *New York Times*, 9/29–30/97; Richard N. Haass, "Sanctioning Madness," *Foreign Affairs*, 76, 6, 1997.

46. *New York Times*, 1/23/96, 9/15/96, 4/18/97, 11/9/98; editorials by Rosenthal, 2/11/97, 9/16/97; editorial by Netanyahu, 11/4/95; William Martin, "The Christian Right and American Foreign Policy," *Foreign Policy*, 114, Spring 1999.

47. Ali A. Mazrui, "Between the Crescent and the Star-Spangled Banner: American Muslims and U.S. Foreign Policy," *International Affairs*, 72, 3, 1996, 493; *New York Times*, 10/30/96; *Washington Post*, 7/6/97.

48. Hedrick Smith, *The Power Game: How Washington Works* (New York: Random House, 1988), 230.

49. Liebman and Cohen, 41; Goldberg, ch. 11; Mitchell Geoffrey Bard, *The Water's Edge and Beyond: Defining the Limits to Domestic Influence on United States Middle East Policy* (New Brunswick, NJ: Transaction Books, 1991), 10ff.

50. Rees.

51. Bard, 31ff; Ball and Ball, 215ff; Mansour, 240ff.

52. Goldberg, 254.

53. Goldberg, 231.

54. Mansour, 241f.

55. Michael Barnett, "Identity and Alliance in the Middle East," in Peter J. Katzenstein, ed., *The Culture of National Security: Norms and Identity in World Politics* (New York: Columbia University Press, 1996), 432ff.

56. Tivnan, 71ff; Goldberg, ch. 7.

57. Ben-Zvi, ch. 4.

58. Charles McC. Mathias Jr., "Ethnic Groups and Foreign Policy," *Foreign Affairs*, 59, 5, 1981, 993.

59. Tivnan, 104, 119f; Goldberg, 209f.

60. Smith, 217; Tivnan, ch. 6; Bard, chs. 10–11; Schoenbaum, 280f.

61. *Washington Post*, 4/8/92, 8/11/92; *New York Times*, 9/13/91, 9/19/91, 3/18/92; *Congressional Quarterly Almanac*, 1992, 539ff; Goldberg, prologue.

62. Rees; AP Online, 6/23/98; *Congressional Quarterly*, 1/10/98, 1/24/98; *Journal of Commerce*, 12/15/97.

4. E Pluribus Unum or Ex Plures Uno?

1. "In 1991, 13 percent of the whites in the United States said that they had generally 'unfavorable' opinions about black Americans . . . In Czechoslovakia that same year 49 percent of the Czechs had 'unfavorable' attitudes toward the Hungarian ethnic minority living within the boundaries of their country. Likewise 45 percent of West Germans disliked the Turks living in Germany; 54 percent of East Germans regarded Poles negatively; 40 percent of Hungarians frowned on the Romanians who lived among them; and 42 percent of the French disdained Arab

immigrants from North Africa." Stephan and Abigail Thernstrom, *American in Black and White: One Nation Indivisible* (New York: Simon and Schuster, 1997), 530.

2. For an eloquent expression of this concern, see Arthur M. Schlesinger Jr., *The Disuniting of America: Reflections on a Multicultural Society* (New York: Norton, 2nd ed., 1998), epilogue.

3. Alan Rosenthal, *The Third House: Lobbyists and Lobbying in the States* (Washington: Congressional Quarterly Press, 1993), 6; Helmut Norpoth, "National Opinion Ballot Report, 1998," included with *Great Decisions* published by Foreign Policy Association (New York) 1998, with an essay by Sanford J. Ungar, "Special Interests: Is U.S. Foreign Policy for Sale?"

4. See, e.g., *U.S. News and World Report*, 9/8/97.

5. Michael Walzer, *What It Means to Be an American* (New York: Marsilio, 1992).

6. Seymour Martin Lipset, *American Exceptionalism: A Double-Edged Sword* (New York: Norton, 1996), 281ff; Robert D. Putnam, "Bowling Alone," *Journal of Democracy*, 6, 1, 1996.

7. Walzer, 47, 45, his emphasis.

8. Walzer, 39f, 67, 96ff, 100. In *On Toleration* (New Haven: Yale University Press, 1997), Walzer offers some further "Reflections on Multiculturalism," arguing that many of the discomforts of modern life—the decline of the family and organized labor, for example—might be remedied by stronger ties of cultural association. He makes no mention of the tensions between national life and these cultural units, however.

9. Michael Sandel, "The Procedural Republic and the Unencumbered Self," *Political Theory*, 12, 1, 1984, 82; compare to Walzer, 18.

10. Walzer, 23f, 27ff, 36ff.

11. Richard Rorty, "The Unpatriotic Academy," *New York Times*, 2/13/94; also Rorty, "The Dark Side of the Academic Left," *Chronicle of Higher Education*, 4/3/98, and *Achieving Our Country: Leftist Thought in Twentieth Century America* (Cambridge, MA: Harvard University Press, 1998).

12. See, e.g., Yael Tamir, *Liberal Nationalism* (Princeton: Princeton University Press, 1993), 30ff, 90ff; David Miller, *On Nationality* (New York, Oxford: Oxford University Press, 1995).

13. Stephen D. Krasner, *Defending the National Interest: Raw Materials Investments and U.S. Foreign Policy* (Princeton: Princeton University Press, 1978); Hans J. Morgenthau, *In Defense of the National Interest* (New York: Knopf, 1951); Peter Trubowitz, *Defining the National Interest: Conflict and Change in American Foreign Policy* (Chicago: University of Chicago Press, 1998).

14. Mona Harrington, "Loyalties: Dual and Divided," in Stephan Thernstrom, ed., *Harvard Encyclopedia of American Ethnic Groups* (Cambridge, MA: Harvard University Press, 1980).

15. Fenian Brotherhood, *Proceedings of the Second National Congress* (Philadelphia: James Gibbon Printer, 1865).

16. Martha Nussbaum, *For Love of Country: Debating the Limits of Patriotism* (Boston: Beacon Press, 1996).

17. Yasemin N. Soysal, *Limits of Citizenship: Migrants and Post-national Membership in Europe* (Chicago: University of Chicago Press, 1994), 1. See in much the

same vein David Jacobson, *Rights across Borders: Immigration and the Decline of Citizenship* (Baltimore: Johns Hopkins University Press, 1996).

18. Soysal, ch. 8, 163.

19. Soysal, 3, 136f.

20. *Afroyim v. Rusk, United States Reports*, 387, October Term, 1966, 253ff; Reed Ueda, "Naturalization and Citizenship," in Thernstrom, ed., *Harvard Encyclopedia of American Ethnic Groups;* Patricia McGarvey-Rosendahl, "A New Approach to Dual Nationality," *Houston Journal of International Law*, 8, 2, Spring 1986; David S. Gordon, "Dual Nationality and the United States Citizen," *Military Law Review*, 102, Fall 1983; *Los Angeles Times*, 4/6/98; Peter H. Schuck, *Citizens, Strangers, and In-Between: Essays on Immigration and Citizenship* (Boulder, CO: Westview Press, 1998), ch. 10.

21. Milton J. Esman, "The Chinese Diaspora in Southeast Asia," in Gabriel Sheffer, ed., *Modern Diasporas in International Politics* (New York: St. Martin's, 1986).

22. Igor Zevlev, "Russia and the Russian Diasporas," *Post-Soviet Affairs*, 12, 3, 1996.

23. Sections 301 and 205 of "Libertad," the Helms-Burton bill.

24. *New York Times*, 12/10/96, 12/30/96.

25. Walzer, 17.

26. Peter Brimelow, *Alien Nation: Common Sense about America's Immigration Disaster* (New York: Random House, 1995), xv; and see the discussion of Brimelow's book in Schuck, ch. 14.

27. George J. Borjas, "The New Economics of Immigration," *Atlantic Monthly*, Nov. 1996; Kevin McCarthy and Georges Vernez, "Immigration in a Changing Economy: California's Experience" (Santa Monica, CA: Rand Corporation, 1997).

28. Walzer, 17.

29. Peter Skerry, *Mexican Americans: The Ambivalent Minority* (Cambridge, MA: Harvard University Press, 1993), 297ff.

30. *Los Angeles Times*, 6/16/97; *Washington Post*, 5/10/97; George Vernez et al., *How Immigrants Fare in U.S. Education* (Santa Monica, CA: Rand Corporation, 1996); Vilma Ortiz, "The Mexican-Origin Population: Permanent Working Class or Emerging Middle Class?" and Roger Waldinger, "Ethnicity and Opportunity in the Plural City," in Waldinger and Mehdi Bozorgmehr, eds., *Ethnic Los Angeles* (New York: Russell Sage, 1996); Lawrence E. Harrison, *The Pan-American Dream* (New York: Basic Books, 1997), ch. 11; Linda Chavez, *Out of the Barrio: Toward a New Politics of Hispanic Assimilation* (New York: Basic Books, 1991), 113ff; John J. Miller, *The Unmaking of Americans: How Multiculturalism Has Undermined America's Assimilation Ethic* (New York: Free Press, 1998); Michael Lind, *The Next American Nation: The New Nationalism and the Fourth American Revolution* (New York: Free Press, 1995).

31. Center for Immigration Studies, "Remaking the Political Landscape: How Immigration Redistributes Seats in the House of Representatives," Washington, 10/6/98.

32. David Kennedy, "Can We Still Afford to Be a Nation of Immigrants?" *Atlantic Monthly*, Nov. 1996.

33. Rodolfo Acuña, *Occupied America: A History of Chicanos* (New York: Harper and Row, 2nd ed., 1981), 2.

34. Skerry, ch. 1; Ignacio Garcia, *Chicanismo: The Forging of a Militant Ethos among Mexican Americans* (Tucson: University of Arizona Press, 1997).

35. Rodolfo O. de la Garza et al., "Will the Real Americans Please Stand Up: Anglo and Mexican American Support of Core American Political Values," *American Journal of Political Science*, 40, 2, May 1996.

36. *New York Times*, 10/13/96.

37. Schuck, xv, 8.

38. Schuck, 76ff, chs. 5–7, 211ff, 244ff, 344ff.

39. Gabriel Sheffer, "A New Field of Study: Modern Diasporas in International Politics," and Milton Esman, "Diasporas in International Relations," in Sheffer, ed., *Modern Diasporas in International Politics* (New York: St. Martin's, 1986).

40. Walzer, 24f.

41. Dimitri C. Constas and Athanassios G. Platias, *Diasporas in World Politics: The Greeks in Comparative Perspective* (London: Macmillan, 1995), esp. foreword by James Rosenau. See also Thomas Risse-Kappen, *Bringing Transnational Relations Back In: Non-State Actors, Domestic Structures, and International Institutions* (Cambridge: Cambridge University Press, 1995); Gabriel Sheffer, "Ethno-national Diasporas and Security," *Survival*, 36, 1, 1994.

42. See, e.g., *Thesis*, published quarterly by the Hellenic Ministry of Foreign Affairs; Michael Jones-Correa, "New Directions for Latinos as an Ethnic Lobby in U.S. Foreign Policy," *Harvard Journal of Hispanic Policy*, 9, 1995–96; and esp. several of the essays in Rodolfo O. de la Garza and Jesus Velasco, eds., *Bridging the Border: Transforming Mexico-U.S. Relations* (Lanham, MD: Rowman and Littlefield, 1997).

43. Serge Schmemann, "A New Collision of East and West," *New York Times*, 4/4/99; also *New York Times*, 3/25/99.

44. For a book that finds virtually no problems for the nation in ethnic groups' involvement in foreign policy, see Yossi Shain, *Marketing the Democratic Creed Abroad: Diasporas in the U.S. and Their Homelands* (Cambridge: Cambridge University Press, 1999). For works that point out the dangers of diasporas as international networks that spread ethnic conflict, see David A. Lake and Donald Rothchild, eds., *The International Spread of Ethnic Conflict* (Princeton: Princeton University Press, 1998). On the risks to American foreign policy that ethnic influence can pose, see Charles McC. Mathias Jr., "Ethnic Groups and Foreign Policy," *Foreign Affairs*, 59, 5, 1981.

45. J. J. Goldberg, *Jewish Power: Inside the American Jewish Establishment* (Reading, MA: Addison Wesley, 1996), 6; Charles S. Liebman and Steven M. Cohen, *Two Worlds of Judaism: The Israeli and American Experiences* (New Haven: Yale University Press, 1990), 40f; Lipset, 172; Peter Novick, *The Holocaust in American Life* (Boston: Houghton Mifflin, 1999), 171. See also a book sponsored by the American Jewish Committee, Charles Herbert Stember et al., *Jews in the Minds of America* (New York: Basic Books, 1997); Alan M. Dershowitz, *Chutzpah* (Boston: Little, Brown, 1991), intro. and ch. 10; David Biale, *Power and Powerlessness in Jewish History* (New York: Schocken, 1986), ch. 8.

46. Renae Cohen and Jennifer Golub, "The Israeli Peace Initiative and the Is-

rael-PLO Accord: A Survey of American Jewish Opinion in 1994," American Jewish Committee, 1995, 44f.

47. Noam Chomsky, *The Fateful Triangle: The United States, Israel and the Palestinians* (Cambridge, MA: South End Press, 1993), 16; Goldberg, 69f.

48. Will Kymlicka, *Multicultural Citizenship* (Oxford: Oxford University Press, 1995), 94ff; Amitai Etzioni, *The New Golden Rule* (New York: Basic Books, 1996), ch. 7.

49. William A. Galston, "A Public Philosophy for the 21st Century," *Responsive Community*, 8, 3, 1998; Etzioni, 197. See also Charles Taylor, "The Dynamics of Democratic Exclusion," *Journal of Democracy*, 9, 4, 1998; and Tamir.

50. Paul Watanabe, *Ethnic Groups, Congress, and American Foreign Policy: The Politics of the Turkish Arms Embargo* (Westport, CT: Greenwood Press, 1984), 155ff. The terms of abuse aimed at Henry Kissinger by members of the Greek American community at the time of the Turkish invasion of Cyprus may serve as a case in point.

51. Ann Louise Bardach, "Our Man in Miami," *New Republic*, 10/3/94; Bardach and Larry Rohter, "Key Cuba Foe Claims Exiles' Backing," *New York Times*, 7/12–13/98; Human Rights Watch, *Dangerous Dialogue: Attacks on Freedom of Expression in Miami's Cuban Exile Community* (New York: Americas Watch, The Fund for Free Expression, vol. 4, issue 7, Aug. 1992); *Economist*, 11/19/97.

52. Ball and Ball, 217f, 221ff; Paul Findlay, *They Dare to Speak Out: People and Institutions Confront Israel's Lobby* (Chicago: Lawrence Hill, 1985).

53. Howe cited in Mathias, 998; Linda Chavez, "What to Do about Immigration," *Commentary*, March 1995; Harold Isaacs, *Idols of the Tribe: Group Identity and Political Change* (Cambridge, MA: Harvard University Press, 2nd ed., 1989), 211. In this vein, see Keith B. Richburg, *Out of America: A Black Man Confronts Africa* (New York: Harcourt Brace, 1997); Eddy L. Harris, *Native Stranger: A Black American's Journey into the Heart of Africa* (New York: Simon and Schuster, 1992).

54. Judith N. Shklar, *American Citizenship: The Quest for Inclusion* (Cambridge, MA: Harvard University Press, 1991).

Index